Microsoft Dynamics AX 2009 Programming: Getting Started

Get to grips with Dynamics AX 2009 development quickly to build reliable and robust business applications

Erlend Dalen

BIRMINGHAM - MUMBAI

Microsoft Dynamics AX 2009 Programming: Getting Started

First published: December 2009

Production Reference: 1091209

Published by Packt Publishing Ltd.
32 Lincoln Road
Olton
Birmingham, B27 6PA, UK.

ISBN 978-1-847197-30-6

www.packtpub.com

Cover Image by Harmeet Singh (singharmeet@yahoo.com)

Credits

Author
Erlend Dalen

Reviewers
Harish Mohanbabu

Mohammed Rasheed

Acquisition Editor
Douglas Paterson

Development Editor
Darshana Shinde

Technical Editors
Mayuri Kokate

Aaron Rosario

Indexer
Hemangini Bari

Editorial Team Leader
Akshara Aware

Project Team Leader
Priya Mukherji

Project Coordinator
Ashwin Shetty

Proofreader
Jeff Orloff

Graphics
Nilesh R. Mohite

Production Coordinator
Dolly Dasilva

Cover Work
Dolly Dasilva

About the Author

Erlend Dalen started working as a developer with the first version of Axapta in 1998. He was then working with some of the first Axapta implementations in Norway and was also part of a team who created an advanced product configurator for Axapta. From 2000 to 2002 he worked on developing eCommerce, mobile, and integration solutions in Java for a Norwegian IT consultancy company. He has worked for Columbus IT since 2002, first as a senior developer in Norway and in USA and now as the technology manager of the Norwegian branch, where his responsibilities have been to implement new technology areas, creating an eCommerce solution for Dynamics AX, and being the technology solution architect in internal and customer projects.

Columbus IT is one of the largest Dynamics resellers in the world. With offices in 30 countries and more than 1100 employees, Columbus IT provide 6000 customer hours every day.

I would like to thank my wife Benedikte for backing me up on this project. When I have felt that things moved slowly, she has motivated me to push forward to finish the project.

I would also like to thank Columbus IT Norway for letting me take some time off to write the book and my co-workers at Columbus IT Norway for helping me out whenever I had a question.

Last but not least, I would like to thank my daughter Ellinor for forcing me to take play-breaks every now and then. You put a smile on my face when I was struggling with the book.

About the Reviewers

Harish Mohanbabu is a technical architect who has been working on Dynamics AX since version 2.5. He has 11 years of experience in software engineering, consulting, and management; the last 7 years were spent on Dynamics AX. His focus is architecture, design, and development, including quality assurance activities. Harish lives in Hertfordshire, England with his wife Chelvy and his children Swetha and Rahul.

Mohammed Rasheed (BE, Msc) is a Senior Technical Consultant at Junction Solutions UK (www.Junctionsolutions.co.uk) where he is responsible for the delivery of integrations and customizations involved in Junctions Solutions UK projects.

Junction Solutions are the most exciting Microsoft Dynamics AX Partner for retail, with over 40 successful implementations across the world and a retail solution that has been certified by Microsoft for quality. Junction Solutions' innovative multi-channel retail software was built on Dynamics AX to resolve the unique challenges of 21st century retailers who trade across many channels including stores, online, mail order, franchise, wholesale, and direct sales. Junction Solutions bring these channels together and provide modern retailers with a holistic view of their business, enabling them to develop new revenue opportunities, drive better customer service, and deliver improved profitability.

Mohammed is a double master in Dynamics AX with over 8 certifications on Dynamics AX. Though his strengths are rooted in X++ development, Mohammed is a highly regarded generalist and has solid knowledge of both functional and technical aspects of Dynamics AX. His passion for development is evident in the fact that Mohammed takes pleasure from refactoring and optimizing X++ code.

Mohammed lives in Bradford, UK, and in the little free time that he gets he likes to read books or articles on emerging technologies. Mohammed blogs on his website www.dynamic-ax.co.uk.

Table of Contents

Preface

First of all, I would like to thank you for buying this book.

My aim in writing this book has been to try and make the process of learning AX programming easier for developers who are new to AX. There may be several ways of achieving this. I have simply focused on the areas that I feel are most important. I have briefly mentioned, or even left out, areas that you most likely don't need in the beginning of your AX development career.

Another way in which I have tried to simplify the learning process has been to write less about background processes and how things work in theory, instead giving good examples that you can apply in your daily work.

I hope that you will enjoy reading this book and that it will put you on a fast track to become an efficient Dynamics AX developer.

Welcome to the wonderful world of AX programming!

What this book covers

Chapter 1: Getting to know Dynamics AX 2009 - This chapter takes you through the development environment in AX and explains some of the development tools that are included with AX. You will also write your first AX program, if you have never done so before.

Chapter 2: X++ - This chapter covers the basics of AX's programming language X++ and explains in brief how data types, statements and loops, operators, classes and methods, and macros work.

Chapter 3: Storing data - This chapter takes you through the process of creating extended data types, tables, and relations.

Chapter 4: *Data User Interaction* - This chapter shows you how to create forms where users can read, update, insert, and delete data. It also shows you how to create reports, menu items, navigation pages, and menus.

Chapter 5: *Searching for Data* - This chapter explains the different options to use when you need to search and retrieve a set of data from the database. It shows you how to create a query, how to create a view, and how to write different select statements.

Chapter 6: *Manipulate Data* - This chapter shows you how to insert, update, and delete data using table methods to manipulate one record at a time and set based manipulation to manipulate a set of data.

Chapter 7: *Integrate Data* - This chapter shows you how to read and write data to and from different kind of files and to and from a database using ODBC. It also provides an example of how to write a generic import and export program in AX.

Chapter 8: *Integrate with standard AX* - This chapter shows you how some of the main modules in AX (Inventory, Ledger, Account Receivable, and Accounts Payable) are built by looking at their entity schemas and by providing examples of how to perform typical tasks within these modules.

Chapter 9: *Creating a New Module* - This chapter shows you how to create a new module in AX by creating number sequences, parameter tables, license codes, configuration keys, and security keys.

Chapter 10: *Working with .NET and AX* - This chapter explains how you can use .NET classes in AX with the Common Language Runtime and how you can write .NET code that uses AX classes by using the .NET Business Connector for AX.

Chapter 11: *Web Services* - This chapter shows you how to create a web service that expose AX logic, how to publish the web service to Internet Information Services (IIS), and how to make AX consume a web service.

Chapter 12: *Enterprise Portal* - This chapter takes you through an example of how to expose AX data to web by using the Enterprise Portal and SharePoint.

Appendix A: Links - This appendix will provide you with references to websites and help files in AX, so that it easier for you to find them again later.

Appendix B: Debugger - This appendix will act as a quick guide on how to use the debugger tool.

What you need for this book

All of the examples in this book have been created using the Virtual PC (VPC) image called Pre-Sales Demonstration Toolkit For Microsoft Dynamics AX 2009.

I would recommend that you either use the VPC or an AX installation that is not in use by anyone else when you follow the examples in this book so that you don't step on anyone's toes.

The VPC can be downloaded here if you are a Microsoft Partner with access to Microsoft PartnerSource: `https://mbs.microsoft.com/partnersource/ deployment/documentation/howtoarticles/presalesdemokitmdax2009. htm?printpage=false&stext=AX 2009 VPC`

If you have access to the Microsoft CustomerSource instead:

`https://mbs.microsoft.com/customersource/downloads/servicepacks/ vpcimageax2009sp1.htm?printpage=false&stext=ax2009 vpc`

If you prefer to install MS SQL Server, Dynamics AX 2009, Visual Studio 2008, and all the other required software to follow all the examples in this book, you should take a look here to find the standard system requirements for Dynamics AX 2009:

`http://www.microsoft.com/dynamics/en/us/using/ax-system- requirements-2009.aspx`

Who is this book for

This book is targeted at developers who are new to Dynamics AX, and at consultants who know the functional side of AX but would like to learn how AX works behind the scenes. Experienced AX developers might also pick up some good pointers here and there.

Conventions

In this book, you will find a number of styles of text that distinguish between different kinds of information. Here are some examples of these styles, and an explanation of their meaning.

Code words in text are shown as follows: "You can find information about global functions here such as `strlen()`."

A block of code is set as follows:

```
static void HelloWorld(Args _args)
{
  print "HelloWorld";
  pause;
}
```

New terms and **important words** are shown in bold. Words that you see on the screen, in menus or dialog boxes for example, appear in the text like this: "Under the **Development** tab page, you can enable the **Sort alphabetically** checkbox to sort the properties alphabetically".

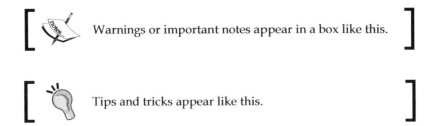

Warnings or important notes appear in a box like this.

Tips and tricks appear like this.

Reader feedback

Feedback from our readers is always welcome. Let us know what you think about this book—what you liked or may have disliked. Reader feedback is important for us to develop titles that you really get the most out of.

To send us general feedback, simply send an email to feedback@packtpub.com, and mention the book title via the subject of your message.

If there is a book that you need and would like to see us publish, please send us a note in the **SUGGEST A TITLE** form on www.packtpub.com or email suggest@packtpub.com.

If there is a topic that you have expertise in and you are interested in either writing or contributing to a book on, see our author guide on www.packtpub.com/authors.

Customer support

Now that you are the proud owner of a Packt book, we have a number of things to help you to get the most from your purchase.

Downloading the example code for the book
Visit http://www.packtpub.com/files/code/7306_Code.zip to directly download the example code.
The downloadable files contain instructions on how to use them.

Errata

Although we have taken every care to ensure the accuracy of our content, mistakes do happen. If you find a mistake in one of our books—maybe a mistake in the text or the code—we would be grateful if you would report this to us. By doing so, you can save other readers from frustration, and help us to improve subsequent versions of this book. If you find any errata, please report them by visiting http://www.packtpub.com/support, selecting your book, clicking on the **let us know** link, and entering the details of your errata. Once your errata are verified, your submission will be accepted and the errata added to any list of existing errata. Any existing errata can be viewed by selecting your title from http://www.packtpub.com/support.

Piracy

Piracy of copyright material on the Internet is an ongoing problem across all media. At Packt, we take the protection of our copyright and licenses very seriously. If you come across any illegal copies of our works, in any form, on the Internet, please provide us with the location address or web site name immediately so that we can pursue a remedy.

Please contact us at copyright@packtpub.com with a link to the suspected pirated material.

We appreciate your help in protecting our authors, and our ability to bring you valuable content.

Questions

You can contact us at questions@packtpub.com if you are having a problem with any aspect of the book, and we will do our best to address it.

Getting to know Dynamics AX 2009 **1**

By reading this chapter, you will learn how the development environment is structured and what tools are accessible to the developer in AX. The famous HelloWorld code will be a piece of a cake for you to understand after the first step-by-step walkthrough of this book, and you will know what the different nodes in the application object tree represent.

Here are some of the topics that you can learn more about in this chapter:

- Creating a job that prints something on to the screen
- A tour of the development environment
- A look at the tools available
- An overview of the AX architecture

Development environment

Let's have a look at the main features of the AX development environment:

- The AX programming language
- The Application Object Tree
- The X++ code editor
- The compiler
- The labels

Programming language

The programming language in AX is called **X++**, and its syntax is similar to Java and C#. In addition to being an **object-oriented programming (OOP)** language, it also includes embedded SQL. This means that writing SQL statements in AX is very easy, because you, as a developer, do not need to create a connection to the database, create a statement that is executed on the connection, and so on. Instead, you can write the SQL statements directly into the X++ code much like you now can with LINQ for .NET.

You will get to know the syntax, features, and how the X++ language works in general in Chapter 2, *X++ language*.

MorphX

In addition to the programming language, Dynamics AX provides an integrated development environment called **MorphX**. MorphX is all of the visual development in AX, and it lets the developer create code elements in a graphical way much like Visual Studio by dragging and dropping, and setting properties on elements.

Application Object Tree

The **Application Object Tree (AOT)** is where you find all code elements in AX.

You can open it by clicking on the icon from the top-menu shown below or by pressing *Ctrl + D* from anywhere in AX.

You will then see the AOT presented in a tree view as shown on the right-hand side in the following screenshot:

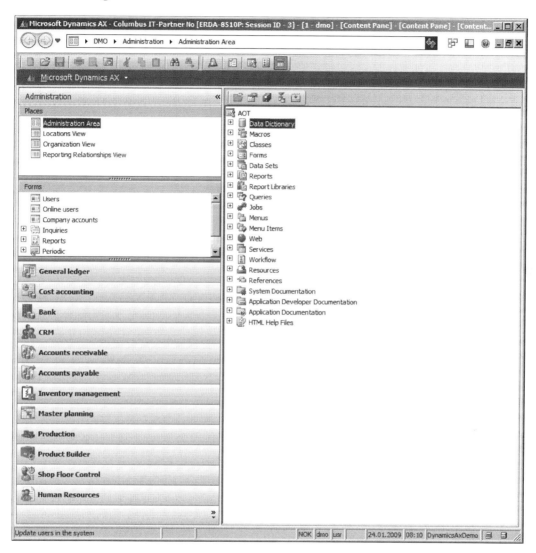

Data Dictionary

The AOT is organized to contain all elements that relate to how the data is stored in the database and those that relate to security, such as the Security Keys, Configuration Keys, and License Keys, under the node called **DataDictionary**. Under this node, you will find tables, maps, views, extended datatypes, base enums, license codes, configuration keys, security keys, table collections, and perspectives.

Macros

Macros are predefined values used throughout the solution and are present just as a best practice tool. You won't have to hardcode values into the code, but rather reference a macro-element within a macro.

Classes

Classes in AX are classes in the same sense as you are used to from C# or Java or whichever object-oriented programming language you already know. They are blueprints of how objects should look at runtime.

Forms

Forms are the end users' way of communicating with the system. They can open forms to search for data, view data, change data, create new records, or delete records. In addition, forms very often contain buttons that link to other forms, reports, and classes that execute business logic.

Data Sets

Data Sets are new in AX 2009 and are used by Visual Studio components, such as Reporting Services reports and AX User Controls, as you will see in later chapters. The data sets define the tables that are used by these Visual Studio components by adding the tables to the data sets much like you would do with table in a data source.

Reports

Reports are the standard AX reports that will display data in a report form to the users, or write the data to a printer or file.

Report Libraries

Report Libraries are links to reporting projects in Visual Studio. You can't create a reporting library directly from AX. You have to create a reporting project in Visual Studio first and import it into AX. It then becomes a report library.

Queries

Queries in the AOT are predefined static queries that can be reused throughout the whole application. A query contains a hierarchy of data sources that defines the data that should be available for the query. Queries can also be used by other elements in AX such as in forms, reports, and classes.

Jobs

Jobs are static methods intended to directly execute a small piece of code. They work fine for code that is supposed to execute once, but are not intended to be a part of a customer solution.

Menus

Menus present the end user with options to open the most used forms and reports and to start periodic tasks.

Menu Items

MenuItems are pointers to forms, reports, or classes. There are three different types of menu items: **Display**, **Output**, and **Action**. The display menu items are used to open forms; the output is used to open reports and the action is used to execute a class with a main method (start point).

Web

The **Web** node consists of subnodes that in turn hold different types of elements relevant for developing web applications such as the enterprise portal.

Services

Services are used to set up web services that let other applications use AX classes through the **Application Integration Framework** (**AIF**). The AIF is used for electronic communication with trading partners or applications.

Workflow

The workflow framework in AX lets developers create workflows that define certain execution flows depending on certain events. The typical scenario for using a workflow in AX is the purchase requisition where one employee enters a purchase order. If the purchase order is over a certain limit, it has to be approved by a manager. If denied by the manager, a message is triggered to the employee who created the order. If approved, the order is automatically sent to the vendor.

Resources

Resources are files that are imported into the AX database, and can be referenced in the code from the resources node in the AOT rather than using a directory and filename on the disk. These files are typically images, icons, cascaded stylesheets, and XML files. You can preview the files by selecting a resources node in the AOT, right-clicking on it, and selecting **Open**.

System documentation

At the bottom of the AOT, you can find different types of help. The system documentation consists of documentation of the AX core. These are the elements in AX that are not open source. This means that you, as a developer, have to relate to these elements as "black-boxes". This means that only you will know what to put into methods and what you can expect to get back. You can find information about global functions here such as `strlen()`. This function (and most other functions) is documented with an explanation of the input parameters, return value, and an example of how to use the function.

The same goes for core classes and their methods. Typical core classes are Map, Array, AsciiIo, FormRun, XppCompiler, and so on, just to mention a few.

Application Developer Documentation

Application Developer Documentation consists of documentation regarding standard AX tables and classes. This documentation is basically just another way of displaying information that you, as a developer, should be able to find by browsing the AOT, reading code, and looking at properties.

Properties

"So how do I look at properties?" you might ask. Well, at anytime while you are in the AOT you can use a combination of *Alt + Enter* keys, or you can right-click on the AOT and select **Properties**. The next image is a screenshot of the **Properties** window.

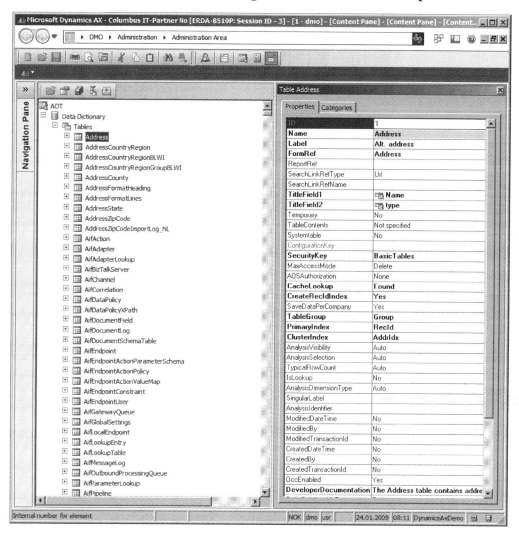

Each element-type in the AOT will have a fixed set of properties that can be changed by the developers. The properties marked with bold text have been changed specifically for the selected element. The pink background that you will see in the **Name** property means that it is mandatory. A yellow background means that it is best practice to have something in that property. The rest of the properties are defaulted by the system.

The properties are by default organized after relevance relative to the element it represents. This sorting, can however, be set to alphabetic order from the user options form. Press the Microsoft Dynamics AX button (*Alt + M*) and navigate to **Tools | Options** to open the user options form. Under the **Development** tab page, you can enable the **Sort alphabetically** checkbox to sort the properties alphabetically, as shown in the following screenshot:

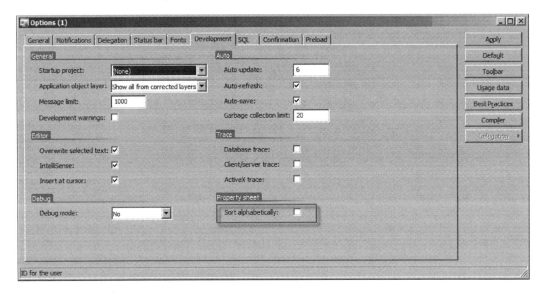

X++ code editor

The X++ code editor is where you will write all code. It consists of three sections: method list, menu bar, and code window.

The method list will show all methods in the selected element if you double-click on an element. If you double-click on a method within an element, you will see only that method in the method list. If you then double-click on another method in the same element, you can see both selected methods in the method list. When you change a method, it will display an asterix after the method name in the method list. This asterisk shows that you a changed method that has not yet been saved.

The code window will obviously show the X++ code for the selected method in the method list, as shown in the following screenshot:

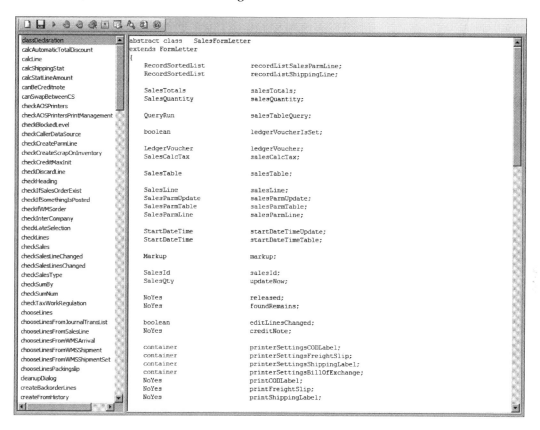

The menu bar has the following buttons, listed from left to right, as shown in the following screenshot:

Description of the menu bar button is as follows:

- **New**: Creates a new method within the selected element.
- **Save**: Saves all the methods open in the method-list.
- **Run**: Executes the method or class if it is executable.
- **Breakpoint**: Sets a breakpoint at the line where the cursor has been placed.
- **Enable/Disable breakpoint**: Enables or disables a breakpoint.
- **Remove all breakpoints**: Removes all breakpoints for the current user.
- **Compile**: Compiles and checks for errors in the code.
- **Lookup properties/methods**: Displays help for the selected text if the cursor is placed over a core-function or method, list methods for a class, available values for enums, and so on.
- **Lookup label/text**: Opens the label editor and searches for the selected text.
- **Scripts**: Opens a context-menu that consists of small code snippets such as do-while loop, header comments, and so on. You can also create your own scripts by creating new methods in the EditorScripts class.
- **Help**: Displays the help file for the selected text in the code window, if such a help file exists. If not, it displays the help file for the X++ code editor.

Compiler

The compiler in AX is in many ways just like any other compiler. It checks for syntax errors and gives the developer error messages if there are any syntax errors found. It can also give warnings if it sees any code that it finds misplaced or not written according to best practice rules.

Though one of the major differences between the AX compiler and other compilers, such as the Visual Studio .NET compiler, is that the AX compiler only requires you to compile the code that you have changed. The problem with this is that the code that you have changed can make classes that consume your changed code not to compile anymore. If they are not recompiled and probably also changed, users will experience a runtime error.

To decide how the compiler should act when compiling you can change the compiler parameters.

First of all, to change the compiler parameters, you have to open the user options form, that is, press the Microsoft Dynamics AX button (*Alt + M*) and select **Tools | Options**.

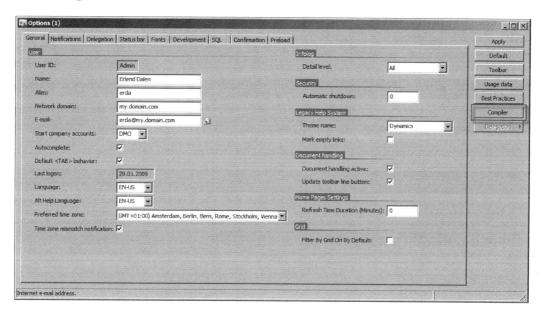

From the user options form click on the **Compiler** button to open the compiler setup form. Here you check the **Cross-reference** flag and you are good to go. Remember that compiling code in AX will take a lot more time when it has to update the cross references as well. See the following screenshot for more information regarding the cross references:

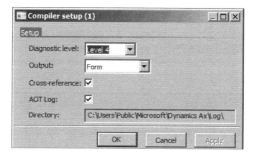

The fields in this form control how the X++ compiler should act. It can be set to give compiler warnings at different levels by changing the **Diagnostic level**. You can select not to receive any warnings about strange looking code, such as having a line of code after a `return` statement in a method. Compiler errors will, of course, still show. **Level 4** means that the compiler will also run best practices checks.

The **Output** defines where the compiler messages should appear. They can appear either in a **Compiler output** form, such as the following one:

Or in a print window, such as the next one:

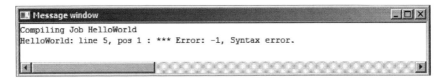

The compiler output form is set as default as it contains more information and has a more standardized look and feel. It is divided into the following tab pages:

- **Status**: Lets you see the overall status of what you have compiled
- **Errors and warnings**: Displays any errors or warnings depending on the diagnostics level set in the compiler setup form.
- **Best Practices**: Shows the best practice warnings as specified in the best practice parameters form.
- **Tasks**: Tasks are added in the code by writing a comment that has the TODO statement as shown below:

```
// TODO: Remember to fix the for-loop
```

Labels

The **labels** in Dynamics AX are a way of translating all user visible text by only referencing to a label ID in the code. Each language is represented by a language-specific label file within each label module. These label files consist of the label ID and the text for that label in that specific language. The label files are stored in the application directory and have the file extension .ald (**Application Label Data**). When opening a label file in a text editor you can see labels listed below:

```
@SYS390 Quantity that is not yet cost accounted in the BOM unit.
@SYS400 Create and compose serial numbers automatically.
```

```
@SYS403 Finish must be greater than start.
@SYS418 Transfer customer information?
```

This means that if you write `@SYS403` in the label-property of a field in AX it will display **Finish must be greater than start.** to the users viewing that field in a form or report, if they are using the language code `en-gb` (as this was taken from the label file `AxSYSen-gb.ald`.)

To create a new label file, simply start the label file wizard from the Microsoft Dynamics AX button (*Alt + M*), navigate to **Tools | Development tools | Label file wizard**, and run through the three self-explaining steps of the wizard.

Your label file will then be named `AxXXXen-gb.ald`, where XXX is a three lettered abbreviation chosen when walking through the wizard.

Creating your first AX program

To make the HelloWorld example, we simply open the AOT by pressing *Ctrl + D* from anywhere in the main Dynamics AX window or by clicking on the AOT button in the top menu, as shown in the first screenshot in this chapter.

Go to the **Jobs** node in the AOT, right-click on it, and select new Job.

Check if the Job opens automatically.

A new X++ editor window will open showing a new Job:

```
static void Job1(Args _args)
{
}
```

As a Job is static and has an input parameter of the `Args` class, it can be run directly. Obviously, the previous example doesn't do anything, it simply edits the job. It will display a HelloWorld message on the **Print WINDOW** while running the job by clicking on the **Go** button or by pressing *F5*.

```
static void HelloWorld(Args _args)
{
  print "HelloWorld";
  pause;
}
```

The pause statement will halt the execution of the program and ask you if you would like to proceed. It is shown in this example just so that you see what the **Print WINDOW** displays. If the pause statement hadn't been put here the **Print** WINDOW would print HelloWorld and just close again in a blink of an eye. This is shown in the following screenshot:

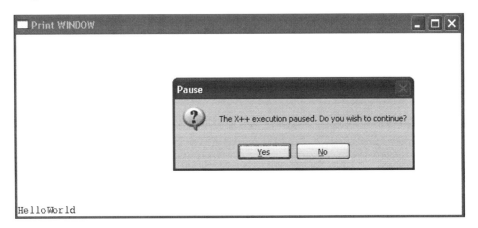

Development tools

AX comes with many different tools that can help developers do their job. Some of these tools are, however, rarely used because they provide little value. We will now have a look at some of the tools you will use on a day-to-day basis when programming in AX. Some of the things you need to know about are:

- Cross references
- MorphX version control
- Debugger

Cross references

The cross references let developers select an element in the AOT and ask the system where the element is used. The result is listed in a form and shows if the element is used for read or write, the name of the elements it is called from methods using it, and where in the methods it is used (line/column). Cross references also enable the developers to see all elements used by the selected element, but of course, the best value for the cross reference tool is to be able to see where one certain element is used.

The following is a screenshot of the form displaying the result:

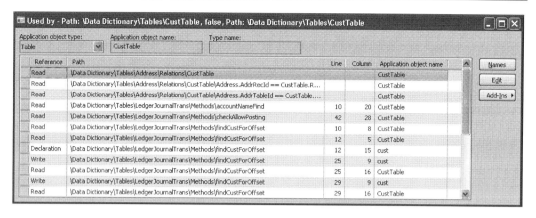

To be able to see the cross references you need to update them on a regular basis, at least if you want to see them in a development environment at a point in time where changes are being done. This can be done by setting up the update to run in batch, or you can set cross references to update every time you change an element. To set it up to update every time you change an element, you need to enable the Cross-reference parameter in the **Compiler Options** form that you find by pressing on the Microsoft Dynamics AX button (*Alt + M*) | **Tools** | **Options** and clicking on the Compiler button. First of all though, you have to run a full cross reference update. This is done by selecting the Microsoft Dynamics AX Button (*Alt +M*) and navigating to **Tools** | **Development tools** | **Cross Reference** | **Periodic** | **Update**. The following screenshot shows the **Update cross-reference** screen:

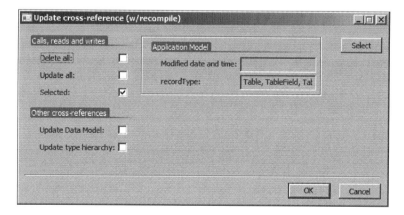

You can choose to delete all existing cross-references before creating them again, update cross-references for all elements in the AOT, or select which elements you would like to have updated by clicking on the **Select** button. You will then get a query where you can filter what kind of elements you would like to update the cross-references for.

In addition, there are two other useful types of cross-references that can be updated from this form. Updating the data model will enable end users to filter queries not only the fields in the query that they are running, but also fields from other related tables. An example of this can be when the end user wants to print the report **Cust** that lists customers. Let's say he would like to limit the report to show only the customers who have ever created an order. He would then have to add the **SalesTable** to the structure of the report, so that it would create an inner join between the **CustTable** and the **SalesTable**.

Updating the **type** hierarchy will enable developers to look at a class or an extended data type and see if it belongs to a hierarchy. This is shown in the following screenshot:

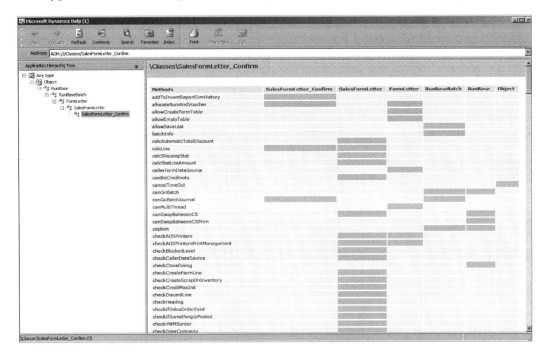

The left-hand side part of the form, that is, the **Application Hierarchy Tree** will show which class hierarchy the **SalesFormLetter_Confirm** belongs to. All classes in AX automatically extend the **Object** class as you can see in the top of the tree. The right-hand side part of the form will show you all the methods in the **SalesFormLetter_Confirm** and where they are implemented in the class hierarchy.

MorphX version control

If you have done development in Visual Studio on projects with multiple developers, you have most likely used a version control tool and know the essentials of it. If not, let me try to explain how a version control tool works. It basically is a repository where you can check elements in and out and track changes done to an element over time. If for some reason you would like to take back an older version of an element, the version control enables you to do that as well.

When you check an element out it is locked to other developers so only you can make changes to it. When you have completed your changes to the element you simply check it in and comment on what kind of changes you have made. It will then be available for other developers to change again. If for some reason one of the changes done to the element creates an unwanted situation you can simply revert the element to the state in which it was before the particular change was made.

Setting up the MorphX Version Control System

To set up the MorphX **Version Control System** (**VCS**) in AX simply press the Microsoft Dynamics AX button (*Alt + M*) and navigate to **Tools | Development tools | Version Control | Setup | Parameters**. You will get the screen shown in following screenshot:

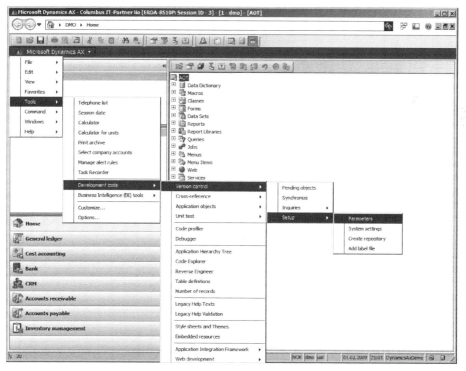

You should then set this form up like I have done in next screenshot. First of all, you have to select **Enable** in the **Source control status**. Then, you need to select the version control type that you would like to use. This book only covers the **MorphX VCS**, as it is the best option for most AX development. The main reason for this is that it doesn't require each developer to have a full AX installation locally like the Visual Source Safe and Team Foundation Server do.

If you are creating a new module for AX, or if you are already using Team Foundation Server, then selecting Team Foundation Server as version control for AX might be a better option.

 When using the MorphX VCS, the repository is actually inside the AX database, so you will always have an access to it as long as you are logged on to your AX solution.

You can also select to have the AOT elements color coded depending on the VCS status and to receive a warning when reverting objects.

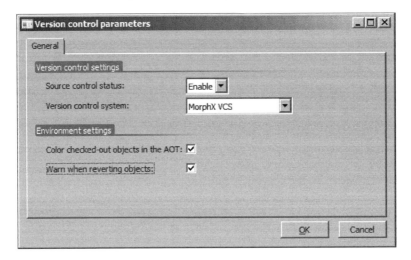

After setting these parameters, you can choose to create a repository by pressing the Microsoft Dynamics AX button (*Alt + M*) and navigate to **Tools | Development tools | Version Control | Setup | Create repository**.

This will basically check in all elements in the AOT with a shared comment at that point of time. If you have a new solution without any modifications to standard AX, this is not needed, as you always have the possibility to go back to the original version in the system layers.

You can also set some rules as to what should be allowed and denied when trying to check in an element into the VCS by pressing the Microsoft Dynamics AX button (*Alt + M*) and navigating to **Tools | Development tools | Version Control | Setup | System settings**. This is shown in the following screenshot:

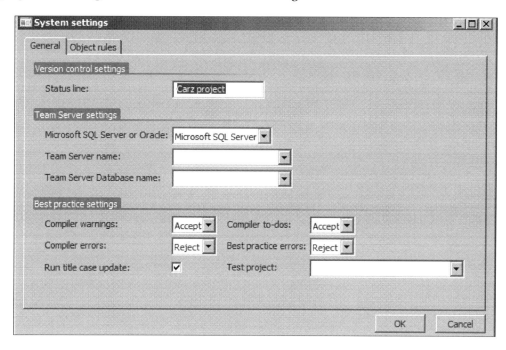

In this form, you can select to set rules so that the developers can't check in code that doesn't compile or have best practices errors.

You can also set up a test project and run the code through that test project successfully before being able to check in code.

Using the MorphX Version Control System

When you have set up the MorphX VCS, you can start adding elements to the VCS as you start working on them.

To add an element to the VCS, simply select the element in the AOT and click on the **Add to version control** button from the AOT menu bar, as shown in the following screenshot, or right-click on the element, and select **Add to version control**:

When an element has been added to the version control, you will be able to check in the element to add your changes to the repository. This is done either by clicking on the **Check in** button from the AOT menu bar, pressing *Alt + I*, or by right-clicking on the element and selecting **Check in**. This screen is shown in the following screenshot:

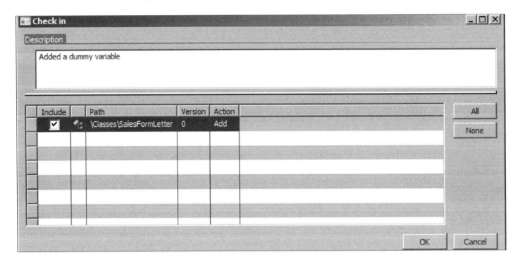

You will then see a form consisting of all elements that are either checked out, or added to the VCS but not yet checked in. You have to type a description of what you have done to the element before clicking on **OK**. The element will then be checked in to the repository.

To see the history of what has been done to this element over time you can select the element in the AOT and either click on the **History** button, or right-click on the element and select **History**.

The history form will show the history of one specific element in the AOT. The history consists of all check ins with comments, user ID, date, time, and version ID.

You can also open the .xpo file from the history form by clicking on the **View File** button.

XPO is the export format that is used by AX to export and import code. It can be used to transfer code from one AX solution to another. The XPO files are in text format and can be opened in a text editor for verification.

To open up the selected version of the element in an AOT window click on the **Open new window** button. If you open a version other than the current one, or one that is checked out by someone else, you will only be able to read the code (no changes allowed).

Selecting two versions of the same element enables the **Compare** button where you can compare the two different versions to track the changes.

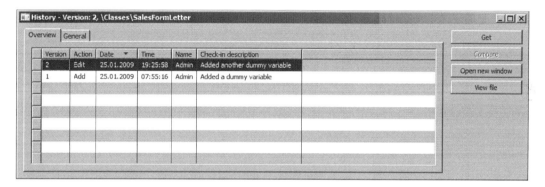

Debugger

The most important developer tool is the debugger. This tool will help you in your search to find what is wrong with your code, if you are one of those developers who write code that doesn't work as expected. Even if you never write code with bugs, you might be lucky enough to find other developer's bugs, and the debugger will then hopefully make you curse and swear a little less.

The debugger contains two main sections—the **code section** at the top and the **information section** at the bottom.

The **code section** is where you see the active code being executed. You can execute the code step-by-step, run from where you are, stop the code execution, step into, step over, and even go backwards in the active method, set breakpoints, toggle breakpoints, and remove breakpoints.

The **information section** contains separate windows for the call-stack, local, global and class variables, breakpoints, output, and variable watch.

Architecture

Now that you have seen some of the development tools in AX, let's have a look at how AX is built from a technical perspective.

We will look at the following concepts:

- Application object layers
- Network tiers

Application object layers

Dynamics AX 2009 consists of sixteen application object layers that contain all the elements you see in the AOT.

These layers can be looked at as an onion with multiple layers. In the middle is the core application in the **SYS** layer and the outermost layer is the user layer **USR**.

Therefore, when any application element is being executed the system will look at the outermost code layer first to see if there is any code for that element; if not, it peels a layer off the onion, and tries the next layer. When it hits a layer where the element exists, it will use the code from this layer, and will not continue to peel off layers to find code for that element in the innermost layers. The following figure shows the multiple layers:

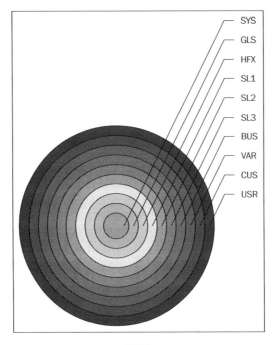

As you might have noticed, the above figure only shows half of the layers. Each of the layers in the illustration, except the **HFX**, **SL1**, **SL2**, and **SL3**, has a patch-layer. The patch-layers are used for service-packs and hotfixes, and exist one layer outside its corresponding main layer. If we look at the **SYS** layer there is actually a **SYP** layer between the **SYS** layer and the **GLS** layer.

The **HFX**, **SL1**, **SL2**, and **SL3** layers are new in Dynamics AX from version 2009, but can be found in previous versions as DIS, DIP, LOS, and LOP.

The list below is taken from the Dynamics AX 2009 SDK and provides an explanation of each layer:

Layer	Description
SYS	The standard application is implemented at the lowest level, the SYS layer. The application objects in the standard application can never be deleted.
GLS	When the application is modified to match country/region-specific legal demands these modifications are saved in a separate layer, the GLS layer. If an application object, for example, a form, is modified in the GLS layer, the modifications are saved in the GLS layer only and the modified version of the form is used.
HFX	HFX is an application object patch layer reserved by Microsoft for future patching or other updates.
SL1, SL2, or SL3	A layer where the distributor can implement vertical partner solutions. SL is an abbreviation for SoLution.
BUS	When a business partner creates their own generic solution, their modifications are saved in the BUS layer and the top-level application objects are used.
VAR	**Value Added Resellers (VAR)** can make modifications or new developments to the VAR layer as specified by the customers or as a strategy of creating an industry-specific solution. Such modifications are saved in the VAR layer.
CUS	The supervisor or administrator of an end user installation might want to make modifications that are generic to the company. Such modifications are saved in the CUS (CUStomer) layer.
USR	End users might want to make their own modifications, such as in their reports. These modifications are saved in the USR layer.

Each of these layers is represented in the application folder with a `.aod` file if there is any code in the solution in the layer. The same goes for the patch layers. This means that the application object file for the **SYS** layer is `AxSYS.aod`, and as the patch layer for **SYS** is called **SYP**, the patch file would be `AxSYP.aod`.

Network tiers

AX 2009 is built as a three-tier solution. This means that it has a **data-tier** where the data is stored, a **logic-tier** where all business logic is executed, and a **presentation-tier** that presents information to the user and receives input from the user.

As an AX developer you can select to have the piece of code you are writing be run on the client or the server. The client will represent the presentation-tier and the server will represent the logic-tier. The AX server is also called the **Application Object Server** or **AOS**. The data-tier consists of either an MS SQL or an Oracle database.

There are also two completely different clients available in AX. The **regular Windows client**, also known as the **rich client**, is the one most users think of when we talk about the AX client, but there is also a business connector client. The **business connector client** can be used by a third-party application to integrate to AX, and it is also used by the enterprise portal.

In addition to these three layers we also often talk about a fourth component in the tier model, the file-server. The **file-server** is not really a tier in itself as it does not execute any code but only stores the code.

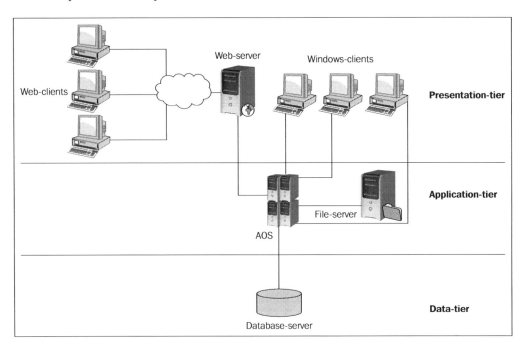

Case Study: Carz Inc.

Most of the examples in this book will be related to a case study where you will be assigned to develop a module in AX for a car rental company called Carz Inc.

Carz Inc. rents out cars and sells cars after they have reached a certain mileage.

They need to store information about their cars and their customers. They also need a booking system within Dynamics AX that enables them to see which cars are available or rented out within different car groups.

The customers should also be able to see availability from an enterprise portal site.

The examples will show you step-by-step how to create extended data types, tables, forms, reports, and everything you need to make the whole module work according to best practices rules and according to the requirements set by Carz Inc.

Summary

Now that you have made it through the first chapter of this book, you have hopefully gotten a good foundation to learn more on how to program in AX.

This chapter has shown you how to write the famous HelloWorld program in AX and taken you through the development environment where you learned about the different elements in the AOT.

You have seen some of the most important development tools that you will get to know very well once you get going with the AX development.

The application object layers and network tiers have shown you the main concepts behind the technical architecture of AX, and finally, you have read a little bit about the case study that we will continue to use throughout the book.

In the next chapter, you will learn the syntax of the X++ language by looking at the different data types you can use in X++, how to write statements and loops such as `if-else` and `while` loops, how different operators are used, and how to create and use classes and methods.

2
X++ Language

After finishing this chapter, you will be able to express yourself using the X++ language. You will know what kinds of data types are available, how to create all kinds of loops, how to compare and manipulate variables, where to find predefined functions, and how to use them.

The chapter will cover the following topics:

- Comments
- Data types
- Statements and loops
- Operators
- Classes and methods
- Macros

Introduction

You have already seen the HelloWorld example and probably thought that this looks pretty easy and yes, it is. The X++ syntax is not very strict as it is case insensitive. However, you should try to follow the naming conventions used in the rest of AX.

Some, but not all, of these naming conventions are listed here:

- Application object names are mixed case. The first letter of the name is uppercase as is the first letter of each word in the name. This is called Camel casing (for example: SalesFormLetter).
- Methods, variables, and functions have mixed case names with a lowercase first letter. This is called Pascal casing (for example: initFromSalesTable).
- Primitive variable types use lowercase names (for example: `str`).

- All names should be in U.S. English.
- Be consistent while naming.
- Only tables, base enums, and extended data types should have the prefix 'DEL_'. This prefix is used to indicate that the element will be removed in the next version, and is used by the data upgrade scripts in AX.

To learn more about the different best practices in AX please check out the Developer Help file.

When writing comments in the code you can either use a one-line comment or a multi-line comment. A one-line comment is written like this:

```
// This is a one line comment
```

A multi-line comment is written like this:

```
/* This comment spans over
multiple lines.
This is the last line of this comment */
```

Comments are color-coded green in the editor window.

Data types

We will now have a look at the different kind of data types you can use in AX.

They can be separated into two main groups:

- Primitive data types
- Composite data types

Primitive data types

Primitive data types are the building blocks of the programming language. They are used to store a single value based on the type in runtime code. The values that we are able to store in each data type vary, depending on which data type is used. If you would like to store a text string you can use the string data type. If you would like to store a date value you can use the `date` data type, or perhaps the `utcdatetime`. You can also use the data type `anytype` if the type of data read into the variable is decided at runtime.

In the next chapter, we will look at how to create extended data types and how they can be used to easily create fields in a table. All of the extended data types extend primitive data types.

The different primitive data types available in AX are:

- String (`str`)
- Integer (`int`)
- Real (`real`)
- Boolean (`boolean`)
- Date (`date`)
- Enum (enum)
- TimeOfDay (`timeofday`)
- UtcDateTime (`utcdatetime`)
- Anytype (`anytype`)

String

The string data type is probably one of the most used data types. It is used to hold text information, and its length can either be set while declaring the variable or it can be dynamic. When using fixed length strings simply add the number of characters you would like to limit the variable to between the variable type and the name of the variable, as shown in the next example.

Also note that the variable type keyword is `str` and not string.

```
static void Datatypes_string1(Args _args)
{
    str 7      fixedLengthString;
    str        dynamicLengthString;
    ;

    fixedLengthString = "Welcome to Carz Inc";
    dynamicLengthString = "Welcome to Carz Inc";
    print fixedLengthString;
    print dynamicLengthString;
    pause;
}
```

 The extra semicolon after the variable declaration is mandatory as long as the first line of code is not a keyword. The semicolon tells the compiler that variable declarations have come to an end. You cannot declare new variables after this semicolon.

The print commands will show the following output:

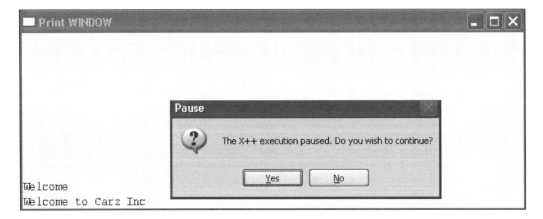

When working with strings there are some functions that are nice to know about, that help you manipulate strings, search for text inside a string, and so on. These functions can be found in the **Application Object Tree (AOT)** under System Documentation\Functions and some under Classes\Global.

I will show just a few of these functions in this chapter but you should get familiar with more of them by browsing the AOT and trying them out yourself.

strfmt

This method is used to format a string and change any occurrences of %n with parameter n.

To illustrate this, the next Job will print **100: Welcome to Carz Inc**

```
static void Datatypes_string_strmft(Args _args)
{
    str     name;
    int     a;
    ;

    name = "Carz Inc";
    a = 100;
    print strfmt("%1: Welcome to %2", a, name);
    pause;
}
```

Notice that the strfmt function also converts any other data types into string.

substr

The `substr` function returns a part of a string. The first parameter is the original string, the second is the start position, and the third is the number of characters to read.

```
static void Datatypes_string_substr(Args _args)
{
    str     carBrand;
    ;

    carBrand = "Volkswagen";
    print substr(carBrand, 6, 5);
    pause;
}
```

The print command from the method will display **wagen** as the substring starts at position 6 of the value of the first parameter, which is **Volkswagen**, and reads 5 characters ahead.

Integer

Integers are numbers without decimals. They are divided into two separate data types in AX: the `int` which is a 32 bit integer, and the `int64` which is a 64 bit integer.

The `int` data type ranges from -2,147,483,647 to 2,147,483,647. The `int64` ranges from -9,223,372,036,854,775,808 to 9,223,372,036,854,775,808, which should be enough for most of us.

You can do any kind of arithmetic with the integers directly in the code, such as the multiplication in the next example that will print **Carz Inc have 24 cars in total**.

```
static void Datatypes_integer1(Args _args)
{
    int     carsInEachOffice;
    int     offices;
    ;

    carsInEachOffice = 6;
    offices = 4;
    print strfmt("Carz Inc have %1 cars in total",
    carsInEachOffice *
    offices);
    pause;
}
```

Dividing two integers will result in a real number unless you are returning the value to an integer. This means that dividing 24/4 gives the result 6.00, but returning the result to an integer and printing it results in 6 as you will see in the next example.

```
static void Datatypes_integer2(Args _args)
{
    int     x = 24;
    int     y = 4;
    int     res = x/y;
    ;

    // Prints a real value
    print strfmt("%1 / %2 = %3", x, y, x/y);
    // Automatically type casted to int
    // to print the integer value
    print strfmt("%1 / %2 = %3", x, y, res);
    pause;
}
```

Real

A `real` variable can consist of decimal number and integers. It spans a range of –(10)127 to (10)127 with a precision of 16 significant digits. It is worth mentioning that even though your locale use comma as decimal separator the code in AX accepts only period as comma separator.

When the code is executed, however, the print will show the decimal separator that is set in your regional settings.

In my Norwegian locale the next Job will print **The car has used an average of 3,61 gallons gas**.

```
static void Datatypes_real1(Args _args)
{
    real    mileage;
    real    mpg;
    ;

    mileage = 127.32;
    mpg = 35.24;
    print strfmt("The car has used an average of %1 gallons gas",
        mileage/mpg);
    pause;
}
```

There are also some useful functions to use with the `real` data type in AX. Some of the most used ones are:

str2num

If you have a string variable representing a number, you can convert the value into a real variable by using the `str2num` function.

```
static void Datatypes_str2num(Args _args)
{
    str     mileage;
    real    mileageNum;
    ;
    mileage = "388272.23";
    mileageNum = str2num(mileage);
    print strfmt("The car has run %1 miles", mileageNum);
    pause;
}
```

num2str

You can also go the other way around by converting the value of a real variable into a string. This operation, however, requires that you know more about how you would like the number represented. Look at the comments in the next code example for an explanation of the parameters.

```
static void Datatypes_num2str(Args _args)
{
    str     mileage;
    real    mileageNum;
    ;
    mileageNum = 388272.23;
    //  num2str(number to be converted,
    //          minimum characters required,
    //          required number of decimals,
    //          decimal separator <1=point, 2=comma>,
    //          thousand separator <0=none, 1=point,
    //             2=comma, 3=space>)
    mileage = num2str(mileageNum,0,2,2,0);
    print strfmt("The car has run %1 miles", mileage);
    pause;
}
```

The above Job will print: **The car has run 388272,23 miles**

Boolean

The `boolean` data type is just a representation of an integer that can only have the values 0 (false) or 1 (true).

```
boolean    isAvailable = true;
```

Date

The `date` data type obviously holds date values. The dates are system formatted as dd\mm\yyyy.

```
date    birthday = 29\01\2008
```

The `date` variable can hold values from 1\1\1900 to 31\12\2154, and you can use integers to add or subtract a date.

To get the session date set in AX you can use the `systemdateget()` function. The session date in AX is automatically set to the machine date on the computer running your AX client when you start the AX client. You can change the session date by pressing the Dynamics AX button (*Alt + M*) and selecting **Tools | Session Date**. In the form that opens, you can change both the session date and time. This is typically done to post a journal as if it was posted on a different date than the actual date.

To retrieve the local machine's date, use the `today()` function.

Enum

Enums are represented in the AOT under **Data Dictionary | Base Enums**. You can use these enums in the code as a list of literals, as it is much more convenient to read and understand than a list of integers. Each enum can have maximum 251 literals.

The first literal in an enum is indexed by the integer 0, the next one is indexed by 1, and so on; each of these integers represent a more understandable value, as shown in the next example.

Here, you can see how you can assign an enum value to an enum variable of type `Weekdays`.

```
Weekdays day = Weekdays::Monday;
```

The value that is stored in the variable day will be the integer 1 since the enum `Weekdays` also has a value 0 that represents the enum "None", but it's a lot easier to read this code instead of the following that does the exact same thing:

```
Weekdays day = 1;
```

To get a list of all base enums while in the code editor simply press *F11*

enum2str

To get the label for one specific enum value, simply use the `enum2str` function as shown in the next example:

```
static void Datatypes_enum2str(Args _args)
{
    SalesType        salesType; // a standard enum in Ax
    ;
    salesType = SalesType::Sales;
    info(strfmt("The name of the current sales-type is '%1'",
        enum2str(salesType)));
}
```

This example will show the following output:

Actually, in the previous example, you don't have to use the `enum2str` as the enum value is automatically converted to a `str` as it is used in a `strfmt()` function. However, trying to use the enum variable directly in the info will result in a compilation error because you cannot add an enum variable to a string. Hence, in this example the `enum2str` method would come in handy.

```
info("The name of the current sales type is " + salesType);
```

 Note that we used the info method in this example instead of the print statement. The info method is a more user friendly way of displaying information to the end user. It is defined as a static method in the Global class and simply adds a new message of type info to the AX information log. Other types that can be put into the information log (also known as the **infolog**) is error and warning. Try them out by using `error()` and `warning()` instead of `info()`.

enum2int

In the same way that you can get the label of the enum value, you can also get the integer that it represents by using the `enum2int` function as shown in the next example:

```
static void Datatypes_enum2int(Args _args)
{
    SalesType         salesType;
    ;

    salesType = SalesType::Sales;
    info(strfmt("The value of the current sales-type element is %1",
      enum2int(salesType)));
}
```

The info method will give the following output:

TimeOfDay

The variable type `timeofday` is an integer representing the number of seconds since midnight. It can have values from 0 to 86400 that is stored in the database. When used in a report or a form, it is automatically converted to values from 12:00:00 a.m. to 11:59:59 p.m.

str2time

The `str2time` function converts a string representation of time to the `timeofday` value as long as the string is a valid time. If it's not a valid time, the method returns -1.

```
static void Datatypes_str2time(Args _arg)
{
    str timeStr;
    timeofday time;
    ;

    timeStr = "09:45";
    time = str2Time(timeStr);
    info(strfmt("%1 seconds has passed since midnight when the clock
      is %2", time, timeStr));
}
```

The example will print the following to the info:

35100 seconds has passed since midnight when the clock is 09:45

Utcdatetime

The utcdatetime data type was introduced in AX 2009, and holds both date and time information (and actually also time zone information although this is not available in X++ code).

One of the really nice things about utcdatetime is that you can store a value in a utcdatetime variable and have it displayed to users around the world in their local time zone and time format.

 UTC is an abbreviation for Coordinated Universal Time.

Anytype

The anytype data type can contain any of the other primitive data types. The type of the variable data is decided by the first value that is set for the variable.

In the next example, the **any** variable will work as a string variable at runtime as the first value is a string. Since the second value is an integer it is actually converted to a string during runtime so the print will show **33** when executing the Job.

```
static void Datatypes_anytype1(Args _args)
{
    anytype any;
    ;
    any = "test";
    any = 33;
    print any;
    pause;
}
```

There has to be a catch with a data type like this, right?

Consider the following code:

```
static void Datatypes_anytype2(Args _args)
{
    anytype any;
    ;
```

```
        any = systemdateget();
        any = "test";
        print any;
        pause;
    }
```

The compiler will not give any errors here because we are using the `anytype` data type so we can assign any value to the variable. However, trying to assign a string value to a date variable will give a runtime error.

As you probably understand, you should try to avoid using the `anytype` data type. The only exception where the `anytype` data type can be useful is for parameters or return values for methods that can take different data types as input or output. Consider an example where a method can be called from different places and with different input. In one situation the method will be called with a string, and in another situation the method will be called with an integer. Instead of creating two methods or one method with two different input parameters, you could use the `anytype` data type as input parameter to the method and have the method check if it's an integer or a string that was passed to it.

Composite data types

Composite data types are data types where each variable can consist of multiple other variables.

The different kind of composite data types are:

- Container
- Class
- Table
- Array

Container

A container can consist of multiple values of any primitive data types mixed together.

You can store containers as fields in tables by using the container field.

Containers are immutable and adding or deleting a value in the container requires the system to actually create a new container, copy the value before and after the new value, and remove the deleted value.

Container functions

In the next example you can see some of the container functions that you will be using to insert values into containers, delete values from containers, read values from containers, and get the number of elements in a container.

Check out the Global class to find other methods.

```
static void Datatypes_container_functions(Args _args)
{
    container    con;
    ;

    //  conins - Insert values to the container
    con = conins(con, 1, "Toyota");
    con = conins(con, 2, 20);
    con = conins(con, 3, 2200.20);
    con = conins(con, 4, "BMW");
    con = conins(con, 5, 12);
    con = conins(con, 6, 3210.44);
    // condel - Delete the third and the fourth element
    // from the container
    con = condel(con, 3, 2);
    // conpeek - Read values from the container
    info(conpeek(con,1));
    info(conpeek(con,2));
    info(conpeek(con,3));
    info(conpeek(con,4));
    // connull - Reset the container
    con = connull();
    // conlen - Get the length of the container
    info(strfmt("Length: %1",conlen(con)));
}
```

Class

In order to access any data stored with an object you need to have a reference to the memory locations where these objects are stored. This is done by using class variables.

When you create an object of a class you also want to be able to reference that object and the data stored with it throughout the scope where you are using the class methods.

See the next example to get a hint on how an object is created from a class and how the object is referenced by a class variable.

```
static void Datatypes_class_variable(Args _args)
{
    // Declare a class variable from the RentalInfo class
    RentalInfo        rentalInfo;
    ;
    // An object is created and referenced by the
    // class variable rentalInfo
    rentalInfo = new RentalInfo();
    // Call methods to set/get data to/from the object
    rentalInfo.setCar("BMW 320");
    info(strfmt("The car is a %1", rentalInfo.getCar()));
}
```

The RentalInfo class is implemented like this:

```
public class RentalInfo
{
    str       car;
}
void setCar(str _car)
{
    ;
    car = _car;
}
str getCar()
{
    return car;
}
```

Table

A table can be used in X++ by creating a table variable.

This means that you can easily insert, update, delete, search, and perform other actions with table data directly without creating a connection and a statement.

In the code, you can simply write a select-statement directly like in the next example.

```
static void Datatypes_table(Args _args)
{
    CustTable        custTable;  // This is the table variable
    CustAccount      custAccount;
    ;
```

```
custAccount = "1000";
select Name from custTable
    where custTable.AccountNum == custAccount;
info(strfmt("The name of the customer with AccountNum %1 is %2",
  custAccount, custTable.Name));
}
```

All tables in the data dictionary are actually classes that extend the system class Common. They can be seen as wrappers for their corresponding tables in the database, as they have all necessary functionality needed read, create, modify, and delete the data stored in the table that they wrap. In addition the developer can of course add more methods than what is inherited by the common class.

You can find a couple of the most commonly used table methods listed below.

find

All tables should have at least one `find` method that selects and returns one record from the table that matches the unique index specified by the input parameters. The last input parameter in a `find` method should be a Boolean variable called 'forupdate' or 'update' that is defaulted to false. When it is set to true, the caller object can update the record that is returned by the `find` method.

See the next example from the InventTable:

```
static InventTable find(ItemId     itemId,
                        boolean    update = false)
{
    InventTable   inventTable;
    ;

    inventTable.selectForUpdate(update);
    if (itemId)
    {
        select firstonly inventTable
            index hint ItemIdx
            where inventTable.ItemId == itemId;
    }
    return inventTable;
}
```

exists

As with the `find` method, there should also exist an `exists` method.

It basically works the same as the `find` method, except that it just returns true if a record with the unique index specified by the input parameter(s) is found.

In the next example from the `InventTable` you can see that it returns true if the input parameter has a value AND the select statement returns a value.

```
static boolean exist(ItemId  itemId)
{
    return itemId && (select RecId from inventTable
                index hint ItemIdx
                where inventTable.ItemId == itemId
                ).RecId != 0;
}
```

initFrom

Tables that are related to each other share the data that make up the relationship and possibly also other information. When creating new records in the 'many' table in a one-to-many relationship you can create `initFrom` methods that set the common fields in the table.

It can also be used to enter the values in fields in a table from another table.

The next example is taken from the BOMTable and shows how it initiates the `ItemId` and `ItemGroupId` fields in the BOMTable from the corresponding fields in the inventTable.

```
void initFromInventTable(InventTable table)
{
    this.bomId          = table.ItemId;
    this.ItemGroupId    = table.ItemGroupId;
}
```

Array

An array is a list of values that are all of the same data type, as opposed to a container that can consist of values of different types.

The list of values starts with element 1. If you set a value to index number 0 of an array, the array is reset.

There are two different ways of using an array. You can either use a fixed-length array if you know how many elements (max) you will have in the array. If you don't know how many elements can be stored in the array at run time, you can use a dynamic array.

In addition to this, you can also specify something called "partly on disk arrays" that specify how many elements that should be loaded into memory when the array is referenced. This might be a good performance optimization if you have arrays with a lot of data.

The next example explains the different usage of arrays:

```
static void Datatypes_array(Args _args)
{
    // Fixed lenght array
    str licenceNumber[10];
    // Fixed lenght array partly on disk.
    // 200 elements will be read into memory when this array
    // is accessed.
    int serviceMilage[1000,200];
    // Dynamic array
    str customers[];
    // Dynamic lenght array partly on disk.
    // 50 elements will be read into memory when this array
    // is accessed.
    Amount prices[,50];
}
```

Statements and loops

Statements and loops are used to control the execution flow of a program, and without them most programming tasks would be impossible.

In AX, you have access to the following statements and loops:

- For loop
- Continue
- Break
- While loop
- Do-while loop
- If, else if, else
- Switch

For loop

A for loop can be used if the code at runtime knows how many times it should loop through a piece of code before the loop starts. The pseudo code of a for loop in AX is the same as any for loops in most programming languages that has a relationship with the C programming language. It is actually called a three expression for loop as it is built up by three steps.

The first thing that happens is that you initiate the variable used to increment the for loopincrementation. Then you set the test statement and the last thing is to set the increment.

As the next example shows, the variable is initiated to 1, then it tells the for loop to keep on looping as long as `i<= 10`. The last thing it does is to increment i by 1 for each loop.

```
int i;
for (i=1; i<=10; i++)
{
   info (strfmt("This is the %1 Toyota", i));
}
```

Continue

If you would like the code to jump straight to the next iteration you can use the `continue` statement inside any loop.

Break

The break statement can be used to jump out of the loop even though there are more iterations to execute according to the loop condition.

In the previous example I use the `info` method instead of the print window from the HelloWorld example. The `info` method is much more convenient and looks much better from a user point of view. The print window should only be used to display messages to the developers when executing a test Job or something similar.

While loop

You can use the while loop to execute a piece of code many times until a certain condition is met. The while loop will only execute if the `while` condition is met.

```
int carsAvailable=10;
while (carsAvailable != 0)
{
   info (strfmt("Available cars at the moment is %1", carsAvailable));
   carsAvailable --;
}
```

Do-while loop

The do-while loop is pretty much the same as the while loop, except that it will execute once even though the `while` condition is not met. In a do-while loop, the loop is executed at least once, as the `while` expression is evaluated after the first iteration.

```
int carsAvailable=10;
do
{
   info (strfmt("Available cars at the moment is %1", carsAvailable));
   i--;
} while (carsAvailable != 0)
```

If, else if, else

The `if` statement checks to see if the condition used in the statement returns true. If it does, it executes the body of the `if` statement.

If the `if` statement returns false, you can check if another condition is true by using the `else if` statement.

The `else` statement can be used directly with the `if` statement or after an `else if` statement. `If` will execute the body inside the `else` statement if the `if` statement (and all `else if` statements) returns false.

```
if (carGroup == CarGroup::Economy)
{
    info("Kia Picanto");
}
else if (carGroup == CarGroup::Compact)
{
    info("Toyota Auris");
```

```
    }
    else if (carGroup == CarGroup::MidSize)
    {
        info("Toyota Rav4");
    }
    else if (carGroup == CarGroup::Luxury
    {
        info("BMW 520");
    }
    else
    {
        info("Standard cars");
    }
```

You can of course add as many `else if` cases as you'd like, and you can also nest them to have another `if` inside the body of an if statement, but this might not be the best way of getting things done. You should instead consider using the `switch` statement. The reason for this is that the condition has to be evaluated for each `if` and `else if` statement, while the switch statement evaluates the condition once and then finds the correct hit.

Switch

The `switch` statement evaluates the variable used in the statement and instantly knows which case to continue to, as opposed to the `if else if` that has to evaluate from top to bottom until the `if` statement returns true.

Notice that you have to use the `break` statement at the bottom of each case. If not, it will continue to execute the next case as well.

The `default` statement can be used in a similar way as the `else` statement to say that if none of the other cases contained the correct value, jump to the default case instead.

```
    switch (carGroup)
    {
        case CarGroup::Economy :
            info("Kia Picanto");
        break;
        case CarGroup::Compact :
            info("Toyota Auris");
        break;
        case CarGroup::MidSize :
            info("Toyota Rav4");
        break;
```

```
    case CarGroup::Luxury
        info("BMW 520");
        break;
    default
        info("Standard cars");
        break;
}
```

Exception handling

As a developer it is always important to expect the unexpected. One way of making sure that your program can handle abnormal situations is by using exception handling. In AX that means using the following statements:

- `try`
- `catch`
- `throw`
- `retry`

The `try` and `catch` statements should always go together. Using a `try` without a `catch` or vice versa will result in a compiler error.

When you use the `try` statement, you are indicating that whatever code is inside the try block might generate an abnormal situation that should be handled.

The handling of the situation is done in the catch block by specifying what kind of exception the catch block is taking care of. The next example shows how to catch an **error exception** and a **deadlock exception**. The deadlock will never occur in this example, but I put it here just to show you how you can use the `retry` statement:

```
static void ExceptionHandling(Args _args)
{
    try
    {
        // Do something
        info("Now I'm here");
        // A situation that causes an error occurs and you would
        // like to stop the execution flow
        if (true)
            throw error("Oops! Something happened");
        info("Now I'm there");
    }
    catch (Exception::Error)
    {
```

```
                // Handle the error exception
                info ("I would like to inform you that an error occurred ");
            }
        catch (Exception::Deadlock)
        {
                // Handle the deadlock exception
                // Wait for 10 seconds and try again
                sleep(10000);
                retry;
        }
        info ("This is the end");
    }
```

See the SDK for a full list of Exceptions and a description of them.

Operators

Operators are used to manipulate or check the values of variables.

There are three different types of operators that we use when working with AX:

- Assignment operators
- Relational operators
- Arithmetic operators

Assignment operators

In order to assign values to variables, you have to use an assignment operator in X++.

The most obvious is of course the = operator that will set the value to the right of = to the variable to the left of =. This means that the variable car in the next example will be assigned the value BMW.

```
    str  car = "BMW";
```

Other assignment operators include ++, --, +=, and -=. You know these already if you have been programming in C#, C++ or Java. See the next example for an explanation:

```
    static void AssignmentOperators(Args args)
    {
        int    carsInStock = 10;
        ;

        carsInStock++;  // carsInStock is now 11
```

```
    carsInStock+=2;   // carsInStock is now 13
    carsInStock--;    // carsInStock is now 12
    carsInStock-=3;   // carsInStock is now 9
}
```

The increment and decrement can also be prefixed instead of postfixed, as shown in this example, but it makes no difference in X++, and it is best practice to write them postfixed.

Relational operators

As you have seen already in the loops and if statements, the two most used relational operators are == and !=. These are used to find out if a variable is equal or not equal to the value to the right.

This means that relational operators are used in statements that return true or false.

Some of the most commonly used relational operators are as follows:

- == returns true if both expressions are equal
- != returns true if the first expression is not equal to the second expressions
- && returns true if the first expression AND the second expression are true
- || returns true if the first expression OR the second expression OR both are true
- ! returns true if the expression is false (can only be used with one expression)
- >= returns true if the first expression is greater than or equal to the second expression
- <= returns true if the first expression is less than or equal to the second expression
- > returns true if the first expression is greater than the second expression
- < returns true if the first expression is less than the second expression

The last relational operator is the like operator, which I have explained in the next example:

```
static void RelationalOperatorLike(Args _args)
{
    str     carBrand = "Toyota";
    ;
    // use the * wildcard for zero or more characters
    if (carBrand like "Toy*")
    {
```

```
        info ("The car brand starts with 'Toy'");
    }
    // use the ? wildcard for one character
    if (carBrand like "Toy??a")
    {
        info ("The car brand starts with 'Toy' and the last character
            is 'a'");
    }
}
```

Arithmetic operators

The last type of operators are the arithmetic operators. These are used to do mathematical calculations like multiplication, division, addition, subtraction, and also binary arithmetic operations on variables.

As binary arithmetic is rarely used in standard AX; I won't go into details here, but you can learn more about it in the SDK.

Here are a couple of examples on arithmetic operators:

```
static void ArithmeticOperators(Args _args)
{
    int x, y;
    ;
    x = 10;
    y = 5;
    info(strfmt("Addition: %1 + %2 = %3", x, y, x+y));
    info(strfmt("Subtraction: %1 - %2 = %3", x, y, x-y));
    info(strfmt("Multiplication: %1 * %2 = %3", x, y, x*y));
    info(strfmt("Division: %1 / %2 = %3", x, y, x/y));
}
```

The above Job will print the following to the infolog:

Message (04:24:11)
Addition: 10 + 5 = 15
Subtraction: 10 - 5 = 5
Multiplication: 10 * 5 = 50
Division: 10 / 5 = 2,00

Classes and methods

One of the core components of an object oriented programming language is classes. The classes are blueprints for objects, and are used to define what an object of a certain type can do and what kind of attributes it has.

Classes in AX are similar to classes in C#, but you don't specify the methods of a class within its curly brackets. Rather, you create new nodes under the class in the AOT for each method.

The class declaration is used to hold variables that are global in the class. These variables are always protected as opposed to private and public. This means that objects of that class or objects of a subclass has direct access to these variables.

While developing you write classes. At runtime the classes are instantiated as objects. So if 'Car' is a class that defines the characteristics and behavior of a car, the specific car with license number DE2223ED is an object (instance) of the Car class.

To get a list of all classes while in the code editor, just press *F12*, or right-click and select **List classes**

Method access

Encapsulation ensures that objects protect and handle its own information. Changes to an object's state can only be done from safe methods.

This is done by using these access modifiers in the beginning of the method definitions:

- Public: These methods can be used from any methods where the class is accessible and can also be overridden by classes that extend this class (subclasses). If no access modifiers are explicitly written in the code, the compiler assumes that they are public and handles them accordingly.

- Protected: These methods can be used from any methods in the same class or subclass.

- Private: These methods can only be used from any methods in the same class.

RunOn property

The code in AX can run on either the client or the server. The server here will be the **Application Object Server (AOS)**. There are two ways of controlling where objects of a certain class should execute. When developing static methods you can select to use the client or server modifier in the method header like in the next example:

```
// This method will execute on the client.
static client void clientMethod()
{
}
// This method will execute on the server.
static server void serverMethod()
{
}
```

You can also set the **RunOn** property on a certain class to make all objects of that class run on either the client or the server. You can also set the **RunOn** property on the class to **CalledFrom**. This will make objects of that class execute on the same layer as the method that created the object.

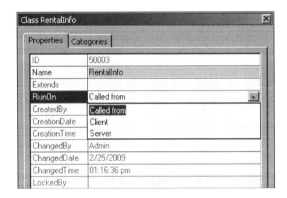

One example where making sure that a method runs on the server or client is when you try to import a file from disk. When referencing to a fixed file location the c drive is obviously the servers c drive when the code is executing on the server and the c:\ drive on the client when the method is executing on the client.

Static methods

In AX, you will see that some methods have a method modifier named `static`. Actually, all the Jobs we have looked at so far have been using the `static` modifier. This means that the method can be called directly without creating an object. This also off course means that the static classes can't access the protected data defined in the **classDeclaration** of the class.

The modifier is used at the beginning of the method definition right after the method access modifier and before the return value as in the next example:

```
public static void main(Args args)
{
}
```

To call a static method you use double colon instead of period as you do in object methods:

```
SomeClass::staticMethod()
```

Default parameter

To set a default value for an input parameter in a method simply add = <default value> like in the next example:

```
void defaultParameterExample(boolean test=true)
```

In this example, the variable test will be defaulted to true if no parameter is given when calling the method. This also means that the parameter is optional. If the method is called with the parameter set to false it will be false when this method executes, but if it's not called with any parameters the test variable will automatically be set to true.

Args

The args class is used extensively throughout AX in order to create a pointer to a caller object for the executing method.

It is used in forms, queries, and reports as the first argument in the constructor. This means that for any forms, queries, and reports, you can get the args class that has been passed to the form, query, or report by using the args() method. Args is also very often used to pass additional information by using the following methods:

- record: Pass a record from a table
- parm: Pass a string value
- parmEnum together with parmEnumType: Pass an enum value
- parmObject: Pass an object of any type

This example demonstrates the effect of using args when calling the main method in a class from a method in another element.

`RentalInfoCaller` is the calling class that calls the main method of the
`RentalInfo` class:

```
public class RentalInfoCaller
{
}
// The main method here is just used
// to be able to execute the class
// directly and show the example.
public static void main(Args args)
{
    RentalInfoCaller          rentalInfoCaller;
    ;

    rentalInfoCaller = new RentalInfoCaller();
    rentalInfoCaller.callRentalInfo();
}
// This is the class that calls the
// main method if the RentalInfo class
void callRentalInfo()
{
    Args      args;
    ;
    args = new Args(this);
    RentalInfo::main(args);
}
// This method is just used as
// a proof that you are able
// to call methods in the calling
// object from the "destination" object
void callBackMethod()
{
    ;
    info ("This is the callBackMethod in an object of the
        RentalInfoCaller class");
}
```

AX has a built in reference to the current object called this as used
in the example above inside the new Args(this).

And this shows the main method of the `RentalInfo` class:

```
public static void main(Args args)
{
    RentalInfoCaller    rentalInfoCaller;
    ;

    rentalInfoCaller = args.caller();
    rentalInfoCaller.callBackMethod();
}
```

When executing the `RentalInfoCaller` class it will start in the main method, create a new object of the `RentalInfoCaller`, and then start the method `callRentalInfo`. The `callRentalInfo` method will then create a new `args` object and pass the `rentalInfoCaller` object executing in as a parameter. This can be done either by passing it as the first parameter in new or by calling the `args.caller()` method after the `args` object has been created. Then the main method of the `RentalInfo` class is called with the newly created `args` object as parameter.

When the main method in the `RentalInfo` class starts, it takes uses the `args.caller()` method to get a reference to the object that called `RentalInfo`. This enables it to call back to the caller object and execute its methods.

So, when executing the `RentalInfoCaller` class, the result will print the following in the info window:

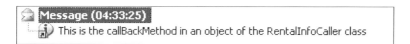

Inheritance

One of the central concepts of object-oriented programming is the possibility to inherit functionality defined at a higher level in the system. This can be done by having a class hierarchy where a method in a subclass overrides a method in the super class (higher level). The method in the subclass can still use the functionality in the same method in the super class by using the super function as in this example:

```
public void sellCar()
{
    ;
    super();
}
```

This method implies that the class that the method belongs to, extends another class where the functionality in the method `sellCar` is already written or that the `sellCar` method is defined at a higher level in the class hierarchy in which this class belong.

In our example, we have a super class called `Car` that extends Object, and then we have we have `Car_Economy`, `Car_Compact`, `Car_MidSize` and `Car_Luxury` who all extend the class Car. Also, they override the `toString` method for all of these classes as shown in the next example done for the `Car_Economy` class:

```
public str toString()
{
    str ret;
    ret = "Economy";
    return ret;
}
```

To make sure that all of the subclasses have the updated information about the super class it is a good idea to compile forward when modifying the class hierarchy. This is done by right-clicking on the super class and selecting **Add-Ins** and **Compile Forward**. To see which methods that your class can use from parent classes, simply right-click on the class in the **AOT** and select **Override Method**. You will then get a list of methods that you can override in this class by clicking on them in this list as shown in the next screenshot:

Construct

As you have seen earlier in this chapter, you can create an object of a class by using the reserved word `new`.

AX has taken the creation of objects to the next level and created a method called `construct`. It is a best practice that all objects should be able to be created from a construct method.

The construct method should consider any parameters sent to it, and based on those, create and then return the correct object. The reason I say "the correct object" here is that a super class should have a construct method that can create objects for all its subclasses and create the correct object based on the parameters sent to it.

Construct methods should always be static, public, and named "construct" like in the next example:

```
public static Car construct(CarGroup carGroup)
{
    Car        car;
    ;
    switch (carGroup)
    {
        case CarGroup::Economy :
            car = new Car_Economy();
            break;
        case CarGroup::Compact :
            car = new Car_Compact();
            break;
        case CarGroup::MidSize :
            car = new Car_MidSize();
            break;
        case CarGroup::Luxury :
            car = new Car_Luxury();
            break;
    }
    return car;
}
```

Main

Classes that should be able to start with the use of a menu item (a button in a form or an element in a menu) need a starting point.

In AX this is done by having a static method called `Main`. The main method always takes one parameter of the `Args` type. This is done to be able to tell where the main method was called from. An example could be that a class is called in a form and you need to know which record in the form the user had selected when pressing the button. This information can be passed on to the class in the `args` object.

The task of the main method is to create an instance of the class by calling the `construct` method (or in some cases where the `construct` method doesn't exist, calling the `new` method), prompting the user for information if needed (`prompt` method), and then calling the method that controls the flow of the class (typically the `run` method).

This is a typical example of a main method taken from the standard AX class `CustExchAdj`:

```
public static void main(Args args)
{
    CustExchAdj custExchAdj = new CustExchAdj();
    ;
    if (custExchAdj.prompt())
    {
        custExchAdj.run();
    }
}
```

RunBase framework

Whenever you write a class that typically asks a user for input and then starts a process based on that input you use the `RunBase` framework as most of the typical methods needed for such a Job is already implemented in the `RunBase` class.

This means that using the `RunBase` framework is done by extending `RunBase` either by directly extending `RunBase` or by extending a class that extends RunBase.

Some of the features implemented in the `RunBase` framework are the following:

- Run: The main flow of the operation
- Dialog: Prompting the user for input and storing that input
- Batch execution: Schedule the Job for later execution

- Query: Used to select data
- Progress bar: Shows the progress of a task
- Pack/unpack with versioning: Remember variable values until the next time the task is executed

 Take a look at the `tutorial_RunbaseForm` to see an example of how the `RunBaseBatch` class can be extended and how all of the above features are used.

Collection classes

In addition to the composite data types we looked at earlier in this chapter, there are also some classes that you can use to store multiple values and even objects in a given way.

These classes are called collection classes and were earlier known as **foundation classes**. They are system classes so you can't change them, but you can extend them to create your own collection classes.

These are the collection classes found in standard AX:

- Array
- List
- Map
- Set
- Struct

Array

I know that this is a bit confusing as there is a composite data type called array as well, but the collection class works a bit different as you will see in the next example. It can also store objects which the array data type can't.

```
static void Collection_Array(Args _args)
{
    // Create a new Array where the
    // elements are objects
    Array   cars = new Array(Types::Class);
    Car  car;
    int i;
    ;
    // Set new elements to the car Array
    // at the given index positions
```

```
        cars.value(1, new Car_Economy());
        cars.value(2, new Car_Luxury());
        cars.value(3, new Car_Compact());

        // Display the content of the Array
        info (cars.toString());

        // Loop through the Array to display
        // each element
        for (i=1; i<=cars.lastIndex(); i++)
        {
            car = cars.value(i);
            info(strfmt("Class: %1", car.toString()));
        }
    }
```

List

A list contains elements of one given type that are accessed sequentially. As you see from the next example you can store elements by using addStart or addEnd at any time, but when you loop through the list using a ListEnumerator they are accessed in the correct sequence.

```
    static void Collection_List(Args _args)
    {
        // Create a new list of type string
        List names = new List(Types::String);
        ListEnumerator  listE;
        ;
        // Add elements to the list
        names.addEnd("Lucas");
        names.addEnd("Jennifer");
        names.addStart("Peter");

        // Display the content of the list
        info (names.toString());

        // Get the enumerator of the list
        // to loop through it
        listE = names.getEnumerator();
        while (listE.moveNext())
        {
            info (strfmt("Name: %1", listE.current()));
        }
    }
```

Map

The map is used to index a value using a key value. Both the key and the value can be of any types specified in the `Types` enum.

```
static void Collection_Map(Args _args)
{
    // Create a new map with a key and value type
    Map cars = new Map(Types::Integer, Types::String);
    MapEnumerator     mapE;
    ;
    // Insert values to the map
    cars.insert (1, "Volvo");
    cars.insert (2, "BMW");
    cars.insert (3, "Chrysler");

    // Display the content of the map
    info (cars.toString());

    // Get the enumerator to loop
    // through the elements of the map
    mapE = cars.getEnumerator();
    while (mapE.moveNext())
    {
        info(strfmt("Car %1: %2", mapE.currentKey(),
            mapE.currentValue()));
    }
}
```

Set

A set can contain of one of the valid types in the `Types` enum. The values in the set are unique, and they are sorted automatically. As you can see, by executing the next example the values will be stored in the following order:"Ford", "Mazda", "Toyota".

```
static void Collection_Set(Args _args)
{
    // Create a new set of type String
    Set cars = new Set(Types::String);
    SetEnumerator     setE;
    ;
    // Add elements to the set
    cars.add("Toyota");
    cars.add("Ford");
    cars.add("Mazda");
    // Check to see if an element
```

```
        // exist in the set
        if (cars.in("Toyota"))
            info ("Toyota is part of the set");

        // Display the content of the set
        info (cars.toString());

        // Get the enumerator of the set
        // to loop through it
        setE = cars.getEnumerator();
        while (setE.moveNext())
        {
            info(setE.current());
        }
    }
```

Struct

A struct can be viewed upon as a class with no method, only attributes. It can store several values of different data types, but one struct can only hold one set of values.

```
    static void Collection_Struct(Args _args)
    {
        // Create a struct with two fields
        struct myCar = new struct ("int ModelYear; str Carbrand");
        int i;
        ;
        // Set values to the fields
        myCar.value("ModelYear", 2000);
        myCar.value("Carbrand", "BMW");

        // Add a new field and give it a value
        myCar.add("Model", "316");

        // Loop through the fields of the struct
        for (i=1; i<=myCar.fields(); i++)
        {
            info(strfmt("FieldType: %1, FieldName: %2, Value: %3",
                    myCar.fieldType(i),
                    myCar.fieldName(i),
                    myCar.value(myCar.fieldName(i))));
        }
    }
```

Macros

Macros are constants, or pieces of code, that are being taken care of by the compiler before the rest of the code to replace the code where the macro is used with the content of the macro. There are three different types of macros: stand alone macros, local macros, and macro libraries.

Macros are typically constant values that are only changed by developers. They are used so that developers don't have to hardcode these kind of values in the X++ code, but rather refer to the macro.

The macro libraries can be found in the AOT under `Macros`. Each of them can contain multiple macros that can be used throughout the rest of AX.

To use the macros from a macro library in AX, simply include them in the scope that you would like to use them. The next example shows how to use two different macros from the same macro library in a Job.

First we create a macro library that consists of two macros:

```
#define.Text('This is a test of macros')
#define.Number(200)
```

Then we use these macros from within a Job:

```
static void Datatypes_macro_library(Args _args)
{
// Referencing macro library has to be done in the class declaration
// or in the  declaration like in this example
    #MacroTest
    ;
    info(strfmt("Text: %1.  Number: %2", #Text, #Number));
}
```

This Job will print the following to the infolog:

A local macro is defined in the class declaration of a class or in the variable declaration of a method like in the next example:

```
static void Local_Macro(Args _args)
{
    // Define the local macro
    #localmacro.WelcomeMessage
    {
        info("Welcome to Carz Inc.");
        info("We have the best offers for rental cars");
    }
    #endmacro;
    // Use the local macro
    #WelcomeMessage
}
```

Standalone macros are the same as the macros used in macro libraries, except that they are defined in a method's variable declaration or in the class declaration of a class.

Summary

In this chapter you have learned about the basic building blocks of AX programming. You have read about the different data types you can use to store data and have also seen some of the functions you can use to manipulate the variables.

You have also seen how you can use conditional statements and loops to control the flow of the code and how to use operators to analyze, assign, and manipulate data.

In the section that explained how classes and methods work you gained knowledge on how to create an object of a class, how inheritance works in AX, the RunBase framework, and you also learned how static methods work.

At the end of the chapter you saw how the different types of macros can be used to replace X++ code.

In the next chapter we will look at how to create tables, fields, and relations so that we get a data model in the third normal form that can store the data in the AX database.

3
Storing Data

You should always try to store data and relate it to the other data in the best possible way as it will reduce the time spent on coding. It will also make sure that the solution you are building will be more stable and perform better.

This chapter will show you how to create tables where you can store data, how to create relations between tables, and how to enforce referential integrity by creating unique indexes and using delete actions.

You will learn more about the following topics in this chapter:

- Extended data types
- Tables
- Relations

Extended data types

In order to understand how data is stored in AX, you need to get an understanding of the extended data types.

As you have read in the previous chapter, there are certain primitive data types you can use when programming in AX. All of these primitive data types can be defined more specifically and with more information to help you when you program in AX. An example of how this is done is saying that you would like to use a real data type for a quantity field. If you don't use an extended data type for the quantity, you will have to set the label, help text, number of decimals, and other relevant information on all the tables where the field is used.

Imagine the effort you then would have to put down to change the information on all quantity fields in a system such as AX. Luckily, you don't have to do this, because AX uses extended data types, and there is, of course, already an extended data type for quantity called Qty. So if you would like to make a change in all quantities in AX, you simply edit the properties on the extended data type Qty.

Creating an extended data type

To create an **Extended Data Type** (EDT), open the AOT and expand the node **Data Dictionary | Extended Data Types**. Then, right-click on **Extended Data Types** and select **New**. You will then get this submenu:

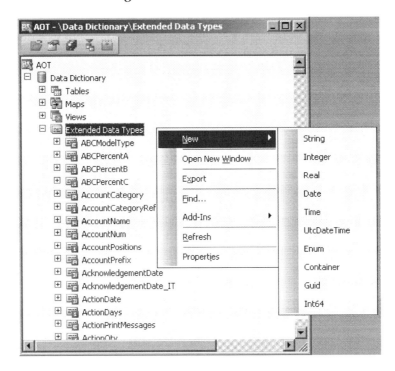

The following are the different data types you can use as a base for your extended data type:

Data type	Information
String	A string can contain all kinds of characters and the length is decided in the properties of the EDT.
Integer	An integer can contain integer values from -2,147,483,647 to 2,147,483,647.
Date	A date can hold a date value and the value will be stored in this format: 3/23/2009.
Time	A time value can hold the time of a day from 12:00:00 am to 11:59:59 pm. The value stored in the database is, however, as an integer specifying the seconds after midnight where the range spans from 0 to 86400.
UtcDateTime	Combines the date and time types into one data type. In addition, it also holds information regarding time zone. Value from 1900-01-01T00:00:00 to 2154-12-31T23:59:59.
Enum	Should always be linked to a Base Enum by the property Enum type.
Container	A list of values with different data types.
GUID	The **GUID** type is a **Globally Unique Identifier** that is a number which is 16 bytes. It is written in text as a sequence of hexadecimal digits like this: {5EFB37A3-FEB5-467A-BE2D-DCE2479F5211}.
	An example of its use in AX is the WebGUID field in the SysCompanyGUIDUsers table.
Int64	An Int64 is a 64 bit integer that can contain integer values from -9,223,372,036,854,775,808 to 9,223,372,036,854,775,808.

In the next example, we will use a string; so go ahead and select **String**. To open the property window, either press *Alt + Enter*, or right-click on it and select **Properties**.

The property window will then look something like the following screenshot:

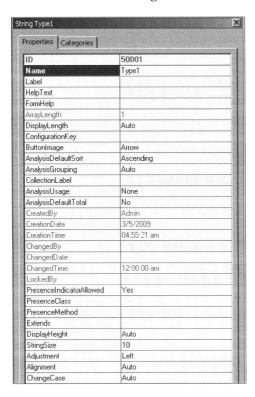

As you will see, some of the properties have a yellow background color. This means that it is best practice to have these properties filled out.

Also notice that if you change any of the properties that have a default value, the value entered will be bold. This is only done to make changes more visible. If you see properties with a red background color, they are mandatory.

You will also see a categorized list of properties in all property windows by clicking on the **Categories** tab. The categories will vary depending on what kind of element is active. The following image shows the categories for the extended data type we created above:

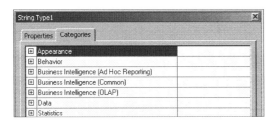

The first thing you would want to change is of course the name of the EDT. In our example we will call it **Car Id**. You should also give the EDT a label that users see throughout the solution. So open the label editor by clicking on the square icon to the right in the label field. Create a label with text **Car Id**. Do the same in the **FormHelp** and create a label with text **Unique identifier for a record in the CarTable**. The last thing you want to check now is the length of the field. By default, a string will be set to 10 characters, which is fine for our example.

There will of course be other times where you would want to check more properties as well and if you are creating an EDT of type integer. It obviously has a different set of properties than a string, but these are at least the basics.

Here is a list of some of the most used properties for all kinds of extended data types. I won't explain all the properties here, as that is beyond the scope of this book, so if there are properties you want to know more about that haven't been explained in this book, take a look at the developers help file.

Property	Information
ID	The ID is set by the AX core according to a number sequence for each of the object layers and cannot be changed by the developer.
Name	The name is the system name that you will use when writing code that references to this extended data type.
Label	The label is the name of the field that the users will see in forms and reports.
Help text	The help text is shown in the lower left corner of a window when the field is active in a form.
FormHelp	Can be used to specify a specialized lookup form when the user does a lookup action on this field.
DisplayLenght	Maximum number of characters shown in a form or report.
Extends	Used to inherit another extended data type.

Tables

The **Tables** node under the **Data Dictionary** in the **AOT** corresponds to tables in the database. When a table is created in the **AOT** it is automatically synchronized down to the SQL server. The synchronization process runs scripts in the background to make sure that the SQL table is created or updated to reflect the table in the **AOT**.

A table in AX should *always* be created from the AOT, never by running an SQL script or by creating a new table using the SQL Server Management Studio. AX also creates additional system fields in the tables and keeps references to the tables and its fields in system tables.

Creating a table

To create a new table, open the **AOT**, expand the **Data Dictionary** node and then the **Tables** node. Right-click on the **Tables** node and select **New Table** as shown in the following screenshot:

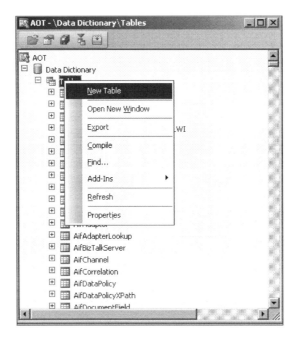

Now that a table has been created, the first thing you want to do is to give the table a descriptive name. Let's call our table **CarTable**.

 You can find information regarding the naming conventions in AX in the SDK here: http://msdn.microsoft.com/en-us/library/aa632638.aspx

To change the name of the table, right-click on the **Table** and select **Properties**. Then change the name property to **CarTable**.

You will now see a red line to the left-hand side of the name of the node in the AOT.

This red line next to **CarTable(usr)** indicates that a change has been made to the element, but the element has not yet been saved. Select the **CarTable** in the AOT and press *Ctrl + S* to save the element. Notice that the red line will be gone now.

Before we start adding fields, indexes, relations, and so on, let's have a look at the properties of our table.

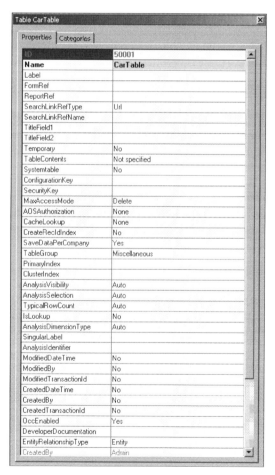

The important properties here are:

Property	Information
ID	The ID is set by the AX core according to a number sequence for each object layers and cannot be changed by the developer.
Name	The name is the system name that you will use when writing code that references to this extended data type.
Label	The label is the name of the table that the users will see in forms and reports.
FormRef	Link to a display menu item to be executed when a reference is done to the current table by the **Go to main table** functionality in AX. It is also used in reports that have a primary index field from the table in the report to link to the form.
ReportRef	Link to an output menu item to be executed when the **Main Table Report** is being created. Typically, when clicking on the print button in a form, the table referenced by the active data source will have a link to a report in the **ReportRef**. If not, the default report is created using the fields in the **autoreport** field group.
TitleField	**TitleField1** and **TitleField2** are used in the title bar in the main form to give some brief information regarding the selected record.
Temporary	If a table is temporary, it will never be synchronized to the database. The data inserted into a temporary table will only exist in memory in the tier and the programming scope in which it was inserted.
ConfigurationKey	The configuration key that the table is connected to. If the configuration key is switched off, the table and all its data will be removed from the database.
SecurityKey	The security key that the table uses to ensure correct user access setup.
TableGroup	Grouping of tables in AX is done by selecting one of the following table groups: **Miscellaneous**, **Parameter**, **Group**, **Main**, **Transaction**, **Worksheet Header**, and **Worksheet Line**
PrimaryIndex	When you have set up multiple indexes for a table you should specify which one is the primary one. This is done to optimize the data fetching done from this table.
ClusteredIndex	Specify which index to be clustered. Clustered indexes should always be set on tables that have the **TableGroup** property set to **Group** or **Main**.
Modified, Created By/Date Time/ TransId	To store information about who created the record, when it was created, who modified it last, and when it was modified last. There can also be a transaction ID attached for the create transaction and another one for the modified transaction.

If the content of a temporary table exceeds 128 KB, the data will be written to a file on disk. This will have significant impact on performance. This means that temporary tables should only be used with relatively small datasets.

There are other properties available, and you can find out more about them in the **Developer Help**. Here we've described only the most commonly used properties.

Adding fields to a table

A table without any fields doesn't do any good, so let's look at how we can add fields to our newly created table.

To add fields to a table you can open two AOT windows and drag an extended data type into the fields of a table. You can also add a new field by right-clicking on the **Fields** node in a table and select **New**. Under **New** you will get a submenu where you can select what kind of field you would like to create.

1. Create the **CarId** field

    In the following example, we will use the extended data type called **CarId** that we created in the previous section of this chapter.

    To add it to the table just drag-and-drop it onto the **Fields** node of the **CarTable**.

    Your result should look something like this:

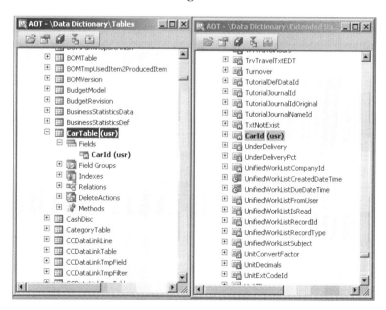

2. Create the **ModelYear** field

   The next thing we will do now is to create a new **Integer** field directly. Simply right-click on the **Fields** node under the **CarTable** and select **New | Integer**.

3. Set properties for the **ModelYear** field

   Then, right-click on the **New field** and select **Properties** (or press *Alt + Enter*). Change the name of the field to **ModelYear**. Also, set the property **Extended data type** to **Yr**, which is the standard AX data type for **Year**. The label and form help will now be inherited from the extended data type **Yr** so we don't have to fill out anything here (unless we are not satisfied with the standard label and form help).

4. Create the rest of the fields

   We will also add two other fields in the **CarTable** so that the table contains the following fields:

Field	Extended data type	Label	Key
CarId	CarId		PK, UIdx
ModelYear	Yr	Model Year	
CarBrand	Name	Brand	
Model	Name	Model	

PK means that it should be a **primary key** and **UIdx** means that the field is included in the **unique index**. You will learn how to create the primary key and unique index later in this chapter.

5. Create the **RentalTable** table

We will also create another table called **RentalTable** that will have the following fields.

Field	Extended data type	Label	Key
RentalId	RentalId		PK, UIdx
CustAccount	CustAccount		
CarId	CarId		
FromDate	FromDate	From date	
ToDate	ToDate	To date	

Adding fields to a field group

In all standard AX forms, fields are grouped into collections of fields that are related to each other, and it is best practice that all fields exist in at least one field group.

To add a field to a field group, simply drag the field from the **Fields** and drop it on the **Field Group** that you want to add the field to.

All tables in AX have two **Field Groups** called **AutoLookup** and **AutoReport**. The field group **AutoLookup** is used when the users want to select a value in a foreign key field. We will look more into this in the Chapter 4, *Data-User Interaction*.

The **AutoReport** field group is used to automatically create a report based on a standard report template in AX containing the fields in the **AutoReport** field group.

The report is generated when the users click on the print icon , or pressing *Ctrl + P* in a form where the table is used as the main data source.

In our example, we will add the following fields to these table groups:

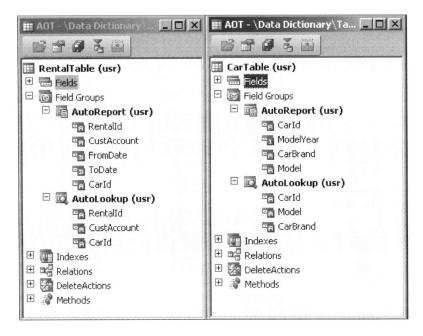

Creating an index

Indexes in AX are used to maintain uniqueness and to speed up the table search.

When a `select` statement in AX executes it is sent to the database query optimizer that analyzes the statement and decides which index will be the best to use for the statement before it is executed in the database and records are returned to AX.

 All tables in AX should have at least one unique index. This index should consist of the fields that make up the primary key of the table.

To find out which other index a table should have and which fields they should be made up of, you need to look at the `select` statements that use the table, and look at how they select data. Fields that are often used in ranges, in joining tables, or in grouping or sorting are candidates for indexing. You should, however, limit the number of indexes in a table as each index will have to be updated whenever a record is inserted, updated, or deleted from the table. This can become a performance bottleneck, especially for transactional tables.

You can create an index for a table by right-clicking on the **Index** node under the **Table** in the AOT and selecting **New Index**. A new index called **Index1** will then be created. Right-click on **Indexes** and select **Properties** (or *Alt + Enter*) and change the name of the index. The best practice for naming indexes is to use the name of the fields in the index postfixed with **Idx** unless the last field ends with ID. In that case, we just add an **x** at the end; so in the example, I have created an index called **CarIdx**.

The next thing to do is to add a field to the index. This is done by dragging the field from the **Fields** node in the table and dropping it onto the newly created index.

As the **CarId** is the primary key in the table it is also the obvious candidate for the unique index. To make the index unique simply set the property **AllowDuplicates** on the index to **No**.

The **CarTable** should now look like this:

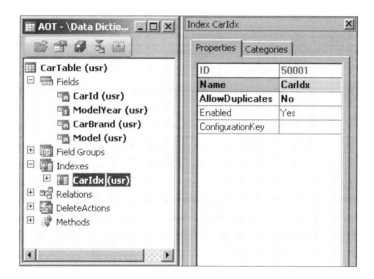

Now you can try to add a unique index on the **RentalTable** on your own. It should consist of the **RentalId** field only.

Creating a relation

One of the ways of creating a relation between two tables is to do this directly on the foreign key table.

You can see an example of how a table relation looks like by taking a look at the table **SalesTable** in the AOT and expanding the **Relations** node. Open the relation called **AddressCounty** and look at the fields used in the relation. The same fields are the fields that make up the primary key in the table that the relation points to. Look at the property called **Table** in the relation to see which table the relation points to (select the relation and press *Ctrl + Enter* to open the property window). Then find that table in the AOT and notice that the same fields make up the unique index in that table.

Each of the fields that make up the relation can be put into the relation as two different types. So far, we have only seen the type called **normal relations**. The other type is called **conditional relations**. These relations are used together with **normal relations** to add a condition on the related data. To better understand how this works, let me try to explain with an example.

Take a look at the table in AX called **InventTrans**. It consists of all transactions that can be done to an **Item** in AX. Now open its relations and look at the relation called **CustTable**. Its field's are as follows:

- One of the fields in the relation is the **CustVendAC**, which holds a reference to an ID in the table that it relates to, in this case the **AccountNum** in the **CustTable**.
- The other field is the **TransType**, which is a fixed enum value for each relation, in this case 0. The base enum used in this case is the **InventTransType** and its value 0 indicates the enumeration **Sales**. The **TransType** is the conditional relation and is also called a fixed field relation in this example. The opposite would be a related fixed field relation and in that case, the enum field would exist in the related table instead of in the table hosting the relation.

In this case, it means that all records in **InventTrans** where the **TransType** equals 0 can be related to a record in the **CustTable** through the **CustVendAC** field.

 It is best practice to only use table relations when the relation consists of more than one field. For relations that consist of only one field you should use relations on extended data types.

You can also create relations that are used for navigation purposes between forms. These kinds of relations are called **Navigational Relations**. These relations are used for tables where there are no constraints on integrity like we have between foreign and primary keys. The relation we saw in **InventTrans** is a navigational relation. It is used so that the user can select a record in the **CustTable** form, open the **InventTrans** form, and automatically have it only to select the transactions where the **CustVendAC** is equal to the **CustAccount** in the record that was selected in **CustTable** form. In other words, it will enable the users to filter the records in **InventTrans** based on where the **InventTrans** form was called from.

Creating a delete action

To enforce referential integrity, it is crucial to add a delete action for all tables that have a foreign key pointing to the current table.

This will make sure that we delete any references to any record being deleted so that we are not left with records that point to other records that no longer exist.

To illustrate this, let's say you have a table called **RentalTable** and another table called **CarTable**. A record in **RentalTable** will always have a link to one (and only one) record in **CarTable** and a record in **CarTable** can exist in many records in **RentalTable**.

This scenario is visualized in the simple data model shown below:

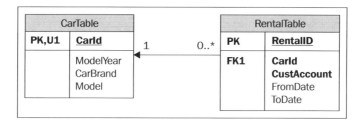

We then have a one-to-many relationship between the **RentalTable** and the **CarTable**. It is then important that if a record in the **CarTable** is about to be deleted either one of two actions take place—either all the records in **RentalTable** with a link to the record in **CarTable** are also deleted or the user is not allowed to delete the record in **CarTable** because it has referencing records in **RentalTable**.

Follow these steps to create a delete action in **CarTable**:

1. Open the **delete actions** tab under the **CarTable.**
2. Right-click and select **New | Delete Action.**
3. Open the **Properties** window (*Alt + Enter*).
4. Change the table that it should point to. In our case the **RentalTable.**
5. Decide which action should take place when a record in the **CarTable** is deleted according to the list below.

The options are:

Delete Action	Information
None	No action will take place on related records in the **RentalTable** when you delete a record in the **CarTable.**
Cascade	All records in **RentalTable** related to the record being deleted in **CarTable** will also be deleted.
Restricted	The user will get a warning saying that the record in the **CarTable** cannot be deleted because transactions exist in table **RentalTable**. The user will be unable to delete the record in **CarTable** if one or more related records exist in the **RentalTable.**
Cascade + Restricted	This option is used when deleting records through more than two levels. Let's say that another table existed that had a cascade delete action against **CarTable** and the **CarTable** had a **Cascade + Restriced** delete action against **Rental Table**. If the record in the top level table was about to be deleted it would also delete the related records in **CarTable**. In turn, all the records in **RentalTable** related to the records being deleted from **CarTable** would also be deleted. If only a record in **CarTable** was about to be deleted, the user would get the same message as when using the **Restricted** method.

Table browser

If you want to see all the data that exists for all fields in a table, you can open the table browser. In earlier versions of AX you would have to right-click on the table and select **AddIns | Table browser**, but in AX 2009 you can simply select the table

in the AOT and press *Ctrl + O*, or click on the **open** button .

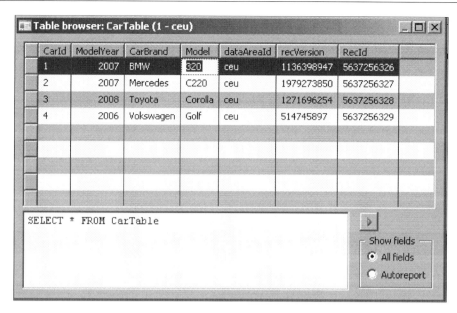

You will also notice that it lists some fields that you haven't added. These are system fields.

Field name	Information	Optional
dataAreaId	This field will store the company account the record was created in.	No
recVersion	The first time a record is created it will have record version = 1. Any changes done to the record will cause the **recVersion** to get a new random integer value. The field is used to make sure that two processes cannot overwrite the same record.	No
RecId	The **RecId** is a unique identifier set by the system for each table in AX. In older versions, the **RecId** was unique per company account but from version 4.0 it was changed to be unique per table.	No
Modified, Created By/Date Time/ **TransId**	As described in the *table properties* section, these system fields can be added to a table to see when a record was created or modified and who created or modified it. A transaction ID can also be added for both the creation and modification. Only the last change to the record will be stored by the modified fields.	Yes

Relations

There are two different ways of creating primary and foreign keys in AX. One of them is to create a relation on an extended data type. This can be done only if the primary key consists of only one field and it should always be used when the key consists of only one field.

The second option was already explained under the *Tables* section in this chapter.

To create a primary key that consists of one field, you have to create an extended data type that will be used for the field in the key. In our example, we will use the EDT created in the previous section.

Expand the extended data type node in the AOT, right-click on the **Relations** node, and select **New | Normal**.

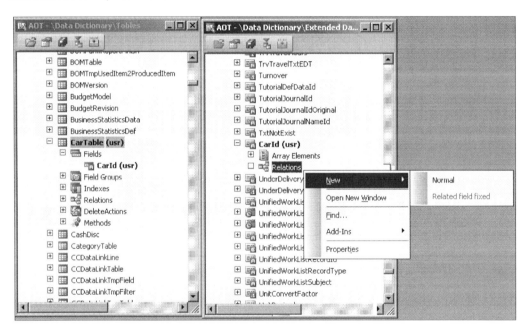

Open the **Properties** window and select the table that will host the field as a primary key and the field that represents the primary key as shown below:

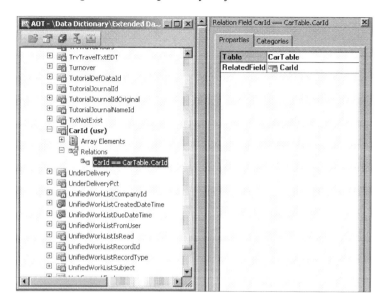

Now you can save the extended data type. You have now created a primary key as the field in the table that refers to an extended data type and the extended data type refers back to the field in the table. All other tables that have fields that use this extended data type will now have foreign keys pointing to this primary key. However, these foreign keys will not be shown in the **Table relations** list.

Summary

In this chapter, you have read about how tables are created in AX, how to set up an extended data type, and how to create fields in tables based on extended data types.

You have also read how to enforce referential integrity by adding delete actions, how to create indexes to ensure uniqueness of data, and how to create relations between tables to link related information.

You should now be ready to create data storage for your tables in AX and set them up according to best practices.

In the next chapter, you will learn how to create forms that enable users to see data from tables and enter and update data and navigation pages that are used to display data. You will also learn how to create reports in both X++ and by using the .NET and Reporting Services integration in AX. Finally, you will learn how to create menu items to be used as buttons in forms and as items in menus, and how to create new menus.

4
Data-User Interaction

Data is no good unless it can be entered by, and shown to, the user. In this chapter, you will learn how to create tools for user interaction by creating a form that has both one data source and two data sources related to each other, showing data from both data sources, and linking the report to the selected record in the form by using menu items. You will also be able to create a menu and a navigation page consisting of menu items that will open the form and the report.

The chapter will also show you how to create Reporting Services reports in Visual Studio using the new Reporting Service extensions.

We will look at the following topics in this chapter:

- Forms
- Reports
- Menu items
- Navigation pages
- Menus

Forms

A form in AX is used for basic user interactions, to display data to users, and retrieve data from users. Additionally, users can also start actions from a form. Starting an action from a form compared to starting the same action from a menu can be very different as the user can have a record active while inside a form. This can enable the user to open a new form or report with data related to the record selected. This is available through standard functionality in AX when the tables used in the two forms are related to each other. This functionality is achieved through the args class, which we previously discussed in Chapter 2, *X++ Language*, and through *Relations* as you read about in the previous chapter.

Main components of a form

A form has three subnodes:

- Methods: Enable the developer to write code that is relevant only to the current form
- Data sources: Link to tables and is used to fetch data from the database, thus making that data available to the form
- Designs: Specify the look and feel of the form

Methods

All forms in AX extend the system class `FormRun`. This means that they all have standard methods that they use when executing. These methods can be overridden in the **Methods** subnode. To override a standard method, right-click on the **Methods** subnode and select **Override**. You will then get a list of all the methods that can be overridden in the root of the form. Once you override them you can see that they all call a method called `super`. This is basically just a call to the method with the same name in the class that the form extends (`FormRun`).

 Executing a parent method by using the `super()` call can be done in any method that is overridden from an extended class. It is a standard feature in many object-oriented languages.

The most common methods to override in a form are listed in the following table. A complete list of form methods can be found in the SDK.

Method	Comment
init	Executed when a user opens the form. It creates the runtime object of the form, and is used to initialize variables and form controls that are used by other methods in the form.
run	Executed immediately after the `init` method. The super call in run opens the form and runs the data selection defined by the data sources in the form.
close	Executed by `closeOk` or `closeCancel`. Closes the form and, writes any data in the form that hasn't been updated yet if the `closeOk` flag is set.
closeCancel	Executed when the user presses the *Esc* key or a *Cancel* button. Makes sure that data is not updated when entering the `close` method.
closeOk	Executed when the user presses an OK button. This method will set the `closeOk` flag to true so that the `close` method will actually close the form.

These methods enable you to write code in forms to control its behavior. You are of course free to write any kind of code in the form methods, but you should bear in mind that all forms execute on the client. Writing code in forms that call methods on the server will generate client-server traffic that will cause decreased performance.

 It is best practice to write code in classes and tables because of the ability to reuse the code in other elements.

Data sources

The easiest way to display data from the AX database in a form is to add at least one data source to the form. The data source is actually a table variable that is used to fetch data from the database and hold the data in the table variable as long as the form is active or until an action in the form forces the data source to refresh the data from the database.

The following is a list of some of the properties you will change when adding a data source in a form. The complete list of properties can be found in the SDK:

Property	Comment
Name	The name of the data source should be the same as the table used by the data source.
Table	The name of the table used by the data source.
Index	Sets the index defined on the table to be used as the default sorting for the data source.
AllowEdit	If set to false, none of the fields from this data source will be editable in the form.
AllowCreate	If set to false, users are not allowed to create new records in the table used by this data source.
AllowDelete	If set to false, users are not allowed to delete records from the table used by this data source.
JoinSource	The join source is used to link two related tables to each other in the form. Can only be used if two or more data sources exist in the form. The join source should be set on the secondary data source.
LinkType	Maintains the link between the joined data sources. See the SDK for the different options.
DelayActive	If set to **Yes**, it will delay the execution of the active method so that scrolling down a grid will cause the active method to execute only for the final record selected.

Each data source also has some standard methods that you can override. The methods are defined by the system class named FormDataSource. Some of the methods most commonly overridden are listed below. A complete list of data source methods can be found in the SDK.

Method	Comment
init	Executed by `super()` in the forms `init` method. Creates the query specified by the properties on the data source. This is where you initialize any variables you want to use to override the default query.
executeQuery	Executed when the form opens, and every time the data is sorted, filtered, or refreshed. The method is used to fetch data from the table and make it available for the form. If you want to use a dynamic query in the form that changes the records fetched based on a user input, you should remove the call to `super()` in this method and write your own query.
create	Called when the user creates a new record by pressing *Ctrl + N* or pressing the **New** button in the menu.
active	Executed when the user selects a record in the form. It fetches data from the joined data sources (if any) when the user selects a new record.
write	Executed when a record is either inserted or updated from the form. It will call the `validateWrite` method to make sure that the insert or update is valid, before passing the command to the server to actually execute the insert/update operation in the database.
delete	Executed when a user deletes a record in the form. Passes the handle to the server, which in turn will delete the actual record from the database.
validateWrite	Executed by the `write` method to make sure that all data is valid (mandatory fields are filled out) and no keys are violated.
validateDelete	Executed by the `delete` method. Asks the user to confirm the deletion.
reread	Rereads the active record from the database.
refresh	Refreshes the view of all the records currently held in the data source.
research	Refreshes the complete query defined in the data source.

Designs

The following is a list of some of the properties of the **Design** node that you find under the **Designs** node. You can find the complete list of these properties in the SDK.

Property	Comment
Left/top	Defines the x and y coordinates where the form will open on the screen.
Width/Height	The width and height of the form. If you would like the users to be able to resize the form, set these parameters to column width and column height.
Caption	The name of the form that you want to present to the users. The caption is shown in the top line of the form.
TitleDatasource	The TitleField1 and TitleField2 of the selected table in this property will be displayed to the left of the caption.
WindowType	Should be set to standard except for lookup forms where this property should be set to popup.

Each of the visual components that you can use within a form also has a set of properties and methods, so you have a lot of options as a developer. Most of the time, you won't have to change any of these properties, at least as long as you have done a good job defining the elements in the data dictionary.

Creating a form with one data source

We will now create a form that allows the users to create, read, update, and delete data from the **CarTable** that we created in the previous chapter.

Creating the form

Open the AOT and expand the **Forms** node.

Right–click on the **Forms** node and select **New Form**. A new form will be created called **Form1**. Change the name of the form to **CarTable,** so the name of the form will be the same as the table it will represent.

 It is best practice to name the form the same as the data source if it represents a main form for the table used.

Adding the data source

The next thing to do is add the data source. This can be done either by dragging and dropping the table `CarTable` to the **Data Dictionary** node in the form, or by right–clicking on the **Data Sources** node and selecting **New Data Source**. If you choose the latter, you will have to change the `Table` property of the **Data Source** to **CarTable**. The name of the **Data Source** will automatically be the same as the table it is representing, and it is also best practice to keep it that way as long as you don't have multiple data sources using the same table.

Creating a form design

Forms in AX that consist of one data source where the table used as data source is not a parameter table, is mainly built using the following schema:

Design | Tab | TabPage | Grid | Fields

If the form has any buttons that open other related or unrelated forms, reports, or start classes, these buttons should be put into a button group so that the schema is extended with the following:

Design | ButtonGroup | Buttons

In our example I have created a form that looks like this:

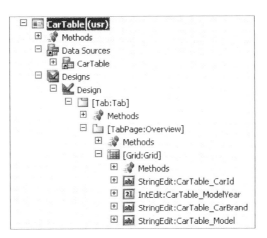

The parameters that I have changed are:

TabPage:Overview

Name=Overview

Caption=Overview (Use the label find tool to find a label with this text.)

Grid:Grid

DataSource=CarTable

To add the fields, I simply dragged them from the **Fields** node under the **Data Sources CarTable** and dropped them onto the **Grid**.

Once this is done, you can take a look at the form in design mode by double-clicking on the **Design** node.

You will then see the form in design mode and also have a toolbar available that you can use to add other fields or graphical components. It should look something like the next screenshot of the `CarTable` form:

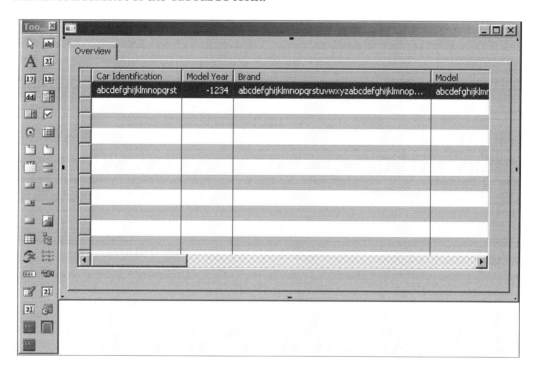

To get a full list of all the different graphical components that you can add to a form, check out the SDK.

Take a look at the tutorial forms located under the **Forms** node in the AOT. Search for forms starting with `tutorial_Form`. These forms will show you how to set up forms for all kinds of form controls.

To test the form and see if it holds any data simply select the form in the AOT and press *Ctrl + O*, or press the **Open** button in the toolbar.

The form should then look something like the next screenshot:

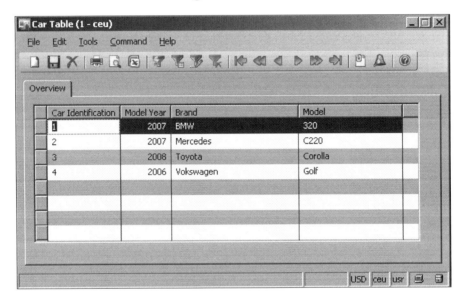

Notice that you can now also see the standard toolbar at the top of the form. This is standard functionality, so you don't have to worry about it unless you want to remove it.

In that case, you can change the property **HideToolbar** on the design node from **No** to **Yes**.

You should also create a similar form for the RentalTable that we will use later in this book.

Creating a form with two data sources

The next thing we would like to do now is to create one form with two data sources. The basics are the same as if we were to use one data source, but under the **Data Source** node we obviously add two data sources instead of one. In our example, and in most cases in AX, these two data sources are linked together through a relation either in the extended data type or in the table.

Either way, you will need to change the **JoinSource** property in the data source that is the "many" node in the one-to-many relationship.

Take a look at `tutorial_Form_Join` to see examples of how to use the **JoinSource** property.

In our example, we will use the **CarTable** as the main data source and have the **RentalTable** joined to **CarTable** as the **RentalTable** is the "many" node in this relationship. It should look like the next screenshot, when the data sources are joined together in the form.

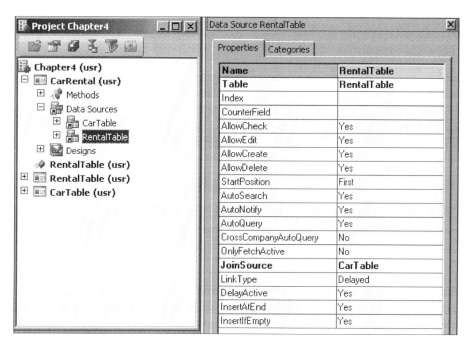

We will now take a look at the design of this form.

Separating the design using a FormSplitter

As the purpose of this form is to show data from both tables we will divide the form into two parts in same way that the **SalesTable**, **PurchTable**, and a lot of other standard AX forms are built when showing a parent-child relationship.

This means that under the **Design** node we will add a group node for the car information and another group node for the rental information. In addition, we will add a group that will work as a form splitter. The purpose of the form splitter is to enable the users to resize the different parts of the form.

To make the form splitter work we need to add some code in the form. First of all, we will add a variable in the classDeclaration:

```
public class FormRun extends ObjectRun
{
    SysFormSplitter_Y _formSplitterVertical;
}
```

We also have to initialize this variable to point to the `formSplitter` in the form and link it to the first group in the design. This means that when you move the form splitter, the first group in the design will resize accordingly. We do this in the `init` method:

```
public void init()
{
    super();
    _formSplitterVertical    = new
        SysFormSplitter_Y(ctrlSplitVertical, CarGroup, this);
}
```

Note that the variables `ctrlSplitVertical` and `CarGroup` will give a compilation error here because they don't exist. To make it work, we will change the property `AutoDeclaration` on both the splitter group itself and on the first group (the group that holds the Car information. I have called this group `CarGroup` in my example) in the design node to **Yes**.

We also have to override three methods under the `ctrlSplitVertical` group in the design:

```
int mouseUp(int x, int y, int button, boolean ctrl, boolean shift)
{
    int ret;
    ret = super(x, y, button, ctrl, shift);
    return _formSplitterVertical.mouseUp(x, y, button, ctrl, shift);
}
int mouseMove(int x, int y, int button, boolean ctrl, boolean shift)
{
    int ret;
    ret = super(x, y, button, ctrl, shift);
    return _formSplitterVertical.mouseMove(x,y,button,ctrl,shift);
}
int mouseDown(int x, int y, int button, boolean ctrl, boolean shift)
{
    int ret;
    ret = super(x, y, button, ctrl, shift);
    return _formSplitterVertical.mouseDown(x, y, button, ctrl,
        shift);
}
```

This is done to make sure that the variable we declared in the classDeclaration and initialized in the `init` method is changed when the user moves the form splitter in the form up or down. To understand why we have to do this, simply remove all the code in the form and see what happens when you open the form and try to drag the form splitter up or down.

In addition to creating a form splitter, we will also change the width and length on the groups, tabs, tab pages, and grids in the form to 'Column Width' and 'Column Height' (except from the form splitter which will be set to a fixed height).

Another important thing to remember is to change the **Data Source** property on the grid that will hold the records from the `RentalTable` from `CarTable` (which is the default as it is the first data source in the form) to `RentalTable`.

You then add fields to the grid the same way you did in the first form by dragging the fields from the **Data Source** and dropping them under the **Grid**.

The form should now look something like the next screenshot of the AOT:

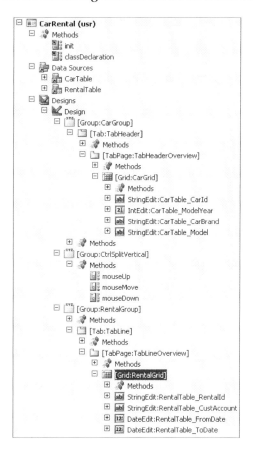

When you open the form, it should look like the next screenshot:

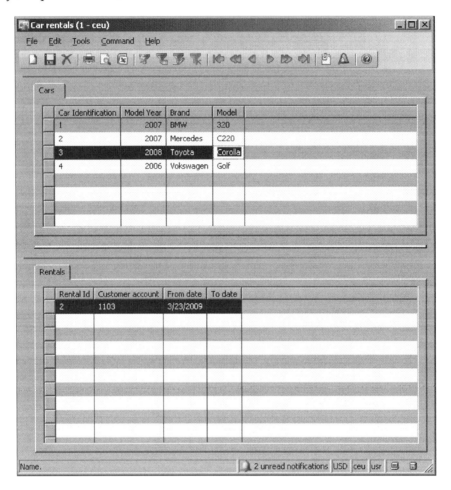

The rental part of the form will now only show records related to the record selected in the car part of the form. The **CarId** field in the **RentalTable** was not added to the grid as the information is obsolete (the **Car Identification** already shows in the **Cars** part of the form).

Display and edit methods

You would sometimes like to present data from two different data sources in one grid in a form. Let's say you have a form that only shows the records in the rental table. The grid in the form will look similar to the next screenshot:

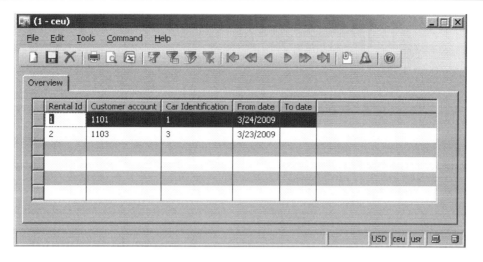

The end users may say that the field **Car Identification** doesn't tell them anything, and they would like to be able to see the **Brand** and **Model** from the **CarTable** in the grid as well.

This is not a problem as one record in the **RentalTable** will always point to only one record in the **CarTable**.

What you need to do then is to create two display methods on the table **RentalTable**.

Display and edit methods should preferably be written on tables and not in data sources or elsewhere in forms or reports, although this is possible.

The methods should be written as follows:

```
display Name brand()
{
    Name        ret;
    ;
    ret = CarTable::find(this.CarId).CarBrand;
    return ret;
}

display Name model()
{
    Name        ret;
    ;
    ret = CarTable::find(this.CarId).Model;
    return ret;
}
```

The display modifier in the beginning of the method will make the fields read-only in forms, and will enable you to drag-and-drop the method from the table to the grid in the form. So the next thing to do is to drag these methods from the **RentalTable** and drop them under the grid in the **RentalTable** form. They will then become fields in the grid. You will also have to set the data source property on these fields to **RentalTable** as they are defaulted empty.

The form will now look like this:

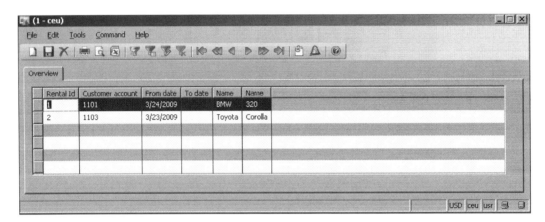

We can now see that we have done something foolish while designing the **CarTable**. The fields **Brand** and **Model** were set to use the extended data type called **Name**. Although the correct label has been set in the table itself, they will not show when you fetch the fields using display and edit methods. To fix this, you could create new extended data types for **Brand** and **Model**, set the correct label on the extended data types, and change the **Extended Data Type** properties on these two fields in the **CarTable**. You would then also have to change the variable type in the display methods (and any other methods) where the fields are used. This would be the correct way of dealing with the problem, but it is also the most time consuming. For a quick-fix you could change the **Label** property on the fields in the form, but that would not help if you had to use the display methods in other forms or reports.

Edit methods

Edit methods are basically the same as display methods, except that users can also write data to the fields. Instead of using the `display` modifier in the method header you use the `edit` modifier. In addition, the first input variable should be of type Boolean and called `set`. This variable will be set to true if the user changes the value in the field in the form. The second input parameter should hold the value that the user types in the field in the form.

To give an example of an edit method, we will create a new field in the **CarTable** to hold the mileage of the car and have an edit method in **RentalTable** that enables the users to be in the **RentalTable** form and still edit the field in **CarTable**.

We'll create an extended data type of type integer for the new field and call it `Mileage`. Then we'll add the field to the **CarTable**.

The edit method in **RentalTable** will then look like this:

```
edit Mileage mileage(boolean set, Mileage value)
{
    CarTable          carTable;
    Mileage           ret;
    ;
    carTable = CarTable::find(this.CarId, set);
    if (set)
    {
        ttsbegin;
        carTable.Mileage = value;
        carTable.update();
        ttscommit;
    }
    else
    {
        ret = carTable.Mileage;
    }
    return ret;
}
```

The first thing we do in this method is that we find the record in **CarTable** by using the **carId** in the record that is selected in the form. If the field is edited, the set parameter is true; we can use that parameter to decide if the record we select from **CarTable** should be selected for update or not.

If the set variable is true we then tell the server to lock the record so that only this process can update the record by using the `ttsbegin` statement. You will learn more about manipulating data later in the book, so I won't go into details here, but the `Mileage` field in **CarTable** is set to be equal to the value that the user entered in the **RentalTable**. The `ttscommit` will make sure that the record is written to the database, and will also unlock the record so that it can be updated by other processes.

If the set variable is false we simply return the mileage value from the selected **CarTable** record.

Considerations

There are a couple of things to consider when using display and edit methods:

- When a display or edit method from one table returns data from another table, then it is best practice to manually activate record level security in this method.
- In a grid within a form users generally click on the field's title to sort the form. If a field is bound to display or edit method, then sorting will not work.
- Using display or edit methods in a grid has performance implications. Caching display methods will however help in optimizing performance.

Caching display methods

In order to speed up the performance of display methods, we can add it to the cache. Data retrieved by the display method is then put into the cache and fetched from the cache in consequent requests until the `reread` method on the data source is called.

Follow these steps to add the display method brand to the cache in the **RentalTable** form:

1. Find the **RentalTable** form in the AOT.
2. Right–click on the **RentalTable Data Source** and select **Override method | init.**
3. Add the following code after `super()` in the **init** method:

   ```
   RentalTable_ds.cacheAddMethod("brand");
   ```

The `cacheAddMethod` also has a second parameter that is automatically set to true. If it's set to false, the value of the display method will not be refreshed when a record is written to the database.

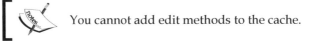 You cannot add edit methods to the cache.

Creating a lookup form

In Chapter 3, *Storing Data*, you learned that there are two standard table groups in all tables in AX. One of these table groups is the **AutoLookup**. This table group is used to create a lookup form when users press the lookup button in a form.

However, you may sometimes need a lookup that has extended functionality. Maybe it only shows a limited set of records from the table based on some logic, or maybe, in some cases, you have to present additional fields in the lookup form.

In these cases, you will have to create a customized lookup form. This can be achieved in two different ways.

Adding a new form in the AOT

To create a lookup form by adding a new form in the AOT, simply create a form the way you would like to have your lookup form look like and then set the **WindowType** property to **Popup** on the **Design** node. Before super() in the run method (or after super() in the init method) of the form; you use the selectMode() method to set the field that should return a value to the form that opened the lookup form.

In the form where you want to use this new specialized lookup you will have to change the lookup method on the lookup field in the **Data Source**.

We will create a lookup form like this for the **CarTable** so that the lookup can sort by the mileage when the user is in the **RentalTable** form.

First, we create the new form in the AOT and call it **CarIdLookup**. We add the **CarTable** in the data sources and add a piece of code in the init method of the data source to make sure that the form will sort by mileage.

```
public void init()
{
    super();
    this.query().dataSourceTable(tablenum(CarTable)).
    addSortField(fieldnum(CarTable, Mileage), SortOrder::Ascending);
}
```

This method basically uses the standard method addSortField() on the data source table in the current query to set the Mileage as the sort field, and tells it to sort in an ascending order.

The next thing we do is create a grid under the design node of the form, and add the fields we would like to display in the lookup form to the grid.

The last thing we have to do with the form is to tell the form to return the CarId to it's calling form. To do this you first have to set the property **AutoDeclaration** to **True** on the **CarTable_CarId** field in the **Grid**. Then you have to add the selectMode() call in the run or init method or the form:

```
public void init()
{
    super();
    this.selectMode(CarTable_CarId);
}
```

Now we have to change the **RentalTable** form and add this code to the lookup method on the field **CarId** in the **RentalTable** data source:

```
public void lookup(FormControl _formControl, str _filterStr)
{
    Args      args;
    FormRun formRun;
    ;
    args = new Args(formstr(CarIdLookup));
    formRun = classfactory.formRunClass(args);
    formRun.init();
    this.performFormLookup(formRun, _formControl);
}
```

This code creates a new `FormRun` class and uses the `Args` class to point to the new lookup form we just created. It then calls the forms `init` method, and finally calls a method on the field called **performFormLookup** with the `FormRun` object as parameter. It will then open the **CarIdLookup** form and wait for the user to select a record in the lookup form and return the value set in the field set by `selectMode` as described previously.

Creating a lookup in the lookup method

You can also have a lookup form being created by only writing code in the lookup method. Let's have a look at how we could have done the previous example using this method.

```
public void lookup(FormControl _formControl, str _filterStr)
{
    SysTableLookup   sysTableLookup;
    Query                    query = new Query();
    QueryBuildDataSource    queryBuildDataSource;
    ;
    //Create an instance of SysTableLookup with the form control
    //passed in
    sysTableLookup =
    SysTableLookup::newParameters(tablenum(CarTable), _formControl);
    //Add the fields to be shown in the lookup form
    sysTableLookup.addLookupfield(fieldnum(CarTable, CarId));
    sysTableLookup.addLookupfield(fieldnum(CarTable, CarBrand));
    sysTableLookup.addLookupfield(fieldnum(CarTable, Model));
    sysTableLookup.addLookupfield(fieldnum(CarTable, Mileage));
    //create the query datasource
    queryBuildDataSource = query.addDataSource(tablenum(CarTable));
    // Clear any existing sort fields and add the new sort field
    queryBuildDataSource.sortClear();
    queryBuildDataSource.addSortField(fieldnum(CarTable, Mileage),
```

```
            SortOrder::Ascending);
      //add the query to the lookup form
      sysTableLookup.parmQuery(query);
      // Do the lookup
      sysTableLookup.performFormLookup();
  }
```

I have noticed that in some versions of AX there is a bug that will make the sorting fail in this example, because the first field set using the addLookupfield will always have sort priority one. You would then have to put the Mileage field first instead to make the sorting work.

Reports

Reports in AX are used to display data to users in a format which is suitable for the way that the information is read.

If a report is to be printed on paper and sent to customers it should have a neat layout and maybe also have your company logo at the top of the report. These kinds of reports are still a lot easier to create in the AOT using MorphX.

If the report is to be used internally and only on the intranet it would probably be a good idea to create the report in Reporting Services as Reporting Services reports are more flexible, and can use diagrams, pivot and key performance indicators, as well as standard two-dimensional report layouts. It is also very easy to use data from cubes instead of directly from the AX database using Reporting Services.

Dynamics AX 2009 is integrated with Reporting Services in such a way that developers can write code in Visual Studio that can access business logic within AX.

AX reports

AX reports are the reports that are generated in AX using MorphX. They exist in the AOT under the **Reports** node and can be created either from scratch in the AOT or from the report wizard. This book will not show you how to use the report wizard as it should be intuitive enough for developers to understand.

When writing a report in AX you should always consider the strategy of how to make sure that the report should:

- Show the data needed for the report
- Interact with the users
- Perform well, even with a large amount of data

For reports that print data with a lot fields that are calculated when the report runs it can be an advantage to create a temporary table that holds all the fields the report will display. You can have a class that populates this temporary table before executing the report with the temporary table as the only data source. Look at the report **InventBalanceAccount** and the class **InventReport_Balance** to see an example on how to achieve this. Note that this line in the `fetch` method of the report has to be executed to be able to transfer the data in the temporary table from the scope of the class to the scope of the report:

```
queryRun.setRecord(inventReport_Balance.tmpInventBalance());
```

Main components of a report

All the AX reports have three subnodes and they are the same as for forms. Although they are similarly built, there are several important differences as you can see below.

Methods

The methods in the report are used to control the look and feel of the report.

Some of the most important methods in reports are listed below:

Method	Comment
Init	Executed when a user start the report. It creates the runtime object of the report, and is used to initialize variables and report controls that are used by other methods in the report.
Run	Executed immediately after the `init` method. The `super()` in run calls `prompt()`, generates the design, calls `fetch()`, and calls `print()`.
Fetch	Creates an object of the query defined in the data sources, presents the query prompt to the user and fetches the records from the database.
Send	Called by the `super()` in fetch for each record that is fetched. Sends this record to the body section in the report that uses the same table as the fetched record.
dialog	Override this method to add options that displays when the user executes the report.
Prompt	Prompts the user for printer options such as where to print the report (mail, printer, screen, and so on).
Print	This method is called to print the report to the selected print medium as selected in the `Prompt` method.

Data sources

Data sources in reports are built differently than data sources in forms. As mentioned earlier in this chapter, using multiple data sources in a form places all the data sources as a list right under the **Data Sources** node. In reports, a **Data Source** also has a subnode called **Data Sources**, where joined data sources can be placed.

This is because the **Data Sources** node in a report consists of a query and queries are built in a tree style to visualize the joins better. In Chapter 5, *Search For Data*, we will learn more about queries.

Designs

A report can have multiple designs so that the code can decide at runtime which design to use. The designs can be totally different, but they would share the same data sources and form methods.

In addition, each of these designs can have two different kinds of specifications. Examples of the report dialog that opens when executing the report is shown for each of the specifications:

- AutoDesignSpecs: Automatically generated and based on the query in the data sources of the report. Limits the possibilities for the developer.

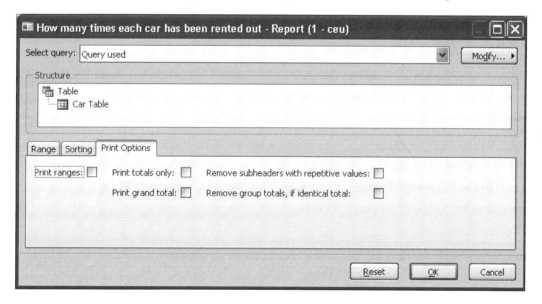

- Generated Design: The developer is in full control of the design, but the print options tab page and its options are removed when executing the report.

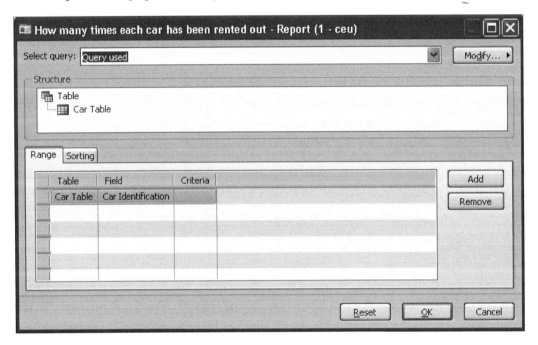

Creating an AX report using MorphX

Let's now create a report that will show the cars and how many times they have been rented out.

Creating the report

1. Start-off by right-clicking on the **Reports** node in the AOT and selecting **New Report**.

2. Change the name of the report to **CarsTimesRented**.

3. Open the **Data Sources** node and the **Query** node under it. Drag the **CarTable** from a new AOT window and drop it into the **Data Sources** node under the **Query** node.

It should then look similar to the next screenshot:

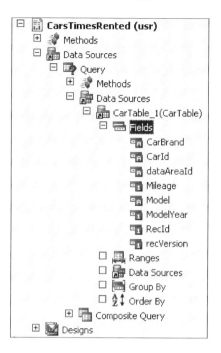

All fields in the **CarTable** are now available to the design of the report. If you would like to add a range or sorting you can do that under the **CarTable_1(CarTable)**. Also, if you would add another data source joined to this one, you would add that in the **Data Sources** under **CarTable_1(CarTable)**. In the related data source you should then switch the property **Relations** to **Yes** so that the relations between the tables always are kept up to date for this report.

In our example, we'll only use one data source so the next step now is to take a look at the design of the report.

Creating the design of the report

These are the steps needed to create the design of the report:

1. Right-click on the **Designs** node and select **New Report Design**. A new report design called **ReportDesign1** is then created.

2. Select the **ReportDesign1**, open the property window, and set the caption that would like to be shown in the report header.

3. Select a **ReportTemplate**. We'll use the **InternalList** in our example. This report template will provide header info that consists of the company name, report caption, time and date when the report was printed, and the page number.

4. Expand the **ReportDesign1**, right-click on **AutoDesignSpecs**, and select **Generate Specs From Query**. All the necessary body nodes will now be created under the **AutoDesignSpecs**. As we only use one data source in our example, we also only get one body section in the report.

5. You can now drag the fields from the **CarTable_1(CarTable)** data source and drop them under the **Body:CarTable_Body**.

The only field missing now is the field that tells how many times a car has been rented. To create this, we simply make a display method on the **CarTable** called `timesRented` that counts how many records exist for the current **carId** in the **RentalTable**.

```
display int timesRented()
{
    int         ret;
    RentalTable         rentalTable;
    ;
    select count(recId) from rentalTable
        where rentalTable.CarId == this.CarId;

    ret = rentalTable.RecId;

    return ret;
}
```

You will learn more on how these `select` statements work in the next chapter so we won't dwell more on that now.

You can now simply drag this method from the **CarTable** in the AOT and drop it under the body section in the report. Remember to add a label to the field as well.

The report in the AOT should now look like the next screenshot:

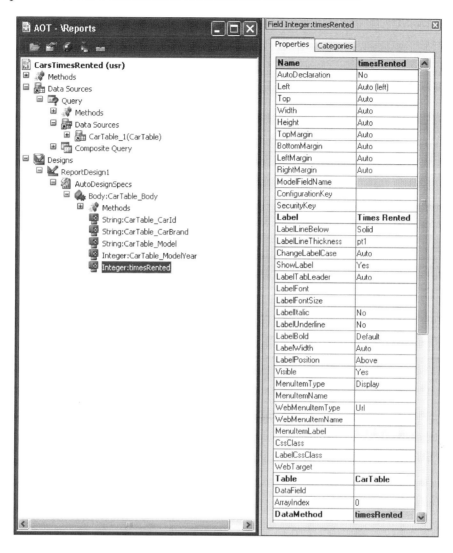

If you run the report now and print it to screen, it should look something like the next screenshot:

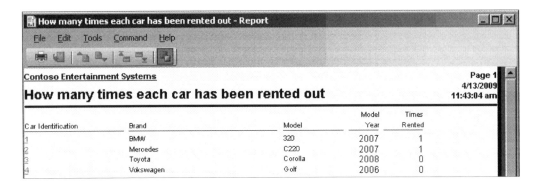

Reporting services

Microsoft SQL Server Reporting Services (SSRS) is a report generation software that is a part of Microsoft SQL Server. It enables users to execute reports using a web interface or even as embedded reports in applications by using a web services interface.

Developers typically use Microsoft Visual Studio with the **Business Intelligence Projects** plugin installed to develop reports for reporting services. Very basic reports (reports created by end users) can also be created using the Report Builder tool that is included.

The reporting services reports are stored as XML files following a standard called **Report Definition Language (RDL)**. When executed, they can be transformed into Excel, PDF, XML, and even as images such as TIFF.

Dynamics AX comes with extensions for Reporting Services and Visual Studio reporting tools for AX that integrates Dynamics AX with Reporting Services and Visual Studio. This enables developers to create Reporting Services reports in Visual Studio that display data from Dynamics AX. The developers can also call business logic inside AX from the reporting project in Visual Studio.

Creating an AX report using Visual Studio

We will now go through the steps needed to create a simple Reporting Services report in Visual Studio that displays AX data:

1. Open Visual Studio and select **New | Project**.
2. In the **Project Types** window, select the **Visual C#** (or Visual Basic under **Other Languages** if you prefer to write the code in Visual Basic).

3. Then select the Dynamics type and the **Dynamics AX Reporting Project** from the **Visual Studio installed templates**.

4. Name the project **CarRentalReports**.

5. Click on **OK** to create the project.

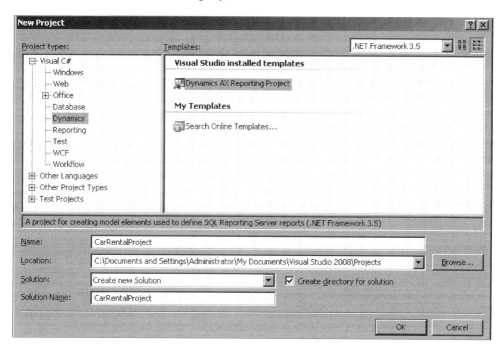

6. When the project opens a new report named **Report1** (the filename is named Report1.moxl) has been created. We will rename this report and call it **CarList** instead. This is done by right-clicking on the report and selecting properties and changing the **Name** property to **CarList**.

7. Also set the **Title** of the report to **Car List**.

8. The next step is to create a dataset to use in the report. A dataset can have either one of two different data source types in the report. The data source can be a query defined in the AOT in AX, or business logic, which is data returned from a method written in the current report project.

9. We will only use a query called CarList in our example, defined later in Chapter 5, *Search for Data*. Jump to the next chapter if you would like to see how it's created.

10. Right-click on **Datasets** in the report and select **Add Dataset**. Name the dataset **Cars** and open its properties. Go to the **Query** property and click on the lookup button to the right in the field.

11. In the window that opens, select the query called **CarList** (if you have jumped to the next chapter and created the query in AX). Then click on **Ok** to go back to the report again. Notice that the **Query** property now has the value: SELECT * FROM CarList. This means that this dataset will select all records that the CarList query returns.

12. If you now expand the **Cars** dataset you will see all the fields from the query that you now can use in the report.

13. The Visual Studio window should now look like this:

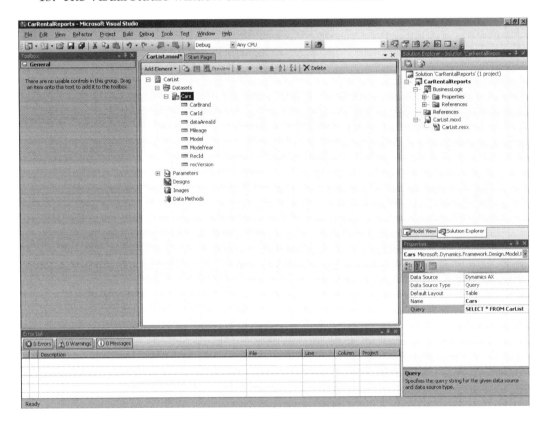

14. We will also create a parameter for our report where the user can enter a maximum mileage. We will use this parameter as a filter in the design of the report later, so that the report will only show cars with less mileage than selected in this parameter.

15. Right-click on the **Parameters** node and select **Add parameter** to add the parameter. Rename it to **MaximumMileage**. Also, change the data type of the property from System.String to System.Int32 as this is the data type of the mileage field that we will compare it to later.

16. Now add a **Auto Design** to the report by right-clicking on **Designs** and selecting **New | Auto Design**. An Auto Design named **AutoDesign1** will be created. Right-click on **AutoDesign1** and select **Add | Table**.

17. To add fields from the **Datasets** to the table in the design drag them and drop them onto the **Data** node in the table like this:

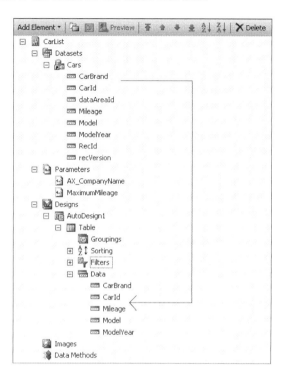

18. You can now have the report sort by mileage by dragging the **Mileage** field from the **Data** node in the table and dropping it on the **Sorting** node.

19. Do the same to add the filter. Also, to make the filter work against the parameter you just created; you have to modify its parameters, as shown in the next screenshot:

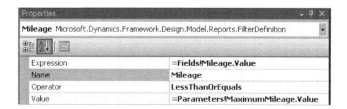

20. You can now preview the report by right-clicking on the **AutoDesign1** node and selecting **Preview**. Enter a value in the **MaximumMileage** parameter and select the **Report** tab page to view the report.

21. It should now look like this:

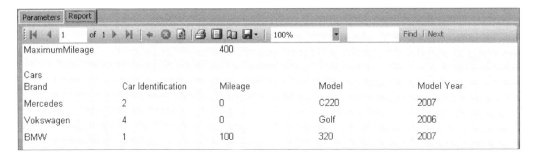

22. If you want to change the layout of the report to have bold labels, other fonts, and so on, you would have to create a precision design instead of an auto design.

23. Now that your report project is ready to be used in AX you should send it to the AOT. This is done by right-clicking on the **CarRentalReports** project in the solution explorer in Visual Studio and selecting **Save to AOT**.

24. To be able to run the report from AX though, it must be deployed to the Reporting Services server. Again you have to right-click on the **CarRentalReports** project in the solution explorer and select **Deploy**.

The report will then be compiled and sent to the Report Services server, and can now be executed from AX by adding a menu item that points to it, as shown in the next section.

Menu items

Menu items are basically classes that are used to start forms, reports, and classes. They can be used as visual components in forms, as buttons, or in menus as links.

There are three types of menu items:

- Display: Used to start forms
- Output: Used to start reports
- Action: Used to start classes that have a main method

Creating a menu item

The easiest way of creating a menu item is to drag a form into the **Display** node, report into the **Output** node, or a class into the **Actions** node under menu items in the AOT.

After the drag-and-drop operation you have to add a label to the menu item.

You can also create output menu items that point to **SQL Reporting Library** reports. You will then have to create an output menu item by right-clicking on the **Output** node under menu items and selecting **New Menu Item**. The next thing to do is to change the **Object Type** property to **SQLReportLibraryReport** and select the report from the drop-down list in the object property. It is best practice to postfix the SQL report menu items with a *.

Add an output menu item for the report you created in Visual Studio by right-clicking on the **Output** node under menu items. in the AOT and selecting **New | Menu Item**. Change the name of the menu item to **CarList** and label to **Car List ***. Then set the object type to **SQLReportLibraryReport** and the object to **CarRentalReports.CarList. AutoDesign1 (<ReportLibrary>.<ReportName>.<DesignName>)**.

Now create menu items for the **CarTable**, **RentalTable** and **CarRentals** forms, and the **CarsTimesRented** report by dragging them onto the **Display** and **Output** nodes under **MenuItems** in the AOT. Set the label for all of them.

Now that you have created menu items for these objects you should also go back to the tables you created in the previous chapter and set the `FormRef` property, so that the table **CarTable** points to the form **CarTable** in the `FormRef` property and the **RentalTable** table points to the **RentalTable** form.

Using a menu item as a button in a form

You can also add a menu item to a form and make it open another form. This is done simply by dragging the menu item and dropping it onto a form design.

To do this as our example, you should first add a button group under the **Design** node of the **CarTable** form. Then just drag the **RentalTable** menu item from one AOT window and drop it onto the button group in the **CarTable** form. A new button will then be created that will open the **RentalTable** form, but in order to get only rentals for the selected car in the **CarTable** form, you have to set the **Data Source** property on the button to **CarTable**.

The form will then look like this:

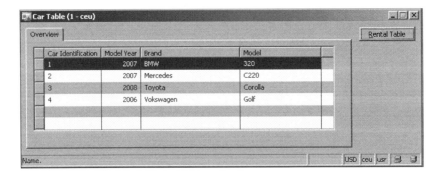

And the form in the AOT, with the properties of the button, should look something like the next screenshot:

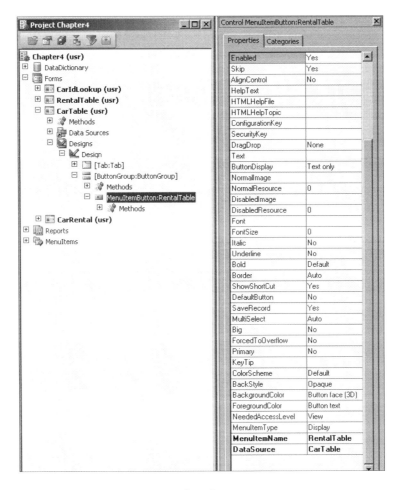

Navigation pages

Navigation pages are a new feature in Dynamics AX 2009 that is used to provide links to the most common operations, reports, and forms that users need for each area in the solution.

There are three different kinds of navigation pages:

- List pages: Contains a list of records in the content pane and has buttons that start actions on one or many of the records.

- Content pages: Used for navigation, and is placed inside the content pane. Can contain records in another format than a list. An example is the organization view (Main menu\Administration\Organization View).

- Area pages: The content of a menu defined in the AOT under Menus is displayed as area pages. The area pages open inside the client content page.

List pages

We will look more into how list pages work, as they are the most advanced and interesting of the three kinds of navigation pages.

List pages typically contain a collection of other user interface elements to display data and to perform actions on those data.

The next screenshot is an example of a list page and the different UI elements used:

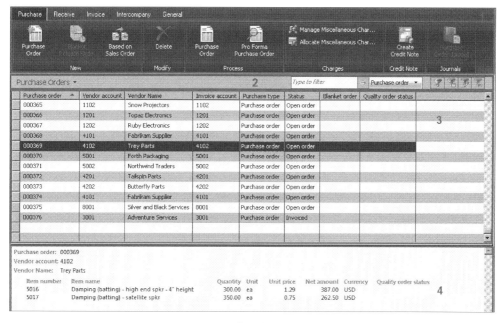

- Action pane: The action pane is like a tab, only with tab pages that contains different kind of actions. Changing to another ActionPane Tab will only change the actions inside the action pane and not the rest of the list page.

- Filter pane: The filter pane is used to filter the data in the content pane. The filter pane will appear automatically in your list page.

- Content pane: The content pane consists of a grid with fields from the data source of the list page.

- Preview pane: The preview pane is a HTML component that is generated at runtime based on fields in certain groups in the form design, and is an optional component in the list pages.

Creating a list page

We will now create a list page that show records in the `CarTable` and add an action in this list page that opens the `RentalTable` form.

1. Right-click on the **Forms** node in the AOT and select **New | Form**.

2. Change the name of the form to **CarsListPage**. (See information box below.)

3. On the **Design** node (under the **Designs** node) you must change the **WindowType** property to **ListPage**. This will make the rest of the form understand that this is a ListPage and will treat it accordingly. Also, it will set a caption for the form `Cars` in our example.

4. Now, add the data source by dragging the **CarTable** and dropping it onto the **Data Source** node in the form. You will now see that the **AllowEdit** and **AllowCreate** are both set to **No** as **ListPages**.

5. To add an action pane, right-click on the **Design** node and select **New | ActionPane**. Right-click on the newly created **ActionPane** and select **New | ActionPaneTab**. Give this action pane tab a caption. We will call it **Rentals** in our example. Right–click on the action pane tab and select **New | ButtonGroup**. Also give the button group a caption. For lack of anything better, we will call our button group **List**.

 It is best practice to postfix the name of a list page with ListPage to make it easier to find in the AOT.

Open a new AOT window and find the display menu item **RentalTable** that we created earlier in this chapter. Drag this menu item and drop it onto the button group. A new menu item button is now created that will open the **RentalTable** form.

Right–click on the new menu item button in the form and change the **ButtonDisplay** property to **Text & Image above**. Change the **Big** property to **Yes**. Set the **DataSource** property to **CarTable,** and also add an image to the button by setting the **NormalImage** property to an image or icon on your hard drive that you think fits the **RentalTable** button.

Right-click on the button group and select **New | CommandButton**. Change the name of the command button to **ExportToExcel** and set the **ButtonDisplay** property to **Text & Image** above, the **MultiSelect** property to **Yes**, the **Big** property to **Yes**, and the **NormalResource** to **10156** (the id of the embedded Excel icon), and last but not least, set the **Command** property to **Export To Excel**.

If you open the form now, it should look like this:

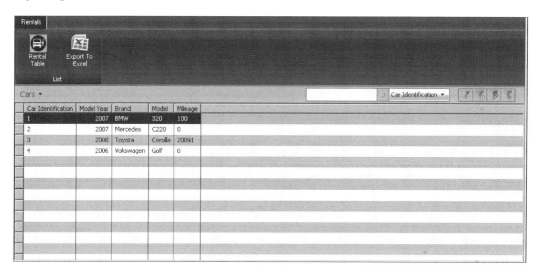

Try out the functionality by pressing the buttons and filtering the records.

Menus

Menus are listed as modules in the navigation pane to the left in a standard AX installation. When selecting a module, the content pane will change to show the contents of the selected menu.

Now that you have created menu items for the forms and reports that you created earlier in this chapter you are ready to add them to a menu.

Create a new menu by right–clicking on **Menus** in the AOT and selecting **New Menu**. Open the properties window for the menu and change the name to **CarRental** and the label to **Car Rental**.

Save the menu; right-click on the menu and select **New | Submenu**. Open its properties window and change the **Name** and **Label** to **Reports**.

Open another AOT window and find the display menu items that you created earlier in this chapter. Drag them from the AOT window and drop them onto the **CarRental** menu in the other AOT window. Do the same for the output menu items you created, but put these menu items in the **Reports** submenu.

You have now created a new menu in AX, but in order to get the menu to show in the main menu, you also have to change the main menu.

Go to the **MainMenu** under **Menus** in the AOT, right-click on it, and select **New | Menu reference**. A new AOT window with all the menus in the AOT will appear. Find the **CarRental** menu in this new AOT window and drag-and-drop it onto the **MainMenu** in the original AOT window so that it looks like this:

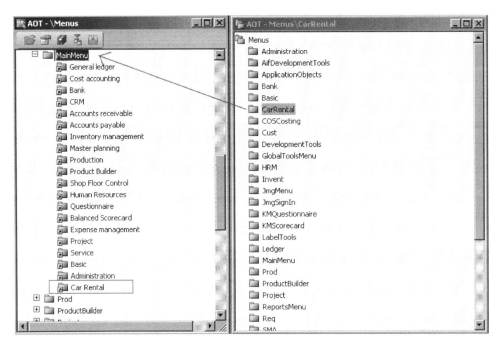

You will now have a menu that looks like the next screenshot when you restart AX:

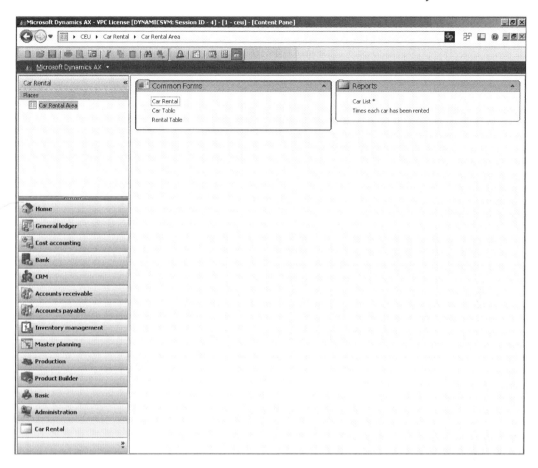

Summary

This chapter has given you an overview of how to create a basic user interface according to best practices, and you have also learned about some of the major new development features in Dynamics AX 2009.

You should now be able to create forms, report, menu items, menus, and navigation pages. Although the examples I have showed you so far are very simple, I hope that they trigger your curiosity to play around and try to change parameters, to see how they affect the result. Basically, this is how you will broaden your knowledge with the possibilities and hopefully few limitations of AX.

In the next chapter, we will look at how to retrieve data using views, queries, and select statements.

5
Searching for Data

In this chapter, you will learn about the different methods of retrieving data from the database. They are as follows:

- **Queries** which are reusable and often used in reports and periodic Jobs
- **Views** that are created in AOT and translated to optimized select statements at runtime
- **Select statements** to use in X++ to fetch data from the database to the application

After reading this chapter you will know how to use these mechanisms and know which one of them to use in different cases.

Queries

Queries are typically used to ask users about ranges and sorting, and then selecting data based on the feedback from the users. A query can consist of one or multiple data sources, and can be created both as static queries in the AOT or as dynamic queries using X++. Most commonly they are used when the ranges or values are not known until runtime. Static queries are defined in the AOT, whereas dynamic queries are defined in X++ code.

Creating a static query using the AOT

Follow these steps to create a static query in the AOT:

1. Open the AOT, expand the **Queries** node, right-click on **Queries**, and select **New Query**. A new query is then created in the AOT.

2. Right-click on the query, select **Properties**, and change the name to **CarList** (or in other cases, to something that describes what kind of data the query is returning).

3. Open a new AOT window, expand the **DataDictionary** node, and then expand the **Tables** node.

4. Drag the **CarTable** and drop it onto the **Data Sources** node of the new query. You can also drag maps or views to the data source of a query.

You have now created the skeleton of the query. Let's now look at how to add sorting and ranges to the query.

Adding a sort order to the query

To add a sorting to the query, just drag the selected field from the **Fields** node under the data source and drop it under the **Order By** node. In our example, we'll use the **Mileage** field. You can then select to have it sort ascending or descending by changing the direction property on the sort field.

When the query prompt is executed in a report, the user has the ability to change the sort order.

Adding a range to the query

You can also add ranges to the data source by dragging a field from the **Fields** node and dropping it onto the ranges. A range can be used to narrow down the result returned by the query, or it can be used as a fixed range that the user cannot change. This is done by adding a value to the value property of the range.

Values in a range can be used like this:

Range operator	Description	Example
,	Selects records where the range field matches any of the values listed	BMW, VW, Volvo
=	Selects records where the range field is a matching value	=VW

Range operator	Description	Example
..	Selects records where the range field is between the values specified including the values used	1000..3000
<	Selects records where the range field is less than the value specified	<2000
>	Selects records where the range field is greater than the value specified	>2000
!	Selects records where the range field is not equal to the value specified	!BMW
?	Selects records where the ? can be any character	Merc??es
*	Selects records where the range field matches the characters before or after the asterisk	Merc*

When the **Status** property is set to **Open**, the users can change the range value. If it's set to **Lock**, the users can see the range value before executing the query, but they are not allowed to change it. If the status property is set to **Hide**, the users won't even be allowed to see the range value.

In our example, we add the **ModelYear** field from the data source **CarTable_1**:

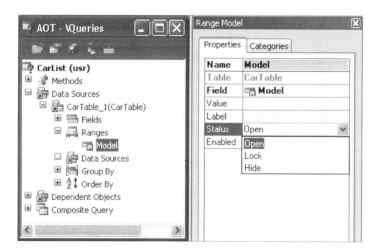

Joining data sources in a query

In order to select data from more than one table, you can join the data sources in your query. Data sources can be joined in a couple of different ways depending on how you would like to link them. This is done by setting the **JoinMode** property to the different values shown in the following table:

JoinMode	Description
InnerJoin	Will return the records where the joined data sources have matching values in the joined fields.
	For example: By using the **CarTable** as the primary data source and using **RentalTable** as the joined data source, the inner join will fetch all records from the **CarTable** where there is a corresponding record in the **RentalTable**. The corresponding records in **RentalTable** will also be fetched.
OuterJoin	Will return all the records from the joined table even if they don't match the joined field.
	For example: Compared to the example using the **InnerJoin**, this will return all records from the **CarTable**, but also records from the **RentalTable** that does not have a match in the **CarTable**.
ExistsJoin	This is just like the **InnerJoin**, except the records from the joined data source are not returned. They are only used to filter the primary data source.
	For example: In our example, it will only return records in the **CarTable** where there is a match in the **RentalTable**. Records from the **RentalTable** will not be fetched.
NotExistsJoin	This is the opposite of **ExistsJoin**. It will select records from the primary data source when matching records in the joined data source does not exist.
	For example: In our example, it will return records from the **CarTable** that did not have any matching records in the **RentalTable**. (Cars that have never been rented).

Follow these steps to add a new data source and join it with the first one:

1. First, we will create a duplicate of the query that we have created so far, as we would like to use the original query in the Reporting Services report (mentioned in the previous chapter). To duplicate any AOT object, right-click on the object and select **Duplicate**. A duplicate is then created with the prefix **CopyOf**.

2. Now rename the new query to **RentalCarList**.

3. Also, change the range under the **CarTable_1** data source to **ModelYear** instead of **Model**. This range will be used later in this chapter.

4. Drag another table, map, or view, and drop it onto the **Data Sources** node below the first data source. In our example, we will add the **RentalTable**. Therefore, open a new AOT window and browse to **Data Dictionary | Tables | RentalTable**. Drag the **RentalTable** and drop it onto the **Data Sources** node under the **CarTable** data source in the query.

5. Open the properties of the **RentalTable** data source in the query and change the **Relations** property to **Yes**.

6. If you expand the **Relations** node under the **RentalTable** data source, you should now see that the **CarTable** data source is linked to the **RentalTable** data source by the **CarId**. Your AOT should look like this:

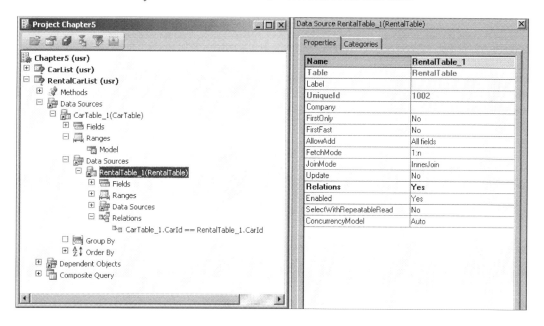

Creating a dynamic query using X++

A query can also be built dynamically using X++ code. This can be the only way of creating the query, if you would like the query to work in one way in some cases and in another way in other cases. An example can be where you would like to join one table if one condition is true and another table if the condition is false. To do this, you need to understand how the query object model works.

The most commonly used classes in the query object model are:

- Query: Contains the definition of the query. Can consist of one data source or several data sources if they are related.

- QueryRun: Class used to execute the query and loop through the result.

- QueryBuildDataSource: Links to one data source in the query. Can be linked to another QueryBuildDataSource object to join linked data sources.

- QueryBuildRange: Enables the end user to limit the result by adding a value in the specified query range.

- QueryBuildFieldList: List of all the fields in data source. One QueryBuildFieldList object for each QueryBuildDataSource. By default the property Dynamic is set to true so that all fields are returned.

- QueryBuildLink: Links two data sources in a join. Is set on the child data source.

The query definition is set up by creating and linking objects from the query object model together. The following example shows how this is done in order to create a similar query as we did in the previous section of this chapter when we created a query called **RentalCarList** in the AOT.

```
static void queryRentalCarList(Args _args)
{
    Query                    query;
    QueryBuildDataSource     queryBuildDataSource1,
                             queryBuildDataSource2;
    QueryBuildRange          queryBuildRange;
    QueryBuildLink           queryBuildLink;
    ;

    // Create a new query object
    query = new Query();
    // Add the first data source to the query
    queryBuildDataSource1 = query.addDataSource(tablenum(CarTable));
    // Add the range to this first data source
    queryBuildRange = queryBuildDataSource1.
    addRange(fieldnum(CarTable, ModelYear));
    // Add the second datasource to the first data source
```

```
queryBuildDataSource2 =
  queryBuildDataSource1.addDataSource(tablen
um(RentalTable));
// Add the link from the child data source to the
//parent data
source
queryBuildLink = queryBuildDataSource2.addLink(fieldnum(CarTable,
CarId),fieldnum(RentalTable, CarId));
}
```

Using a query

Ok, so now we have the query definition. But that doesn't help us much unless we are able to execute the query, right?

This example uses the previous example and just adds the QueryRun object and loops through the result by using the next() method on the QueryRun object.

```
static void queryRunRentalCarList(Args _args)
{
    Query                   query;
    QueryBuildDataSource    queryBuildDataSource1,
                            queryBuildDataSource2;
    QueryBuildRange         queryBuildRange;
    QueryBuildLink          queryBuildLink;
    QueryRun                queryRun;
    CarTable                carTable;
    RentalTable             rentalTable;
    ;

    // Create a new query object
    query = new Query();
    // Add the first data source to the query
    queryBuildDataSource1 = query.addDataSource(tablenum(CarTable));
    // Add the range to this first data source
    queryBuildRange = queryBuildDataSource1.
    addRange(fieldnum(CarTable, ModelYear));
    // Set the range
    queryBuildRange.value("2008..");
    // Add the second datasource to the first data source
    queryBuildDataSource2 =
      queryBuildDataSource1.addDataSource(tablenum(RentalTable));
    // Add the link from the child data source to the parent data
    //source
    queryBuildLink = queryBuildDataSource2.addLink(
      fieldnum(CarTable,CarId),fieldnum(RentalTable, CarId));
```

```
    // Create a new QueryRun object based on the query definition
    queryRun = new QueryRun(query);
    // Loop through all the records returned by the query
    while (queryRun.next())
    {
        // Get the table data by using the get() method
        carTable = queryRun.get(tablenum(CarTable));
        rentalTable = queryRun.get(tablenum(RentalTable));
        info (strfmt("CarId %1, RentalId %2", carTable.CarId,
          rentalTable.RentalId));
    }
}
```

The following result is obtained after running the query:

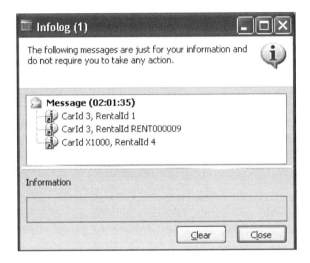

The exact same result will show up if we execute the query that was defined in the AOT in the previous section of this chapter.

The code would then look like this:

```
static void queryRunRentalCarListAOT(Args _args)
{
    Query                   query;
    QueryBuildDataSource    queryBuildDataSource;
```

```
QueryBuildRange          queryBuildRange;
QueryRun                 queryRun;
CarTable                 carTable;
RentalTable              rentalTable;
;
// Create a new query object based on the Query in the AOT called
//RentalCarList
query = new Query(querystr(RentalCarList));
// Find the datasource for the CarTable
queryBuildDataSource = query.dataSourceTable(tablenum(CarTable));
// Find the range that we added to the query in the AOT
queryBuildRange =
   queryBuildDataSource.findRange(fieldnum(CarTable, ModelYear));
// Set the value of the range
queryBuildRange.value("2008..");
// Create a new QueryRun object based on the query definition
queryRun = new QueryRun(query);
// Loop through all the records returned by the query
while (queryRun.next())
{
    // Get the table data by using the get() method
    carTable = queryRun.get(tablenum(CarTable));
    rentalTable = queryRun.get(tablenum(RentalTable));
    info (strfmt("CarId %1, RentalId %2", carTable.CarId,
       rentalTable.RentalId));
}
}
```

Views

Views in AX are objects that are used to retrieve data from the database that is stored in the memory on the layer in which the view is instantiated. The views are actually stored as database views on the SQL server. This means that there are potentially great performance benefits of using views compared to using an equivalent query. This depends of course on the complexity of the query, but in general the performance benefits of using a view compared to a query will increase along with the complexity of the query.

Views can be used throughout AX in all places where tables can be used. This includes forms, queries, reports, and X++ code.

Views in AX can never be used to write data, only to read data from the database. This differs from the SQL implementation that has write-back possibilities for views.

Creating a view

We will now create a view that consists of **CarId**, **CarBrand**, **Model**, **Customer Name**, **FromDate**, and **ToDate** using the following steps:

1. First, we locate the **Views** node under the **Data Dictionary** in the AOT.

2. Right-click on the **Views** node and select **New View**. A new view will be created. You can open its properties by right-clicking and selecting **Properties**.

3. Change the name of the view to **CarCustRental** and give it a label that describes the contents of the view.

4. The views can actually use queries that have already been created as a base for the data selection. This is done in the **Properties** of the view by choosing the query from the **Query** property. However, in our example, we will create the view from scratch.

5. Under the **Metadata** node, right-click on the **Data Sources** node and select **New Data Source**

6. Select the newly created data source and enter **CarTable** in the table property. The name of the data source will automatically change to **CarTable_1**, which is normal.

7. Under the **CarTable** data source, find the **Data Sources** node, right-click on it, and select **New Data Source**. This time, we want to use the **RentalTable** so change the table property to **RentalTable**. Also change the relations property to **Yes** in order to get the link between the two tables active in the view.

8. Do the same to add the **CustTable** as a child data source to the **RentalTable**.

9. The next step is to define the fields that should be made available when this query is executed. Simply drag fields you need to use in the view from the **CarTable_1**, **RentalTable_1**, and **CustTable_1** data source and drop them onto the **Fields** node.

10. You should now have a view that looks like the following screenshot:

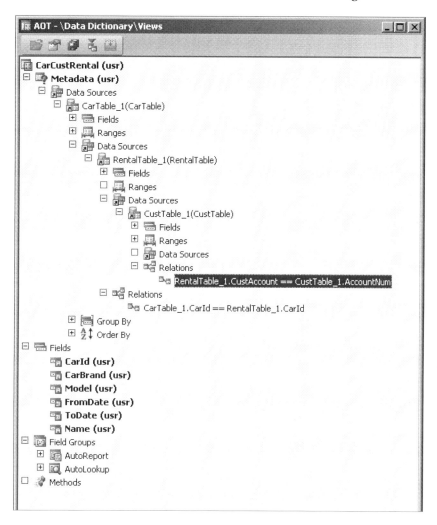

After saving the view, you can browse the contents of the view in the same way as you can with a table by using the table browser. Just open the view and the table browser will display the view with its contents.

You can also take a look at the view in the SQL Management Studio by opening the AX database node, then the **Views** node, and finding the view you just created. Right-click on the view and select **Design** to open it in design view. It should then look something like the following screenshot:

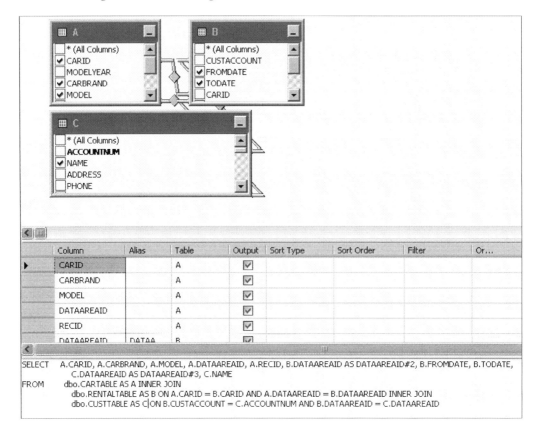

Select statement

One of the great features of Dynamics AX as a development tool is the possibility to write embedded SQL. This basically means that you can write `select` statements that are controlled by the compiler and get results back directly to table variables.

The following list is taken from the SDK and shows the syntax for the `select` statement and the parameters allowed with the `select` statement:

Descipion	Syntax
SelectStatement	`select` Parameters
Parameters	[[FindOptions] [FieldList `from`]] TableBufferVariable [IndexClause] [Options] [WhereClause] [JoinClause]
FindOptions	`crossCompany` | `reverse` | `firstFast` | [`firstOnly` | `firstOnly10` | `firstOnly100` | `firstOnly1000`] | `forUpdate` | `noFetch` | [`forcePlaceholders` | `forceLiterals`] | `forceselectorder` | `forceNestedLoop` | `repeatableRead`
FieldList	Field { , Field } | *
Field	Aggregate (FieldIdentifier) | FieldIdentifier
Aggregate	`sum` | `avg` | `minof` | `maxof` | `count`
Options	[`order by`, `group by`, FieldIdentifier [`asc` | `desc`] { , FieldIdentifier [`asc` | `desc`] }] | [IndexClause]
IndexClause	`index` IndexName | `index hint` IndexName
WhereClause	`where` Expression
JoinClause	[`exists` | `notexists` | `outer`] `join` Parameters

Check out the SDK for a more in-depth explanation of all the different keywords.

In the following examples, we will have a look at how to create different `select` statements depending on what data we would like to have available for the rest of the code.

To have a better understanding of how the different `select` statements work and what data is returned, we will use the following data:

CarTable

The following table shows the test data for the **CarTable**:

CarId	ModelYear	CarBrand	Model	Mileage
1	2007	BMW	320	2299
2	2007	Mercedes	C220	2883
3	2008	Toyota	Corolla	4032
4	2006	Volkswagen	Golf	49902
5	2002	Jeep	Grand Cherokee	65662
6	2003	BMW	Z3	11120
7	2000	Volkswagen	Golf	76322

RentalTable

The following table shows the test data for the **RentalTable**:

RentalId	CustAccount	FromDate	ToDate	CarId
1	1101	24.03.2009	25.03.2009	1
2	1103	23.03.2009	25.03.2009	3
3	1103	02.05.2009	11.05.2009	1
4	1102	10.05.2009	17.05.2009	5
5	1104	10.12.2009	20.12.2009	6

CustTable

The following table shows the test data for the **CustTable**:

AccountNum	Name	CustGroup	Blocked
1101	Forest Wholesales	10	No
1102	Sunset Wholesales	20	No
1103	Cave Wholesales	10	No
1104	Desert Wholesales	30	Yes

Writing a simple select statement

A `select` statement can be written specifically to return only one record or to return many records. If we expect the `select` statement to return multiple records and we would like to loop through these records, we simply embed the `select` statement within a `while` loop.

The following examples will demonstrate how to write simple `select` statements that return different data from the same table.

The first example will select all columns from all records in the `CarTable` as shown in the following Job:

```
static void selectAllRecordsStatic(Args _args)
{
    CarTable        carTable;
    int             records;
    ;
    info("-----------------START-----------------");
    while select carTable
    {
```

```
        info("-------------NEW RECORD-------------");
        info (strfmt("CarId:  %1", carTable.CarId));
        info (strfmt("CarBrand:  %1", carTable.CarBrand));
        info (strfmt("Model:  %1", carTable.Model));
        info (strfmt("ModelYear:  %1", carTable.ModelYear));
        info (strfmt("Mileage:  %1", carTable.Mileage));
        records++;
    }
    info("-----------------END-------------------");
    info(strfmt("%1 records was selected", records));
}
```

Executing this Job will result in the following output to the **Infolog**. Note that only the first records are shown in the **Infolog** window. When executing it yourself, you can scroll down to see the other records at the end line. The **Infolog** screen is shown in the following screenshot:

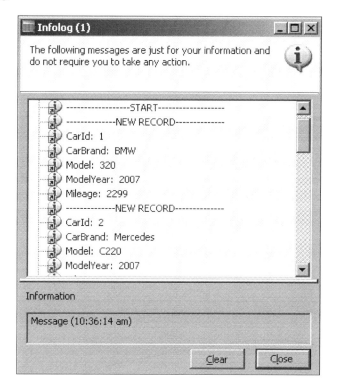

The next example actually does pretty much the same as the first example, but I have added some code to be able to dynamically write the fields in the table. It will also print all the systems fields for each record, but it can be a nice exercise for you to understand how you can use the Dict classes to create dynamic functionality, as shown in the following Job:

```
static void selectAllRecordsDynamically(Args _args)
{
    CarTable        carTable;
    DictField       dictField;
    DictTable       dictTable;
    int             field;
    int             fieldId;
    int             records;
    str             header, line;
    ;

    // Create a new object of type DictTable based on the carTable
    dictTable = new DictTable(tablenum(carTable));

    // Loop through the fields on the table.
    // For each field, store the field-label in the header variable.
    for (field=1; field <= dictTable.fieldCnt(); field++)
    {
        fieldId = dictTable.fieldCnt2Id(field);
        dictField = new DictField(tablenum(carTable), fieldId);
        header += strfmt("%1, ",  dictField.label());
    }
    info(strupr(header)); // strupr changes the string to UPPERCASE

    // Loop through all the records in the carTable
    while select carTable
    {
        line = "";
        // For each record in the carTable, loop through all the
        //fields
        // and store the value of the field for this record in the
        //line variable.
        for (field=1; field <= dictTable.fieldCnt(); field++)
        {
            fieldId = dictTable.fieldCnt2Id(field);
            dictField = new DictField(carTable.TableId, fieldId);
            // Instead of referencing to the fieldname, I reference to
            //field ID
            // to get the fields value.
```

```
                line += strfmt("%1, ",  carTable.(fieldId));
        }
        info(line);
        records++;
    }
    info(strfmt("%1 records were selected", records));
}
```

Executing this Job will result in the following output to the **Infolog**:

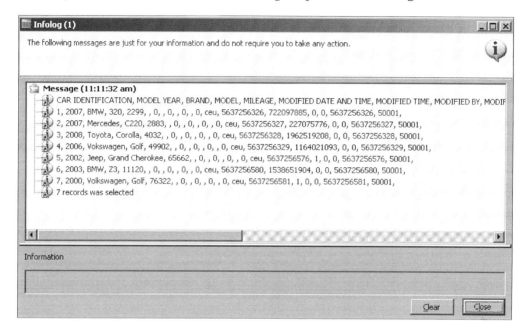

The next example will select all columns from the record in `CarTable` where the `CarId` equals 1. This means that we will only select one record and hence, we do not need the `while` loop:

```
static void selectOneRecord(Args _args)
{
    CarTable          carTable;
    ;
    select firstonly carTable
        where carTable.CarId == "1";

    info (strfmt("Car Brand: %1", carTable.CarBrand));
    info (strfmt("Car Model: %1", carTable.Model));
    info (strfmt("Model Year: %1", carTable.ModelYear));
    info (strfmt("Mileage: %1", carTable.Mileage));
}
```

Executing this Job will result in the following output to the **Infolog**:

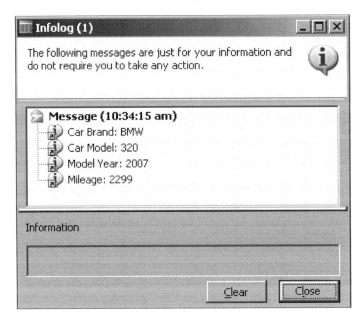

The next example will select only the CarBrand and the Model columns from all records in the CarTable where the ModelYear is greater than 2005:

```
static void selectWhereStatement(Args _args)
{
    CarTable          carTable;
    ;
    info(strupr("CarBrand, Model"));
    while select CarBrand, Model from carTable
        where carTable.ModelYear > 2005
    {
        info (strfmt("%1, %2  ", carTable.CarBrand, carTable.Model));
    }
}
```

Executing this Job will result in the following output to the **Infolog**:

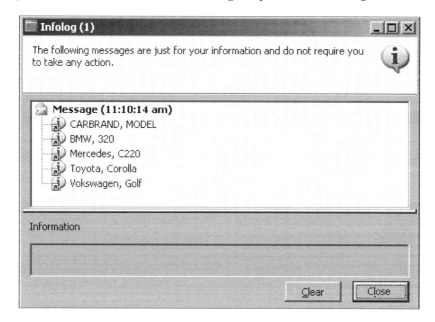

Using sorting in select statements

By default, a `select` statement that returns multiple rows will sort the result in ascending order by the primary index on the table (which can be seen in the first two examples of the previous section).

If you would like to have a statement return the rows in a different order, you have to use the `order by` parameter in the `select` statement and specify the fields you would like to sort the result by. If you have an index that corresponds with the sorting, you can use the name of the index to order by as well, but then you will have to use the statement `index` instead of `order by`. The following example will return the all the records in the `CarTable` sorted in descending order by the `Mileage`:

```
static void selectRecordsSortedDesc(Args _args)
{
    CarTable        carTable;
    int             records;
    ;
    info("-----------------START-------------------");
    while select carTable
        order by Mileage desc
    {
        info("-------------NEW RECORD--------------");
```

```
    info (strfmt("CarId:  %1", carTable.CarId));
    info (strfmt("CarBrand:  %1", carTable.CarBrand));
    info (strfmt("Model:  %1", carTable.Model));
    info (strfmt("ModelYear:  %1", carTable.ModelYear));
    info (strfmt("Mileage:  %1", carTable.Mileage));
    records++;
}
info("-----------------END-----------------");
info(strfmt("%1 records was selected", records));
}
```

Executing this Job will result in the following output to the **Infolog**:

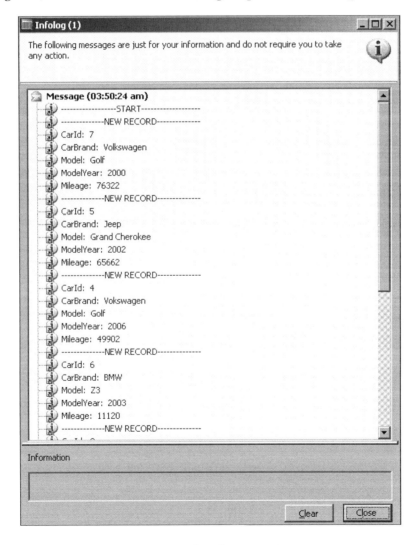

Using joins in a select statement

If you would like to retrieve data from several tables, or at least use ranges from different tables in the `select` statement, you should use one of the join parameters listed next.

Inner join

The inner join is the most common join as it joins two tables that are linked together typically by a one-to-many relationship.

The first table used in the `select` statement should be the "many" part of the relationship. Hence in our example we can say that a record from the `CarTable` can exist many times in the `RentalTable` making the `RentalTable` being used first.

As you might notice, the sorting in a joined select is done first with the innermost table, in this case the `carTable`. When no sorting has been specified AX uses the primary index set on the table. In this case, it uses the `CardIdx` index on the `CarTable` as shown in the following Job:

```
static void selectInnerJoin(Args _args)
{
    CarTable        carTable;
    RentalTable     rentalTable;
    ;

    while select rentalTable
        join carTable // same as writing inner join
            where carTable.CarId == rentalTable.CarId
    {
        info(strfmt("RentalId %1 is a %2 %3", rentalTable.RentalId,
            carTable.CarBrand, carTable.Model));
    }
}
```

Executing this Job will result in the following output to the **Infolog**:

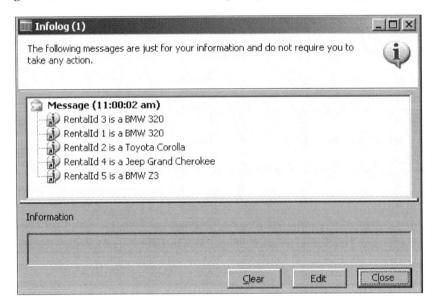

Outer join

An outer join is not only used to join two tables, but also to include the records
that do not have a corresponding match in the joined table. In the following example,
you will see that all records in the CarTable are selected (even though some of the
cars have never been rented):

```
static void selectOuterJoin(Args _args)
{
    CarTable        carTable;
    RentalTable     rentalTable;
    ;

    while select carTable
        outer join rentalTable
            where rentalTable.CarId == carTable.CarId
    {
        if (!rentalTable.RecId)
            info(strfmt("No rentals for the car with carId %1",
            carTable.CarId));
        else
            info(strfmt("RentalId %1 is a %2 %3",
                rentalTable.RentalId, carTable.CarBrand,
                carTable.Model));
    }
}
```

Executing this Job will result in the following output to the **Infolog**:

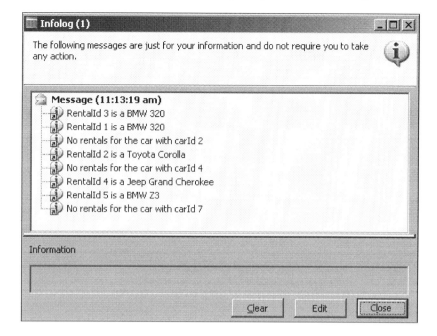

Exists join

An exists join does pretty much the same as the inner join, except one important thing; it does not fetch the records from the joined table. This means that the **RentalTable** variable cannot be used within the while loop in the following example, as it will never have any data:

```
static void selectExistsJoin(Args _args)
{
    CarTable        carTable;
    RentalTable     rentalTable;
    ;

    while select carTable
        exists join rentalTable
            where rentalTable.CarId == carTable.CarId
    {
        info(strfmt("CarId %1 has a matching record in rentalTable",
          CarTable.CarId));
    }
}
```

Executing this Job will result in the following output to the **Infolog**:

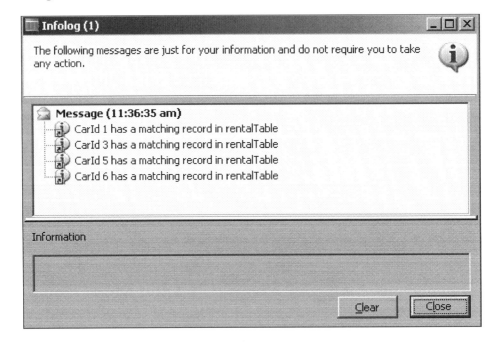

NotExists join

Obviously the `notexists join` is the opposite of the `exists join`. This means that it will return all records from the main table where there does not exist a record in the joined table as described by the `where` clause. This means that the following example will produce the opposite result from the previous example:

```
static void selectNotExistsJoin(Args _args)
{
    CarTable        carTable;
    RentalTable     rentalTable;
    ;

    while select carTable
        notexists join rentalTable
            where rentalTable.CarId == carTable.CarId
    {
        info(strfmt("CarId %1 does not has a matching record in
            rentalTable", CarTable.CarId));
    }
}
```

Executing this job will result in the following output to the **Infolog**:

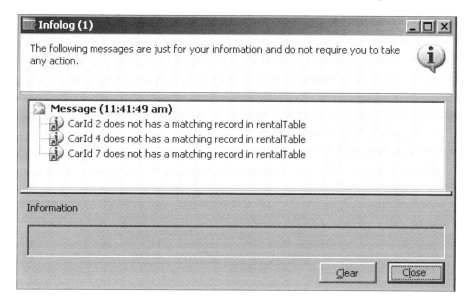

Writing aggregate select statements

In many cases, you would like to write `select` statements that return aggregate data like the sum or average of a field in a set of data. You can also use the `count` aggregate option to count the number of records in a table matching a `where` statement (if any). The `minof` and `maxof` options can be used in the same way to find the minimum or maximum value of a field in a record set that corresponds to the `where` statement.

These examples show how the different aggregate options can be used:

- **sum**

```
static void selectSumMileage(Args _args)
{
    CarTable    carTable;
    ;
    select sum(Mileage) from carTable;
    info(strfmt("The total mileage of all cars is %1",
      carTable.Mileage));
}
```

Executing this Job will result in the following output to the **Infolog**:

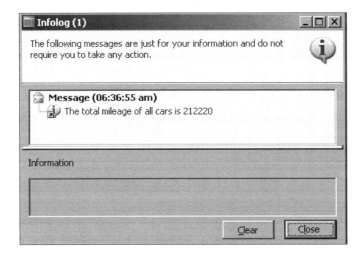

- **avg**

```
static void selectAvgModelYear(Args _args)
{
    CarTable     carTable;
    ;
    select avg(ModelYear) from carTable;
    info(strfmt("The average ModelYear is %1",
      carTable.ModelYear));
}
```

Executing this Job will result in the following output to the **Infolog**:

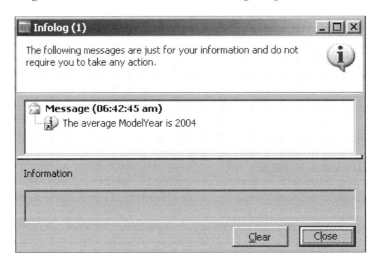

- **count**

```
static void selectCountRentals(Args _args)
{
    RentalTable     rentalTable;
    ;
    select count(recId) from rentalTable;

    info(strfmt("There are %1 rentals registerred in the system",
        rentalTable.RecId));
}
```

Executing this Job will result in the following output to the **Infolog**:

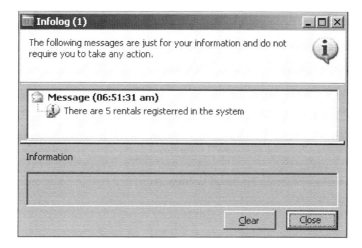

- **minof and maxof**

```
static void selectMinofMileage(Args _args)
{
    CarTable     minCarTable, maxCarTable;
    ;
    select minof(Mileage) from minCarTable;
    select maxof(Mileage) from maxCarTable;

    info(strfmt("The car with the lowest mileage has a mileage of
        %2", minCarTable.CarId, minCarTable.Mileage));
    info(strfmt("The car with the highest mileage has a mileage of
        %2", maxCarTable.CarId, maxCarTable.Mileage));
}
```

Executing this Job will result in the following output to the **Infolog**:

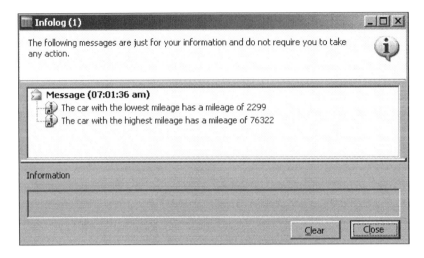

5. Group by

In many cases, aggregate options are used together with the `group by` parameter in order to list the aggregate for each subpart of a table.

In the next example we will find the number of rentals for each customer that has rented cars. I will also demonstrate how to use the `next` command together with the `select` statement instead of the `while select` statement to loop through the records in the result. You will most often see the `while select` statement being used in standard AX, but in case you see the `next` command, you will know it does the same as a `while select` statement. The following example shows how the `group by` aggregate option can be used:

```
static void selectCountRentalsPerCustomer(Args _args)
{
    RentalTable    rentalTable;
    ;
    // Normal while select to loop data
    info ("Using while select:");
    // The result of the count operation is put
    // into the recId field of the tableBuffer
    // since it is an integerfield.
    while select count(recId) from rentalTable
        group by rentalTable.CustAccount
    {
```

```
        info(strfmt("    Customer %1 has rented cars %2 times",
            rentalTable.CustAccount, rentalTable.RecId));
    }


    // Looping the rentalTable cusrsor using the next command
    info ("Using next command:");
    select count(recId) from rentalTable
        group by rentalTable.CustAccount;

    while (rentalTable.RecId)
    {
        info(strfmt("    Customer %1 has rented cars %2 times",
            rentalTable.CustAccount, rentalTable.RecId));
        next rentalTable;
    }
}
```

Executing this Job will result in the following output to the **Infolog**:

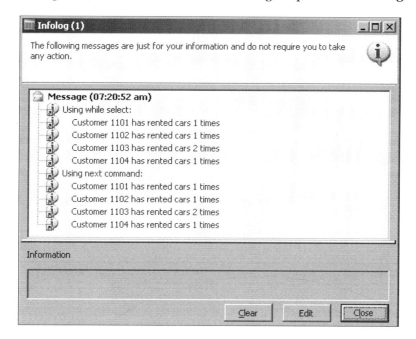

Optimizing the data retrieval

There can be several different steps that you, as a developer, should take in order to optimize the process of fetching data from the database to the application. I will try to cover the most important things for you to keep in mind here.

Using the correct data retrieval method

One important issue, not only for optimization but also for usability, is to select the correct data retrieval method based on what you would like to achieve.

Use queries when you want the users to be able to change the range of data to be retrieved and when the selection criteria are simple enough for the query to handle.

If the selection criteria are complex, and there is no need for the users to be able to change the selection criteria, you should opt for a `select` statement.

If you would like to be able to use the query definition multiple places, you should create a query in the AOT instead of writing it in X++ every time you need to use it. It can also be easier to get a visual overview of a query created in the AOT compared to a query written in X++.

If the selection criteria is complex, there is no need for updating or deleting the data selected and if you would like to be able to use the same selection in many places in the application, then you should consider creating a view in the AOT instead of writing the `select` statement every time.

Field selects

Perhaps the most important thing to do in order to optimize the data retrieval is actually very simple—you should only fetch the data that you need. This means that you should eliminate any `select` statements that you don't need. You should only fetch those fields that the program really needs.

In order to do this you should not use the `select` statement such as the following unless you actually need all fields in the record(s) selected:

```
select carTable; // Is the same as select * from carTable
```

Rather, you should select only the fields needed from the table as follows:

```
select CarBrand, Model from carTable;
```

This will reduce the amount of data that has to be transferred from the database to the application layer; thus reducing the time consumed for the data transfer.

Indexing

Another thing you need to consider is how to use indexes. Additionally, you may also need to consider adding the missing indexes. This part could actually cover a book all by itself, but I'll try to explain the most important things you need to know about the use of indexes in AX.

As covered in Chapter 3, *Storing Data*, all tables should have a unique index that represents the primary key of the tables.

If a lot of data selection is done using constraints other than the primary key, consider creating an index for those constraints as well.

Creating too many indexes on a table to optimize the speed when searching for data may, however, slow down the operation of inserting, updating, and deleting data from the table (as all of the indexes must be updated when one of these operations are performed).

Using views to optimize the data retrieval

When using views the data retrieved is limited to the fields in the **Fields** node of the view. This means that the selected fields can easily be narrowed down when joining several tables. Also, joining several tables will execute faster because the `select` is already compiled and exists on the database layer when the view is executed, (as opposed to queries that have to compile the `select` at runtime).

Other ways to improve data retrieval

There are many different ways of optimizing data retrieval from the database. The most obvious were discussed in the previous sections.

The **CacheLoopup** property on the tables in AX specifies what type of caching is used for the table. If the wrong type of cache is used, it can cause a significant decrease in performance when accessing the table.

Options such as `firstonly`, `forcePlaceholders`, and `forceLiterals` can also give a performance boost on certain occasions.

Please refer to the SDK for more information regarding caching and find operations.

Summary

In this chapter you learned how to write different kind of `select` statements in order to retrieve data from the database, and how to create queries and views.

We also went through the reasons for choosing which of the data retrieval methods to use in different scenarios. We also looked at how to optimize the data retrieval, so that each transfer of data from the database to the application only contains the data necessary for the further operations in the application, and making sure that the correct index was used to find the data.

In the next chapter, we will look at how to manipulate data by inserting, updating, and deleting records.

6
Manipulate Data

Throughout Dynamics AX you can find data manipulation done in code by using the `insert()`, `update()`, and `delete()` methods. An example can be when posting an invoice. When this is done the system has to create records in journals and update data in different tables, all based on the data that already exists in an order and in other base data tables.

In this chapter we will look at the following topics:

- Methods used to validate the data to be inserted, updated, or deleted (`validateWrite`, `validateDelete`, `validateField`)
- The method used for inserting data (`insert()`)
- The method used for updating existing data (`update()`)
- The method used for deleting records (`delete()`)
- The method to send a request to the database to insert a chunk of data (`insert_recordset`)
- The method to send a request to the database to update a chunk of records (`update_recordset`)
- The method to send a request to the database to delete a chunk of records (`delete_from`)
- Direct handling of data manipulation, without running any code within the `update`, `insert`, or `delete` methods

Validate methods

Before manipulating the data it is a good idea to make sure that the data you are inserting, updating, or deleting doesn't break any of the rules you have set for the table you are manipulating.

These rules are typically to check that all mandatory fields have data in the buffer that you are trying to insert, update, or check so that the record you are about to delete doesn't have any related records in tables set up with a restricted delete action.

A validation method should always return a Boolean value true if the validation is ok and false if it's not ok.

If you don't use the validation methods you will be allowed to have records with mandatory fields empty when inserting or updating records from X++. You will also be allowed to delete records that have restricted delete actions against other tables. That means that you are likely to get unreferenced data if you don't use validation methods.

There are three data validation methods used in tables and data sources in AX, and they all have default functionality defined in the system class Common available when they call super():

- validateWrite: Validates records to be inserted or updated. Checks for mandatory fields.
- validateDelete: Validates records to be deleted. Checks for delete actions.
- validateField: Checks if the value of the given field is a legal value.

Validation rules (set using table or form metadata) are automatically triggered when the user creates, updates, or deletes a record using a form. However, if the same actions are performed using X++ code, then the developer needs to write code to validate the action. Another type of validation called aosValidate methods are used to ensure that the user performing the action has the proper access rights according to the user group setup.

Record-based manipulation

The record-based manipulation is used to manipulate one record at a time. The typical usage of record-based manipulation is when you need to manipulate only one record, if you have to manipulate many records and you are unable to use the set-based operators, or would like to commit one record at a time.

In the upcoming sections we will look closer at the following operations:

- Insert
- Update
- Delete

Insert

Perhaps the most common method to manipulate tables in AX is to insert them using the `insert()` method. It is used to insert the data currently held by the table variable into a new record in the database. The `insert()` method in X++ is a table instance method, and hence, it is performed on a table variable, sometimes also referred to as a table buffer.

This means that the `insert()` method will only be able to insert records in the database one at a time.

If you need to insert multiple records you will have to create a loop that calls the `insert()` method multiple times. In turn, this will generate more traffic between the **Application Object Server (AOS)** and the database, more than what is perhaps necessary. An alternative could be to use the `insert_recordset` operator instead (explained later in this chapter).

When inserting multiple records using the `insert()` method it is important that you clear the table buffer each time the loop iterates. This is done by using the table instance method `clear()` at the beginning of the loop. There is an example on how to insert many records in a table by using a loop in Chapter 7, *Integrate Data*.

All tables in AX also have a method called `initValue` that can be used to initialize default values for some of the fields (see the **InventTable** for an example of how `initValue` is implemented). Tables also often have `initFrom` methods that are used to initialize the records if a related record is already known. An example of this is the `initFromSalesTable` method in the **SalesLine** table. The `initFrom` method has to be created manually, whereas the `initValue` method is inherited from the system class Common.

The following example shows how to insert one record into the **CarTable** with fixed values.

```
static void InsertMethod(Args _args)
{
    CarTable            carTable;
    ;
    // Initialize the table variable
    carTable.initValue();

    // Write some values to the table variable
    carTable.CarId = "100";
    carTable.CarBrand = "Audi";
    carTable.Model = "A4";
    carTable.ModelYear = 2009;
    carTable.Mileage = 0;
```

```
    // Check if all values are legal and if so, insert the values of
    //the table variable into a record in the table
    if (carTable.validateWrite())
        carTable.insert();
}
```

Update

In many cases you will of course need to update data in an existing record. In our example, it could be to update the mileage in the **CarTable** each time a car is returned after being rented.

The update() method is used in order to update the selected record with the values of the active table variable.

While updating data it is essential to have a locking system that locks the records that are about to be updated so that no one else can update the same data at the same time. To do this in AX we use the ttsbegin keyword to give a hint to AX that a **transaction scope** should be created in the database when the next select statement, update(), insert(), or delete() methods are executed. Only then will we write the data to the transaction scope of the database instead of to the table itself. When we use the ttscommit keyword the contents of the transaction scope will be written to the actual table in the database. If an error occurs while we are updating a chunk of data we can use the ttsabort keyword to rollback the database transaction. This means that the records that we made updates to are never written to the actual table in the database until the changes are committed.

Another slightly better way of rolling back the transaction is to throw an error message, as the throw statement will call the **ttsabort** implicitly.

It is important that the number of ttscommit statements executed matches the number of ttsbegin statement executed. If they do not match, AX will throw a message saying that an unbalanced X++ TTSBEGIN/TTSCOMMIT has been detected. You will then have to close AX and open it again to reset the **Transaction Tracking System (TTS)** level and to rollback the transactions done within the transaction scope.

Another keyword that we have to use in order to update records in AX is the forupdate keyword. This keyword is used to tell a select statement that the records fetched from the database is going to be updated, and to lock these records so that no one else can update these records until the ttscommit or ttsabort is executed.

The term **rollback segment** is used only in the Oracle databases. MS SQL writes to the logfile(s) and copies the transactions to the datafile(s) when the transaction is committed. As a general term, it can also be called the **transaction scope**.

This means that a single record update would look something like this:

```
static void UpdateMethodSingle(Args _args)
{
    CarTable            carTable;
    ;
    // Start the database transaction
    ttsbegin;

    // Find the record to be updated and flag the record with the
    //forupdate flag
    select forupdate carTable
        where carTable.CarId == "1";

    // Change a value in the table variable
    carTable.Mileage = 23999;
    // Copy the values of the table variable to the actual record
    carTable.update();

    // End the database transaction
    ttscommit;
}
```

In some cases though, you will need to update many records in a table at once. In these cases you should write a `while select` statement, but then another issue arises. If you are updating a huge amount of data the transaction scope will also increase accordingly and become slower and slower to update. To cope with this, you could perhaps commit a smaller chunk of data like in the following example where chunks of 300 records are committed at a time. This option cannot be used if you want to make sure that if one of the records fail none of the records should be updated.

```
static void UpdateMethodMultiple(Args _args)
{
    CarTable            carTable;
    int                 records;
    ;
    // Start the database transaction
    ttsbegin;
```

```
// Find the records to be updated and flag the record with the
// forupdate flag
while select forupdate carTable
{
    // For each 300 records updated, commit the chunk and start a
    // new transaction scope
    if (records mod 300 == 0)
    {
        ttscommit;
        ttsbegin;
    }
    // Change a value in the table variable
    carTable.Mileage = 23999;
    // Copy the values of the table variable to the actual record
    carTable.update();
    // Count how many records have been updated
    records++;
}
// End the database transaction
ttscommit;
info(strfmt("%1 records was updated.", records));
}
```

Delete

When deleting records in a table it is important to also have in mind the effect that delete actions in that table will have on records in other tables.

If a restricted delete action exists and the linked table has records related to the record you are trying to delete, you should not be able to delete the record. This is handled automatically in the user interface (in forms), but when deleting records from X++ you have to add the validateDelete() method first and only perform the delete() if validateDelete() returns true.

However, if a cascade-delete action exists and the linked table has records related to the record you are trying to delete all of the related records will also be deleted when using the delete() method in X++.

Another important thing to remember when deleting a record is to always create a transaction scope using the ttsbegin keyword before selecting the record(s) to be deleted, and ttscommit after the delete method.

The next example shows how to use the delete() method to delete a single record from this table (and all records related to this record where a cascade delete action exists).

```
static void DeleteMethod(Args _args)
{
    CarTable            carTable;
    ;
    // Start the database transaction
    ttsbegin;
    // Find the record to be deleted and flag the record with the
    // forupdate flag
    select forupdate carTable
        where carTable.CarId == "1";

    // Check if this record can be deleted
    if (carTable.validateDelete())
        // Delete the selected record
        carTable.delete();

    // End the database transaction
    ttscommit;
}
```

Set-based data manipulation

As you will see in this section, you can also manipulate a set of data by sending only one command to the database. This way of manipulating data improves performance a lot when trying to manipulate large sets of records. However, there are a couple of things to consider before using set-based data manipulation.

All of the following operators will be converted back to their record-based counterparts runtime if any of the following is true:

- When a record-based method like `insert()`, `update()`, `delete()`, or `aosValidate()` has been overridden

- When AX database logging is set up to log when record-based operations occur, or if the standard AX Alerts are set up to alert when inserts, updates, or deletes occur

- When the cache lookup property on the table is set to entire cache

Insert_recordset

A very efficient way of inserting a chunk of data is to use the `insert_recordset` operator, as compared to using the `insert()` method. The `insert_recordset` operator can be used in two different ways; to either copy data from one or more tables to another, or simply to add a chunk of data into a table in one database operation.

The first example will show how to insert a chunk of data into a table in one database operation. To do this, we simply use two different table variables for the same table and set one of them to act as a temporary table. This means that its content is not stored in the database, but simply held in memory on the tier where the variable was instantiated.

```
static void Insert_RecordsetInsert(Args _args)
{
    CarTable        carTable;
    CarTable        carTableTmp;
    ;
    /* Set the carTableTmp variable to be a temporary table.
    This means that its contents are only store in memory
    not in the database.
    */
    carTableTmp.setTmp();
    // Insert 3 records into the temporary table.
    carTableTmp.CarId = "200";
    carTableTmp.CarBrand = "MG";
    carTableTmp.insert();
    carTableTmp.CarId = "300";
    carTableTmp.CarBrand = "SAAB";
    carTableTmp.insert();
    carTableTmp.CarId = "400";
    carTableTmp.CarBrand = "Ferrari";
    carTableTmp.insert();
    /* Copy the contents from the fields carId and carBrand
    in the temporary table to the corresponding fields in
    the table variable called carTable and insert the chunk
    in one database operation.
    */
    Insert_Recordset carTable
        (carId, carBrand)
        select carId, carBrand from carTableTmp;
}
```

The other, and perhaps more common way of using the `insert_recordset` operator, is to copy values from one or more tables into new records in another table. A very simple example on how to do this can be to create a record in the **InventColor** table for all records in the **InventTable**.

```
static void Insert_RecordsetCopy(Args _args)
{
    InventColor     inventColor;
    InventTable     inventTable;
```

```
    InventColorId    defaultColor = "B";
    Name             defaultColorName = "Blue";
    ;
    insert_recordset inventColor (ItemId, InventColorId, Name)
        select itemId, defaultColor, defaultColorName
           from inventTable;
}
```

The field list inside the parentheses points to fields in the **InventColor** table. The fields in the selected or joined tables are used to fill values into the fields in the field list.

Update_recordset

The `update_recordset` operator can be used to update a chunk of records in a table in one database operation. As with the `insert_recordset` operator the `update_recordset` is very efficient because it only needs to call an update in the database once.

The syntax for the `update_recordset` operator can be seen in the next example:

```
static void Update_RecordsetExmple(Args _args)
{
    CarTable        carTable;
    ;
    info("BEFORE UPDATE");
    while select carTable
        where carTable.ModelYear == 2007
    {
        info(strfmt("CarId %1 has run %2 miles",
          carTable.CarId, carTable.Mileage));
    }
    update_recordset carTable
        setting Mileage = carTable.Mileage + 1000
        where carTable.ModelYear == 2007;
    info("AFTER UPDATE");
    while select carTable
        where carTable.ModelYear == 2007
    {
        info(strfmt("CarId %1 has now run %2 miles",
          carTable.CarId, carTable.Mileage));
    }
}
```

When this Job is executed it will print the following messages to the **Infolog**:

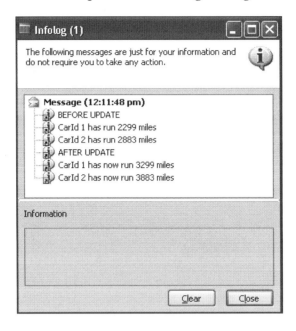

Notice that no error was thrown even though the Job didn't use `selectforupdate`, `ttsbegin`, and `ttscommit` statements in this example. The `selectforupdate` is implicit when using the `update_recordset`, and the `ttsbegin` and `ttscommit` are not necessary when all the updates are done in one database operation. However, if you were to write several `update_recordset` statements in a row, or do other checks that should make the update fail, you could use `ttsbegin` and `ttscommit` and force a `ttsabort` if the checks fail.

 Throwing an `info`, warning, or error inside a transaction scope (between `ttsbegin` and `ttscommit`) will automatically result in a `ttsabort`.

Consider modifying the previous example so that it gets a transaction scope and a check that makes sure to break the update as shown below:

```
static void Update_RecordsetExmpleTts(Args _args)
{
    CarTable        carTable;
    // Change the check to false to make the
    // transaction go through
    boolean         check = true;
    ;
```

```
info("BEFORE UPDATE");
while select carTable
    where carTable.ModelYear == 2007
{
    info(strfmt("CarId %1 has run %2 miles",
      carTable.CarId, carTable.Mileage));
}
ttsbegin;  // Added ttsbegin
update_recordset carTable
    setting Mileage = carTable.Mileage + 1000
    where carTable.ModelYear == 2007;

if (check)
    throw info("This is a test");

ttscommit; // Added ttscommit

info("AFTER UPDATE");
while select carTable
    where carTable.ModelYear == 2007
{
    info(strfmt("CarId %1 has now run %2 miles",
      carTable.CarId, carTable.Mileage));
}
}
```

The update will now never be committed in the database so every time you run this Job the the result will look like the next screenshot:

Delete_from

As with the `insert_recordset` and `update_recordset` operators, there is also an option for deleting a chunk of records. This operator is called `delete_from` and is used as the next example shows:

```
static void Delete_FromExample(Args _args)
{
    CarTable        carTable;
    ;
    delete_from carTable
        where carTable.Mileage == 0;
}
```

Direct handling

In many tables in AX the insert, update, and delete methods have been overridden to include checks or another form of logic. As you can see in the overridden insert method given next, you can put code before or after the `super()` call if you need something to happen before or after the record has been inserted into the record buffer.

```
public void insert()
{
    // Put code to happen before inserting
    // the record here
    super();    // The INSERT INTO statement in SQL is executed
    // Put code to happen after the record
    // has been inserted here
}
```

In some cases though, you will need to be able to insert, update, or delete a record in the table without running the code inside the method. You could then override the method as shown, but you would then always be stuck with the code in the overridden method.

You can then use the doInsert, doUpdate, or doDelete methods that exist on all tables in AX. These methods can never be overridden and can guarantee that the only thing they will do is to insert, update, or delete the record on which you execute the transaction.

This means that calling the doInsert method will do the same as the super() inside the insert method.

The next figure shows a very simplified example of the differences between using insert() and doInsert(). The difference is the same with the update() versus doUpdate().

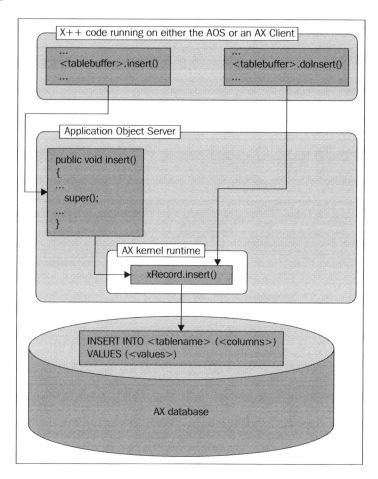

Summary

In this chapter, we have learned how to manipulate data using X++.

We have also looked at how to write code that inserts, updates, and deletes records without breaking the relationship that the record has to data in other tables.

The `ttsbegin`, `ttscommit`, `ttsabort` operators, as well as the `selectforupdate` keyword were introduced to show how to create and handle a transaction scope.

After reading about `insert_recordset`, `update_recordset`, and `delete_from` we learned how to manipulate many records within one database transaction, which is a lot more efficient than using the insert, update, or delete methods.

In addition, we also went through the difference between the insert, update, and delete methods, as well as the `doInsert`, `doUpdate`, and `doDelete` methods.

In the next chapter, we will use the knowledge gained in this chapter to integrate data with other systems. We do this by reading and writing text files and XML files, in addition to other databases using an ODBC connection.

We will also create a class library that can be used for specialized data import and export to and from AX.

7
Integrating Data

As you learned in the previous chapter, the need for data manipulation of a huge chunk of data is more easily achieved by running a periodic Job rather than user data entry. So the data that is being inserted or updated must come from somewhere, right? Let's say you have a semicolon separated file, or maybe even an XML file that contains data that you would like to read into AX. Or, perhaps you need to generate a file in AX, so that it can be read by another system?

In this chapter, you will learn how to:

- Read/write data from/to a character separated file
- Read/write data from/to a binary file
- Read/write data from/to an XML file
- Read/write data from/to a database using ODBC
- Use DictTable and DictField to create generic code for data manipulation
- Create a simple module to export and import data to/from AX

"What is the need for creating import or export routines in code when I can use the standard data import and export functionality in AX?", you might ask. Well, you will notice after a while that the standard data import or export functionality in AX is fairly limited as it treats each table as its own entity while you may also need to include data from several tables.

This chapter focuses on how to generate the different file formats rather than the transportation of the data. We will only generate files that are stored on disk. When integrating data between two systems, you will have to take the data transportation into account as well. If the system that integrates with AX exists in the same domain, storing the files in a shared folder might be sufficient. If the system exists at a different domain, perhaps at a customer or vendor site, you will have to establish a transport link between these two systems. This can be done by using FTP, Web Services, Microsoft BizTalk Server, message queuing, or e-mail to mention a few.

When setting up such a transport you should also consider creating a subsystem that logs data that is being communicated over the transport in order to pick up data that causes errors or unwanted situations.

One way of doing this can be to use the EventWriter that is shown in Chapter 10, *Working with .NET and AX.*

The **Application Integration Framework (AIF)** can be used as a middle layer between AX and the transport links mentioned previously. The AIF is most commonly used in business-to-business integration scenarios where there is a need to exchange electronic business documents.

AIF is not covered in detail in this book, but you can read more about AIF in the SDK available at: `http://msdn.microsoft.com/en-us/library/bb496535.aspx`

Text files

The most common way of integrating data is by reading or writing some sort of text files where the records are separated with a new line and the fields are separated by a certain character. This is typically achieved by using the `TextIo` or `CommaIo` class.

As you can see, in the following figure, these classes belong to a class hierarchy where the `Io` class is the main class.

 Remember to place the code that will read or write data at the correct layer. If it runs on server then the `C:\` drive used by the code will be the `C:\` drive of the AOS server. Also, remember to consider access rights to the folder that you are reading from or writing to.

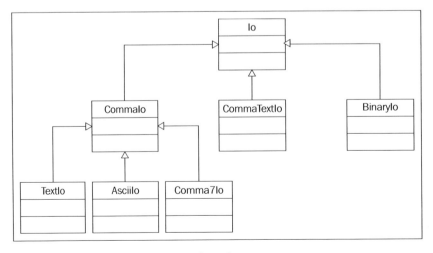

The data in AX is stored using Unicode fields in the SQL database. When this data is exported from AX you need to make sure that the files generated will also be in Unicode. To achieve this, always use the TextIo and CommaTextIo classes.

The AsciiIo and CommaIo classes should only be used if there is an absolute demand for files using the ASCII encoding.

The difference between the TextIo and the CommaTextIo is that by using the CommaTextIo class, the files will by default set the field delimiter to comma and the record delimiter to carriage return + line feed. It will also wrap all of the string fields between " ", while numbers will not be wrapped.

Write data to a text file

Let's look at an easy way to write data from AX to a text file using a Job.

First, we will put all the code in the method inside a try or catch statement to make sure we pick up any errors that are thrown.

We also need to set a filename for the file. We will use this filename when creating a new IO object, but before we do so, we have to ask the system for permission to write the file to the filepath specified. This is achieved by using the FileIoPermission class that extends the CodeAccessPermission class. To learn more about trustworthy computing and how to write secure code, check out the document "Writing Secure X++ Code" from Microsoft. This document can be found at: `http://download. microsoft.com/download/b/6/e/b6e77418-cde2-4ed4-a920-60d7f2d17757/ Microsoft%20Dynamics%20AX%20Writing%20Secure%20X++%20Code.doc`

The second parameter in `new()` specifies whether we want to read, write, or append a file. When using the TextIo class, as shown in the example, we also have the option of setting a third parameter in `new()` that specifies the codepage that we would like to use in the file. This is necessary when writing language-specific characters. You can find a list of these codepages here: `http://msdn.microsoft.com/en-us/ goglobal/bb964653.aspx`

The following table shows how to use the three different options. The Macros used are taken from the #File macro library.

Operation	Code	Macro	Description
Read	R	#io_read	Read data from a file.
Write	W	#io_write	Write data to a file. Overwrite any existing data.
Append	A	#io_append	Write data to a file. Start writing at the end of the file if it already exists.
Translate	T	#io_translate	<not in use>
Binary	B	#io_binary	<not in use>

If the filepath specified doesn't exist, or we do not have permission to write to this folder, a new object would not have been created. We should therefore check to see if a new object of the TextIo was created and throw an exception if the variable is null.

In order to write fields from a table to a file we use a container and put all the field data into the container first. Then, we simply write the container to the file. It is important to remember to empty the container each time by using the connull() method when looping through the records.

The last thing we do is to revert the code access permission by calling the static method revertAssert() that is defined in the CodeAccessPermission class.

Here is an example:

```
static server void WriteTextFile(Args _args)
{
    TextIo                  file;
    // Using the @ before the filename
    // enables us to use single path
    // delimiters. If you don't use it
    // you will have to write the path like this:
    // "c:\\temp\\cars.txt"
    FileName                filename = @"c:\temp\cars.txt";
    CarTable                carTable;
    container               con;
    FileIoPermission        permission;
    #File
    ;
    try
    {
```

```
// Create the permission class
permission = new FileIoPermission(filename, #io_write);
// Add a request for permission before new TextIo()
permission.assert();
// Create the TextIo object
file = new TextIo(filename, #io_write);
if (!file)
    throw Exception::Error;
// Specify the delimiters
file.outRecordDelimiter(#delimiterCRLF);
file.outFieldDelimiter(";");

// Loop through the data source
while select carTable
{
    // Empty the container
    con = connull();
    // Set the data into the container
    con = conins(con, 1, carTable.CarId);
    con = conins(con, 2, carTable.CarBrand);
    con = conins(con, 3, carTable.Mileage);
    con = conins(con, 4, carTable.Model);
    con = conins(con, 5, carTable.ModelYear);
    // Write the container to the file
    file.writeExp(con);
}
}
catch(Exception::Error)
{
    error("You do not have access to write the file to the
        selected folder");
}
// Revert the access privileges
CodeAccessPermission::revertAssert();

}
```

The following screenshot shows how the exported file looks like:

```
1;BMW;2299;320;2007
4;Volksvagen;49902;Golf;2006
5;Jeep;65662;Grand Cherokee;2002
6;BMW;11120;Z3;2003
7;Volksvage;76322;Golf;2000
X1001;Alfa Romeo;29982;166;2005
3;Toyota;4032;Corolla;2008
XX1;BMW;2299;320;2007
2;Mercedes;3883;C220;2007
X1000;Mazda;0;Miata;2009
```

You can now play around by changing the class used from TextIo to CommaIo or CommaTextIo and see the differences in the result, as stated earlier in this chapter.

In the previous example, we used a container to put the data into before writing the content of the container to the file. You can also write the data directly to the file by using the `write()` method instead of the `writeExp()` method. The `while` loop would then look like this:

```
while select carTable
{
    // Write the data to the file
    file.write(carTable.CarId,
               carTable.CarBrand,
               carTable.Mileage,
               carTable.Model,
               carTable.ModelYear);
}
```

Read from file

Reading from a file is very similar to writing to the file, but you now have to change the flow of data by changing the filemode to #io_read instead of #io_write. The methods that set the delimiters also have to change from outDelimiters to inDelimiters.

The `while` loop will now loop through the file content instead of the AX table. In the next example, the information from the file is printed to the infolog. You can, however, play around and find out how to insert and update the data in the `carTable`.

```
static void ReadTextFile(Args _args)
{
    TextIo              file;
    FileName            filename = @"c:\temp\cars.txt";
    CarTable            carTable;
```

```
    container          con;
    FileIoPermission   permission;
    #File
    ;
    try
    {
        // Create the permission class
        permission = new FileIoPermission(filename, #io_read);
        // Ask for permission to write the file
        permission.assert();
        // Create the TextIo object
        file = new TextIo(filename, #io_read);
        if (!file)
            throw Exception::Error;
        // Note that we now use inDelimiters
        // instead of outDelimiters as in the
        // previous example
        file.inRecordDelimiter(#delimiterCRLF);
        file.inFieldDelimiter(";");

        // Write the header info
        info("CarId - CarBrand - Mileage - Model - ModelYear");
        // Read the first record from the file
        con = file.read();
        // Loop as long as the file status is ok
        while (file.status() == IO_Status::Ok)
        {
            // Write the content to the infolog
            info(strfmt("%1 - %2 - %3 - %4 - %5",
                conpeek(con,1),
                conpeek(con,2),
                conpeek(con,3),
                conpeek(con,4),
                conpeek(con,5)));
            // Read the next record from the file
            con = file.read();
        }
    }
    catch(Exception::Error)
    {
        error("You do not have access to write the file to the
                      selected folder");
    }
    // Revert the access privileges
    CodeAccessPermission::revertAssert();
}
```

If you would like to read or write a tab delimited file, change the outFieldDelimiter or inFieldDelimiter to "\t" instead of ";" in the previous examples.

Binary files

Binary files can actually be written and read the same way as text files. The binary files are, of course, not readable in a text editor, but can easily be read back into AX.

The only change you have to make to the two previous examples is to use the BinaryIo class instead of the TextIo class.

The use of binary files to export data from AX is rare as the data will only be readable from AX. You can use it if you don't want the exported data to be readable outside AX.

XML

AX has its own data integration module called the **Application Integration Framework (AIF)** that uses XML documents as a data layer when transporting data. This book does not cover the AIF, as it could probably fill a book on its own. It does, however, cover the same generic base classes that the AIF is based upon, so it can be a good idea to read this part even if you will be using the AIF.

The use of XML files to transport data between systems is increasing rapidly. As you read in the beginning of this chapter, the transport channels used to carry the files are not covered in this chapter. You can, however, learn more on how to use web services as a transport for XML files in Chapter 11, *Web Services*. In this chapter, we simply store and read the XML files to or from the disk, as we did with the text file that we created earlier in this chapter.

Let's now have a look at how we can create an XML document and have it written and read to or from the disk.

I have created a macro library for the following examples that store the tag names so that I don't have to hardcode the text into the code. The name of the macro library is CarsXmlTags and contains the following two tags:

```
#define.CarRootNode("Cars")
#define.CarRecords("CarRecords")
```

Create XML and write to file

The following example shows how to create and write data to an XML file by using the XmlDocument, XmlElement, and XmlWriter classes. It loops through all of the records in the CarTable and find all the fields in the table automatically by using the DictTable and DictField classes.

```
static void WriteXml(Args _args)
{
    XmlDocument  xmlDoc;
    XmlElement   xmlRoot;
    XmlElement   xmlField;
    XmlElement   xmlRecord;
    XMLWriter    xmlWriter;
    CarTable     carTable;
    DictTable    dTable = new DictTable(tablenum(CarTable));
    DictField    dField;
    int          i, fieldId;
    str          value;
    #CarsXmlTags
    ;
    // Create a new object of the XmlDocument class
    xmlDoc = XmlDocument::newBlank();
    // Create the root node
    xmlRoot = xmlDoc.createElement(#CarRootNode);

    // Loop through all the records in the carTable
    while select carTable
    {
        // Create a XmlElement (record) to hold the
        // contents of the current record.
        xmlRecord = xmlDoc.createElement(#CarRecords);
        // Loop through all the fields in the record
        for (i=1; i<=dTable.fieldCnt(); i++)
        {
            // Get the fieldId from the field-count
            fieldId = dTable.fieldCnt2Id(i);
            // Find the DictField object that matches
            // the fieldId
            dField = dTable.fieldObject(fieldId);
            // Skip system fields
            if (dField.isSystem())
                continue;
            // Create a new XmlElement (field) and
            // have the name equal to the name of the
```

```
        // dictField
        xmlField = xmlDoc.createElement(dField.name());

        // Convert values to string. I have just added
        // a couple of conversion as an example.
        // Use tableName.(fieldId) instead of fieldname
        // to get the content of the field.
        switch (dField.baseType())
        {
            case Types::Int64 :
                value = int642str(carTable.(fieldId));
                break;
            case Types::Integer :
                value = int2str(carTable.(fieldId));
                break;
            default :
                value = carTable.(fieldId);
                break;
        }
        // Set the innerText of the XmlElement (field)
        // to the value from the table
        xmlField.innerText(value);
        // Append the field as a child node to the record
        xmlRecord.appendChild(xmlField);
    }
    // Add the record as a child node to the root
    xmlRoot.appendChild(xmlRecord);
}
// Add the root to the XmlDocument
xmlDoc.appendChild(xmlRoot);
// Create a new object of the XmlWriter class
// in order to be able to write the xml to a file
xmlWriter = XMLWriter::newFile(@"c:\temp\cars.xml");
// Write the content of the XmlDocument to the
// file as specified by the XmlWriter
xmlDoc.writeTo(xmlWriter);
}
```

The file that is created looks like the one in the following screenshot(only first part of the file is shown):

```xml
<?xml version="1.0" encoding="utf-8" ?>
- <Cars>
  - <CarRecords>
      <CarId>1</CarId>
      <ModelYear>2007</ModelYear>
      <CarBrand>BMW</CarBrand>
      <Model>320</Model>
      <Mileage>2299</Mileage>
    </CarRecords>
  - <CarRecords>
      <CarId>4</CarId>
      <ModelYear>2006</ModelYear>
      <CarBrand>Volksvagen</CarBrand>
      <Model>Golf</Model>
      <Mileage>49902</Mileage>
    </CarRecords>
  - <CarRecords>
      <CarId>5</CarId>
      <ModelYear>2002</ModelYear>
      <CarBrand>Jeep</CarBrand>
      <Model>Grand Cherokee</Model>
      <Mileage>65662</Mileage>
    </CarRecords>
  - <CarRecords>
      <CarId>6</CarId>
      <ModelYear>2003</ModelYear>
      <CarBrand>BMW</CarBrand>
      <Model>Z3</Model>
      <Mileage>11120</Mileage>
    </CarRecords>
```

As you can see, this file is based on a standard XML format with tags and values only. You can, however, use tag attributes as well. To put the values from the table into tag attributes instead of their own tags, simply change the following code snippet in the example above

```
// Set the innerText of the XmlElement (field)
// to the value from the table
xmlField.innerText(value);
// Append the field as a child node to the record
xmlRecord.appendChild(xmlField);
```

with these lines:

```
// Add the attribute to the record
xmlRecord.setAttribute(dField.name(), value);
```

The file that is created now looks like the one in the following screenshot:

```xml
<?xml version="1.0" encoding="utf-8" ?>
<Cars>
    <CarRecords CarId="1" ModelYear="2007" CarBrand="BMW" Model="320" Mileage="2299" />
    <CarRecords CarId="4" ModelYear="2006" CarBrand="Volksvagen" Model="Golf" Mileage="49902" />
    <CarRecords CarId="5" ModelYear="2002" CarBrand="Jeep" Model="Grand Cherokee" Mileage="65662" />
    <CarRecords CarId="6" ModelYear="2003" CarBrand="BMW" Model="Z3" Mileage="11120" />
    <CarRecords CarId="7" ModelYear="2000" CarBrand="Volksvage" Model="Golf" Mileage="76322" />
    <CarRecords CarId="X1001" ModelYear="2005" CarBrand="Alfa Romeo" Model="166" Mileage="29982" />
    <CarRecords CarId="3" ModelYear="2008" CarBrand="Toyota" Model="Corolla" Mileage="4032" />
    <CarRecords CarId="XX1" ModelYear="2007" CarBrand="BMW" Model="320" Mileage="2299" />
    <CarRecords CarId="2" ModelYear="2007" CarBrand="Mercedes" Model="C220" Mileage="3883" />
    <CarRecords CarId="X1000" ModelYear="2009" CarBrand="Mazda" Model="Miata" Mileage="0" />
</Cars>
```

Read XML from file

The following example will enable you to read a file that is in the same format as the first example in the previous subchapter. You can try on your own to create a Job that reads an XML file that uses attributes such as the second example in the previous subchapter.

```
static void ReadXml(Args _args)
{
    XmlDocument  xmlDoc;
    XmlElement   xmlRoot;
    XmlElement   xmlField;
    XmlElement   xmlRecord;
    XmlNodeList  xmlRecordList;
    XmlNodeList  xmlFieldList;
    CarTable     carTable;
    DictTable    dTable = new DictTable(tablenum(CarTable));
    int          i, j, fieldId;
    #CarsXmlTags
    ;
    // Create an XmlDocument object to hold the
    // contents of the xml-file
    xmlDoc = new XmlDocument();
    // Load the content of the xml-file
    // into the XmlDocument object
    xmlDoc.load(@"c:\temp\cars.xml");
    // Get the root node
    xmlRoot = xmlDoc.getNamedElement(#CarRootNode);
    // Get all child nodes (records)
    xmlRecordList = xmlRoot.childNodes();
    // Loop through the list of records
    for (i=0; i<xmlRecordList.length(); i++)
    {
```

```
        carTable.clear();
        // Get the current record from the
        // record list
        xmlRecord = xmlRecordList.item(i);
        // Get all child nodes (fields)
        xmlFieldList = xmlRecord.childNodes();
        // Loop through the list of fields
        for (j=0; j<xmlFieldList.length(); j++)
        {
            // Get the current field from the
            // field list
            xmlField = xmlFieldList.item(j);
            // Set the matching field in the carTable
            // to be equal to the inner text
            // (the text between the tag and end tag).
            carTable.(dTable.fieldName2Id(xmlField.name())) =
              xmlField.innerText();
        }
        // Insert the record into the carTable
        carTable.insert();
    }
}
```

ODBC

Sometimes, you will need direct access to another database either to read data from tables or in some cases to write data to tables. You can do that in AX by using an ODBC connection to the other database.

In most cases though, I would recommend having AX integrating with the application layer of the other system rather than the data layer to read data from a database. However, sometimes that is not an option, and you will need to read or write data from an external database using ODBC.

The following example shows how to set up a connection to a database using ODBC, how to create an SQL statement, how to execute the statement, and how to retrieve and loop through the result.

The database used in these examples is the AX database itself. Remember to consider access permissions. The user executing the Job should have read access to the database. If the connection is created on the AOS, the user that is set up as the execution account on the AOS should have the appropriate access to the database that you are trying to read from or write to.

Reading from a database using ODBC

The following example shows how to create a connection to another database by using the ODBC API.

These are the steps that the example follows to create a connection and read data from the external database using ODBC.

1. Create an object of the `LoginProperty` class to hold the login information for the external database.

2. Connect to the database by creating an object of the `OdbcConnection` class.

3. Define the SQL statement to be executed.

4. Ensure that the SQL statement is safe by using the `SqlStatementExecutionPermission` class.

5. Create an object of the `Statement` class and execute the SQL statement.

6. Loop through the result of the statement execution.

```
static void ReadOdbc(Args _args)
{
    OdbcConnection                  connection;
    LoginProperty                   loginProp;
    Statement                       statement;
    ResultSet                       result;
    str                             sqlStmt;
    SqlStatementExecutePermission   permission;
    ;

    // Create an object of the LoginProperty class
    loginProp = new LoginProperty();
    // Set the servername and database to the
    // LoginProperty object
    loginProp.setServer("AX-SRV-01");
    loginProp.setDatabase("AX593");

    // Check to see if the executing user has access
    try
    {
        // Create a new connection based on the information
        // set in the LoginProperty object
        connection = new OdbcConnection(loginProp);
    }
    catch
    {
```

```
            error ("You do not have access to the database specified");
            return;
    }
    // Set the select statement to the string variable
    sqlStmt = 'SELECT Dataareaid, AccountNum, Name from
            dbo.CustTable';
    // Check if it's ok to use sql statement
    permission = new SqlStatementExecutePermission(sqlStmt);
    permission.assert();
    // Create and prepare a new Statement object
    // from the connection
    statement = connection.createStatement();
    // Execute the query and retrieve the resultset
    result = statement.executeQuery(sqlStmt);

    // Loop through the records in the resultset and print
    // the information to the infolog
    while (result.next())
    {
        info (strfmt("(%1)  %2:  %3", result.getString(1),
                result.getString(2), result.getString(3)));
    }
    // Revert the permission assert
    CodeAccessPermission::revertAssert();
}
```

Writing to a database using ODBC

The next example shows how to update data in a database using an ODBC connection in AX. The same method can be used to insert or delete data. It can even be used to execute a stored procedure in the database. The steps needed are pretty much the same except that there is no result set to loop after executing the update statement.

```
static void WriteOdbc(Args _args)
{
    OdbcConnection                 connection;
    LoginProperty                  loginProp;
    Statement                      statement;
    str                            sqlStmt;
    SqlStatementExecutePermission  permission;
    ;

    // Create an object of the LoginProperty class
    loginProp = new LoginProperty();
```

```
    // Set the servername and database to the
    // LoginProperty object (consider creating a
    // fixed odbc in windows and reference it here
    // by using setDBS() instead of setServer/setDatabase
    loginProp.setServer("AX-SRV-01");
    loginProp.setDatabase("AX593");

    // Check to see if the executing user has access
    try
    {
        // Create a new connection based on the information
        // set in the LoginProperty object
        connection = new OdbcConnection(loginProp);
    }
    catch
    {
        error ("You do not have access to the database specified");
        return;
    }
    // Set the select statement to the string variable
    sqlStmt = strfmt("UPDATE dbo.CustTable SET Name='test' WHERE
            AccountNum='%1' AND Dataareaid='%2'", "1101", "ceu");
    // Check if it's ok to use sql statement
    permission = new SqlStatementExecutePermission(sqlStmt);
    permission.assert();
    // Create and prepare a new Statement object
    // from the connection
    statement = connection.createStatement();
    // Execute the query and retrieve the resultset
    statement.executeUpdate(sqlStmt);

    // Revert the permission assert
    CodeAccessPermission::revertAssert();
}
```

Import/Export example

As importing and exporting data will most likely be something that you will have to do more than once, it would be nice to have your own little module that you can use every time, one that you feel comfortable using and expanding each time as you find new ways of using it.

I know that the standard import/export tool in AX also lets you do many of these things, but you are a programmer, right? So you probably prefer to write the code yourself.

Anyway, I just wanted to get you started with a simple example that shows how you can have a simple dialog where the user can select what to import/export, the filename, and so on.

The following is the class model diagram of the example:

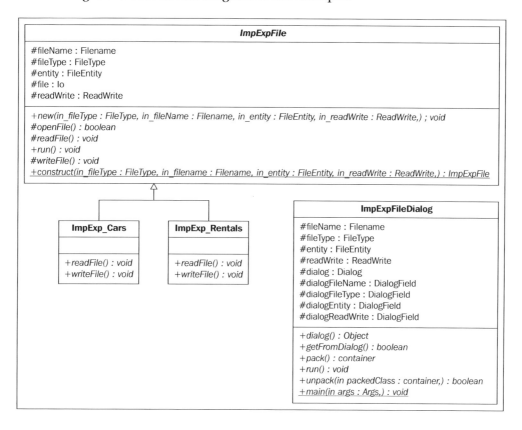

ImpExpFileDialog class

This is the dialog class that is common for all the different import/export entities. You do not need to change this class when adding a new entity class. Change this class only if you would like the dialog to look different or want to add additional fields to the dialog.

classDeclaration

This class provides the starting point for the `ImpExpFile` classes by presenting a dialog for the user, creating an object of the `ImpExpFile` class hierarchy, and then passing control to the created object.

```
class ImpExpFileDialog extends RunBase
{
    // Global variables
    FileName            fileName;
    FileType            fileType;
    FileEntity          entity;
    ReadWrite           readWrite;
    Dialog              dialog;
    // Dialog fields
    DialogField         dialogFileName;
    DialogField         dialogFileType;
    DialogField         dialogEntity;
    DialogField         dialogReadWrite;

    #define.CurrentVersion(1)
    // Macro that contains the global variables
    // to be kept until the next time the user
    // executes this class.
    #localmacro.CurrentList
        filcName,
        fileType,
        entity,
        readWrite
    #endmacro
}
```

dialog

The dialog method defines the dialog that is presented to the user when the prompt method is executed.

```
public Object dialog()
{
    ;
    // Create a new object of the DialogRunbase class
    dialog = new DialogRunbase("Import data from file", this);

    // Add the fields to the dialog and
    // set the initial value to be equal to
```

```
        // the value selected last time.
        dialogReadWrite =
          dialog.addFieldValue(typeid(ReadWrite), readWrite);
        dialogFileName =
          dialog.addFieldValue(typeid(FileName), fileName);
        dialogFileType =
          dialog.addFieldValue(typeid(FileType), fileType);
        dialogEntity = dialog.addFieldValue(typeid(FileEntity), entity);
        return dialog;
    }
```

getFromDialog

This method originated from `RunBase` is initiated when the user clicks on the
OK button in the dialog and is used to store the values the user selected. It is shown
as follows:

```
    public boolean getFromDialog()
    {
        ;
        fileName        = dialogFileName.value();
        fileType        = dialogFileType.value();
        entity          = dialogEntity.value();
        readWrite       = dialogReadWrite.value();

        return super();
    }
```

pack

This method is a standard method inherited from `RunBase`. It is used to save
the values that the user selects and store them until the next time the user executes
the class.

```
    public container pack()
    {
        return [#CurrentVersion,#CurrentList];
    }
```

run

Standard methods from RunBase typically used to start the main execution flow of the class.

```
public void run()
{
    // Create a new object of the ImpExpFile class-hierarchy
    // based on the values selected in the dialog.
    ImpExpFile      impExpFile = ImpExpFile::construct(fileType,
                        fileName, entity, readWrite);
    ;

    // Start the main flow of the ImpExpFile object
    impExpFile.run();
}
```

unpack

Standard method inherited from RunBase and used to fetch the values that the user selected the previous time he executed the class.

```
public boolean unpack(container packedClass)
{
    Version version = RunBase::getVersion(packedClass);
    ;
    switch (version)
    {
        case #CurrentVersion:
            [version, #CurrentList] = packedClass;
            break;
        default:
            return false;
    }

    return true;
}
```

main

This is the class entry point. It is executed when a menu item that points to it is started or if opened directly from the AOT.

```
static void main(Args args)
{
    // Create an object of the ImportFile class
    ImpExpFileDialog    importFileDialog = new ImpExpFileDialog();
    ;
    // Prompt the user with the fields
    // specified in the dialog() method
    if (importFileDialog.prompt())
        // If the user clicks on the OK-button
        // execute the run() method
        importFileDialog.run();
}
```

ImpExpFile class

This is the main class in this class hierarchy. Any code generic to the entity classes that extends this class are set here. The class is abstract, meaning that you can never create an object of this class, only its subclasses can be created (the entity classes).

classDeclaration

This is the class declaration where all the global variables for the class hierarchy are defined as follows:

```
abstract class ImpExpFile
{
    // Use the file macro to set IO flags
    #File

    // Global variables
    FileName        fileName;
    FileType        fileType;
    FileEntity      entity;
    IO              file;
    ReadWrite       readWrite;
}
```

new

Constructor that is used to set default values for some of the global variables.

```
void new(FileType _fileType, FileName _fileName, FileEntity _entity,
    ReadWrite _readWrite)
{
    ;
    fileType = _fileType;
    fileName = _fileName;
    entity = _entity;
    readWrite = _readWrite;
}
```

openFile

This method is used to open the selected file either to read from or write to, as shown below:

```
protected boolean openFile()
{
    boolean ret = true;
    str     rw;
    ;
    if (readWrite == ReadWrite::Read)
        rw = #io read;
    else
        rw = #io_write;

    switch (fileType)
    {
        case FileType::Binary :
            file = new BinaryIo(filename, rw);
            break;
        case FileType::Comma :
            file = new CommaIO(filename, rw);
            break;
        default :
            ret = false;
            break;
    }
    return ret;
}
```

readFile

This method is used to initialize the file to be read as follows:

```
protected void readFile()
{
    if(!this.openFile())
        throw error("Unable to open the selected file");

    file.inFieldDelimiter(';');
    file.inRecordDelimiter('\r\n');
}
```

run

This is the main execution flow of the ImpExpFile. It decides whether to read to or write from file and catch any exceptions that might occur.

```
void run()
{
    try
    {
        // Use this function to make sure that
        // the mouse-pointer changes to a timeglass.
        startLengthyOperation();
        if (readWrite == ReadWrite::read)
            this.readFile();
        else
            this.writeFile();
    }
    catch (Exception::Deadlock)
    {
        retry;
    }
    catch (Exception::Error)
    {
        error(strfmt("An error occured while trying to read the file
            %1 into the %2 entity", filename, enum2str(entity)));
    }

    // Mouse-pointer can switch back
    // to normal again.
    endLengthyOperation();
}
```

writeFile

This method is used to initialize the file to be written to:

```
protected void writeFile()
{
    if(!this.openFile())
        throw error("Unable to open the selected file");
    file.outFieldDelimiter(';');
    file.outRecordDelimiter('\r\n');
}
```

construct

Creates an object of one of the subclasses based on the user input in the dialog.

```
static ImpExpFile construct(FileType _fileType, FileName _filename,
                            FileEntity _entity, ReadWrite _readWrite)
{
    ImpExpFile            impExpFile;
    ;
    switch(_entity)
    {
        case FileEntity::Cars :
            impExpFile = new ImpExp_Cars(_fileType, _filename,
                                          _entity, _readWrite);
            break;
        case FileEntity::Rentalts :
            impExpFile = new ImpExp_Rentals(_fileType, _filename,
                                              _entity, _readWrite);
            break;
    }
    return impExpFile;
}
```

ImpExp_Cars class

This is one of the entity classes that I have created, to demonstrate how to use this example framework. It allows for exporting and importing data from and to the CarTable. Note that, it only supports inserting new records into the CarTable, not updating them. You can of course add that part yourself if you have read the previous chapter.

classDeclaration

This is an empty class declaration as there are no global variables in this class.

```
class ImpExp_Cars extends ImpExpFile
{
}
```

readFile

This example shows a hardcoded way of how to read the file to be used to insert new records into the CarTable. Each line in the file is read into a container. Each field is fetched from the container using the conpeek() function.

```
void readFile()
{
    CarTable        carTable;
    container       con;
    ;
    super();

    con = file.read();

    if (conlen(con) != 5)
        throw error("The file has an illegal format");

    // Read the file as long as the file is ok.
    // The status changes when the cursor hits
    // the end of the file.
    while (file.status() == IO_Status::Ok)
    {
        carTable.clear();
        carTable.CarId = conpeek(con, 1);
        carTable.CarBrand = conpeek(con, 2);
        carTable.Model = conpeek(con, 3);
        carTable.ModelYear = conpeek(con, 4);
        carTable.Mileage = conpeek(con, 5);

        if (carTable.validateWrite())
            carTable.insert();
        con = file.read();
    }
}
```

writeFile

This is used to write information from the carTable to the file.

```
void writeFile()
{
    CarTable        carTable;
    container       con;
    ;
    super();

    while select carTable
    {
        con = conins(con, 1,
                    carTable.CarId,
                    carTable.CarBrand,
                    carTable.Model,
                    carTable.ModelYear,
                    carTable.Mileage);
        file.writeExp(con);
    }
}
```

ImpExp_Rentals class

This entity class is written to export and import all fields from the rental table. It can also be rewritten so that it is generic and work with all tables, but for now, I just wanted to show you how to use the DictTable and DictField classes while exporting and importing.

classDeclaration

This is an empty class declaration as there are no global variables in this class.

```
class ImpExp_Rentals extends ImpExpFile
{
}
```

readFile

This method uses the `DictTable` and `DictField` classes to find all the fields in the `RentalTable` and insert the data from the file to the matching fields in the `RentalTable`.

```
void readFile()
{
    RentalTable     rentalTable;
    container       con;
    DictTable       dTable = new DictTable(tablenum(RentalTable));
    DictField       dField;
    int             i, fields, field;
    ;
    super();

    con = file.read();

    while (file.status() == IO_Status::Ok)
    {
        for (i=1; i <= conlen(con); i++)
        {
            field = dTable.fieldCnt2Id(i);
            dField = dTable.fieldObject(field);
            switch (dField.baseType())
            {
                case Types::Guid :
                    rentalTable.(field) = str2guid(conpeek(con, i));
                    break;
                case Types::Int64 :
                    rentalTable.(field) = str2Int64(conpeek(con, i));
                    break;
                case Types::Date :
                    rentalTable.(field) =
                        str2Date(conpeek(con, i),321);
                    break;
                default :
                    rentalTable.(field) = conpeek(con, i);
                    break;
            }
        }
        if (rentalTable.validateWrite())
            rentalTable.insert();
        con = file.read();
    }
}
```

writeFile

This method uses the `DictTable` and `DictField` to loop through all the fields in `RentalTable` and write their content to the file.

```
void writeFile()
{
    RentalTable      rentalTable;
    container        con;
    int              fields, i, fieldId;
    DictTable        dt = new DictTable(tablenum(RentalTable));
    ;
    super();

    while select rentalTable
    {
        con = connull();
        fields = dt.fieldCnt();
        for (i=1; i<=fields; i++)
        {
            fieldId = dt.fieldCnt2Id(i);
            con = conins(con, i, rentalTable.(fieldId));
        }
        file.write(con);
    }
}
```

Summary

In this chapter, you have learned how to write data from AX to text files, XML files, and binary files and how to read the data back into AX. You have also learned how to read data and how to manipulate data in a database using ODBC.

You have learned the basics of how to use the `DictTable` and `DictField` in order to generate dynamic routines for data manipulation.

You have also seen how to create a simple class hierarchy that can be used for data import or data export in different formats.

In the next chapter, we will look at how to modify standard AX modules such as Inventory, Ledger, Accounts Receivable, and Accounts Payable.

For each of the modules, we will start by having a look at the entity schema and the main class hierarchies before looking at how to perform some of the most common tasks from X++.

8
Integrate with Standard AX

If you have come this far, you are most likely ready to figure out how to change or add functionality in standard AX. This chapter guides you through some of the challenges you face while trying to modify the way some of the standard modules in AX behave.

We will look more into some typical problems you might be faced with when integrating to standard AX in the following main modules of Dynamics AX:

- Inventory
- Ledger
- Accounts Receivable and Accounts Payable

You will also get to know the most important tables within each module, how they are related to each other, and have a look at some of the classes that control the behavior of the module.

One of the main procedural concepts of AX is the way journals and posting of journals work. A journal is like a draft, they do not have any financial transactions related to them until they are posted. Whenever a posting occurs, AX will generate transactions related to the parts of the journal that is being posted. The type of transactions depends on what kind of posting takes place.

Inventory

The inventory module in AX contains the storage and setup of items, and explains how they are stored in the physical inventory. It is also heavily integrated to most of the other modules; the production module has to know which items to produce and which items the production consist of, a sales order in accounts receivable need to know which items to sell, a purchase order in accounts payable need to know which items to purchase, and so on.

InventTable entity schema

The main entity of the inventory is the items, as you have perhaps already figured out. Items in AX are stored in the InventTable and has the following entity schema:

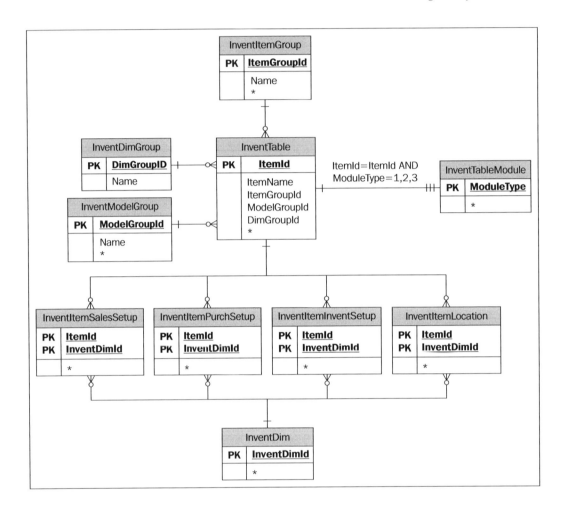

The following list gives a brief description of each of the tables shown in the InventTable entity schema:

TableName	Description
InventTable	The InventTable table contains information about items.
InventItemGroup	The InventItemGroup table contains information about item groups.
InventDimGroup	The InventDimGroup table contains information about a dimension group.
InventTableModule	The InventTableModule table contains information about purchase, sales, and inventory specific settings for items.
InventModelGroup	The InventModelGroup table contains information about inventory model groups.
InventItemSalesSetup	The InventItemSalesSetup table contains default settings for items such as Site and Warehouse. The values are related to sales settings.
InventItemPurchSetup	The InventItemPurchSetup table contains default settings for items such as Site and Warehouse. The values are related to purchase settings.
InventItemInventSetup	The InventItemInventSetup table contains default settings for items such as Site and Warehouse. The values are related to inventory settings.
InventItemLocation	The InventItemLocation table contains information about items and related warehouse and counting settings. The settings can be made specific based on the items configuration and vary from warehouse to warehouse.
InventDim	The InventDim table contains values for inventory dimensions.

 The table descriptions following each entity schema in this chapter are taken from the Dynamics AX SDK also known as the Developer Help.

As you can see, this diagram is very simplified as I have left out most of the fields in the tables to make the diagram more readable. The purpose of the diagram is to give you an idea of the relations between these tables.

The diagram shows that items are grouped into item groups and that they also have tables linked to them that describe their behavior in purchase, inventory, and sales, and also how the items should be treated in regards to financial posting and inventory posting.

InventTrans entity schema

Another entity schema that is important in the Inventory module is the
InventTransaction schema. Again, this is very simplified, with only the main
entities and only the fields that make up the primary and foreign keys shown in the
next diagram.

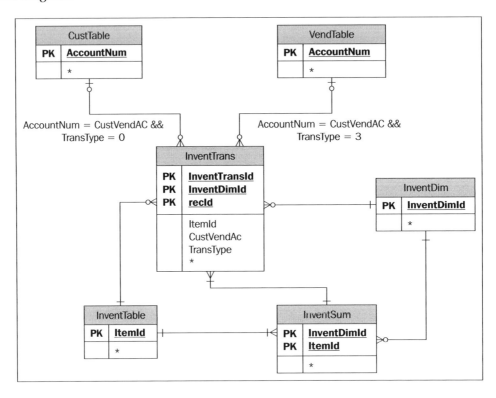

The next table gives a brief description of each of the tables shown in the InventTrans entity schema:

TableName	Description
InventTrans	The InventTrans table contains information about inventory transactions. When order lines such as sales order lines or purchase order lines are created they generate related records in the inventTrans table. These records represent the flow of material that goes in and out of the inventory.
InventTable	The InventTable table contains information about items.
InventSum	The InventSum table contains information about the present and expected on-hand stock of items. Expected on-hand is calculated by looking at the present on-hand and adding whatever is on-order (has been purchased but not arrived yet).
InventDim	The InventDim table contains values for inventory dimensions.
VendTable	The VendTable table contains vendors for accounts payable.
CustTable	The CustTable table contains the list of customers for accounts receivable and customer relationship management.

Main class hierarchies

In addition to the entity schemas it is important to know a little about the main class hierarchies within the Inventory module. We use the classes that they consist of to validate, prepare, create, and change transactions.

InventMovement

The InventMovement classes are used to validate and prepare data that will be used to generate inventory transactions. The super class in the hierarchy is the abstract class called InventMovement. All of the other classes in the hierarchy are prefixed 'InventMov_'.

For example, InventMov_Sales is used to validate and prepare inventory with sales line transactions. Another example is InventMov_Transfer that is used when dealing with inventory transfer journals.

The next screenshot is the **Application Hierarchy Tree** of the **InventMovement** class, and it shows the whole class hierarchy below **InventMovement**.

InventUpdate

The InventUpdate classes are used to insert and update inventory transactions. Whenever a transaction should be posted, the `updateNow()` method in the correct InventUpdate subclass will execute. The super class in the hierarchy is the InventUpdate class, and the other classes in the hierarchy are prefixed 'InventUpd_'.

For example, **InventUpd_Estimated** is used whenever an item line is entered in the system that will most likely generate a physical transaction in the future. A good example can be a sales order line that has the on-order sales status. When a line like this is entered or generated in AX, the **InventUpd_Estimated** is triggered so that the inventory transactions will reflect that the item is on-order.

The next figure shows the **Application Hierarchy Tree** of the **InventUpdate** class and its subclasses:

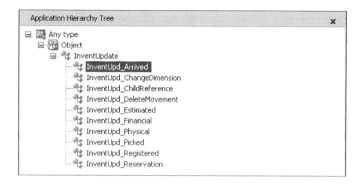

InventAdj

Whenever an adjustment to an inventory transaction takes place, the **InventAdj** classes are used.

The adjustments typically occur when you are doing inventory closing.

The next screenshot shows the **Application Hierarchy Tree** of the **InventAdj** class and its subclasses:

InventSum

The InventSum classes are used to find the on-hand information of a certain item at a certain date. The InventOnHand class is used to find the current on-hand information. The InventSum classes are not structured in a hierarchy as the classes mentioned previously.

Now that you have seen how some of the main tables in the inventory module relate to each other, we will look at how to write code that is integrated to the module.

Inventory dimensions

One thing that you will have to learn sooner, rather than later, is how the inventory dimensions work. Basically, the InventDim table holds information about all the different dimensions that are related to an item. These dimensions can be divided into two types: storage and item dimensions. By default, AX comes with nine dimensions that are listed in the next table:

Dimension	Type	Main table	Description
InventColorId	Item	InventColor	The InventColor table contains information about colors.
InventSizeId	Item	InventSize	The InventSize table contains information about item size.
ConfigId	Item	ConfigTable	The ConfigTable table contains information about available configuration of the various items.
InventBatchId	Storage	InventBatch	The InventBatch table contains information about batches.
InventSerialId	Storage	InventSerial	The InventSerial table contains information about item serial numbers.
InventLocationId	Storage	InventLocation	The InventLocation table contains information about warehouses.
InventSiteId	Storage	InventSite	The InventSite table contains information about sites.
wmsLocationId	Storage	WMSLocation	The WMSLocation table contains information about locations.
wmsPalletId	Storage	WMSPallet	The WMSPallet table contains information about pallets.

Finding an inventory dimension

When combinations of these dimensions are needed in a journal or a transaction we always check to see if the combination already exists. If it does, we link to that record in the InventDim table. If it doesn't exist, a new record in the InventDim table is created with the different dimensions filled out, and we can then link to the new record.

This is done by using a method in the InventDim table called `findOrCreate`. You can see how to use it in the next example:

```
static void findingDimension(Args _args)
{
    InventDim           inventDim;
    ;
    // Set the values that you need for
    // the journal or transaction
    inventDim.InventLocationId = "01";
    inventDim.InventColorId = "02";
    // Use findOrCreate and use the inventDim
    // variable that you have set values into
    inventDim = InventDim::findOrCreate(inventDim);
    // Use the inventDimId to link to the
    // InventDim record that was either
    // found or created
    info(inventDim.inventDimId);
}
```

 The default demo data for AX 2009 has been used by all of the code examples in this chapter.

Finding current on-hand information

Another thing you should know is how to find how many items are available within a certain `InventDim` scope. You do this by setting the InventDim fields into an `InventDim` variable and then specify which of the dimension fields, or combination of dimension fields, you would like to get on-hand information on. In the following example, we search for the on-hand information for an item in a specific color:

```
static void findingOnHandInfo(Args _args)
{
    ItemId              itemId;
    InventDim           inventDimCriteria;
    InventDimParm       inventDimParm;
    InventOnhand        inventOnhand = new InventOnhand();
    ;
    // Specify the item to get onhand info on
    itemId = "1001";
    // Specify the dimensions you want
    // to filter the onhand info on
    inventDimCriteria.InventColorId = "02";
    // Set the parameter flags active
    // according to which of the dimensions
    // in inventDimCriteria that are set
    inventDimParm.initFromInventDim(inventDimCriteria);
```

```
        // Specify the inventDim,
        // inventDimParm and itemId
        inventOnhand.parmInventDim(inventDimCriteria);
        inventOnhand.parmInventDimParm(inventDimParm);
        inventOnhand.parmItemId(itemId);
        // Retrieve the onhand info
        info(strfmt("Available Physical: %1",
          inventOnhand.availPhysical()));
        info(strfmt("On order: %1",inventOnhand.onOrder()));
}
```

You could easily narrow the information down to a specific warehouse by setting a warehouse (InventLocationId) to the inventDimCriteria as we have done for the InventColorId.

Finding on-hand information by a specific date

The next example will let you find the on-hand information of a specific item, with a specific color, on a specific date.

```
static void findingOnHandByDate(Args _args)
{
    ItemId              itemId;
    InventDim           inventDimCriteria;
    InventDimParm       inventDimParm;
    InventSumDateDim    inventSumDateDim;
    ;
    // Specify the item to get onhand info on
    itemId = "1001";
    // Specify the dimensions you want
    // to filter the onhand info on
    inventDimCriteria.InventColorId = "02";
    // Set the parameter flags active
    // accoring to which of the dimensions
    // in inventDimCriteria that are set
    inventDimParm.initFromInventDim(inventDimCriteria);
    // Specify the transaction date, inventDimCriteria,
    // inventDimParm and itemId to receive a new object
    // of InventSumDateDim
    inventSumDateDim =
        InventSumDateDim::newParameters(mkdate(01,01,2009),
                         itemId,
                         inventDimCriteria,
                         inventDimParm);
    // Retrieve the onhand info using the methods
```

```
        // of InventSumDateDim
    info(strfmt("PostedQty: %1",inventSumDateDim.postedQty()));
    info(strfmt("DeductedQty: %1",inventSumDateDim.deductedQty()));
    info(strfmt("ReceivedQty: %1",inventSumDateDim.receivedQty()));
}
```

Entering and posting an inventory journal from code

One of the things you will need to know when dealing with the inventory module is how to automate the journal entry and posting. The next example will show you one way of doing this.

```
static void enterPostInventJournal(Args _args)
{
    InventJournalName       inventJournalName;
    InventJournalTable      inventJournalTable;
    InventJournalTrans      inventJournalTrans;
    InventDim               inventDim;
    InventJournalCheckPost  inventJournalCheckPost;
    ;
    // Specify which invent journal to use
    inventJournalName = InventJournalName::find("IMov");
    // Initialize the values in the inventJournalTable
    // from the inventJournalName and insert the record
    inventJournalTable.initFromInventJournalName(inventJournalName);
    inventJournalTable.SystemBlocked = true;
    inventJournalTable.insert();

    // Insert to records into the inventJournalTrans table
    inventJournalTrans.initFromInventJournalTable
        (inventJournalTable);
    inventJournalTrans.TransDate = systemdateget();
    inventJournalTrans.ItemId = "1003";
    inventJournalTrans.Qty = 3;

    // Find the default dimension
    inventDim.initFromInventTable
        (inventJournalTrans.inventMovement().inventTable(),
          InventItemOrderSetupType::Invent,inventDim);
    // Set additional mandatory dimensions
    inventDim.InventColorId = "02";
    inventDim.InventSizeId = "50";
    inventDim.configId = "HD";
    // See if the inventDim with the selected values
    // allready exist in the InventDim table. If not, it's
    // created automatically
    inventDim = InventDim::findOrCreate(inventDim);
    inventJournalTrans.InventDimId = inventDim.inventDimId;
```

```
        // Offset account is mandatory
        inventJournalTrans.LedgerAccountIdOffset = "401170";
        inventJournalTrans.insert();
        // Use the InventJournalCheckPost class to
        // post the journal
        inventJournalCheckPost =
          InventJournalCheckPost::
            newJournalCheckPost(JournalCheckPostType::Check,
              inventJournalTable);
        inventJournalCheckPost.run();
    }
```

Ledger

The ledger module (also known as General Ledger) is where all financial transactions in AX are controlled and stored. Most of the other modules are connected to the Ledger module in some way as it is the "money central" of AX.

The main entity of the ledger module is the LedgerTable that consists of the chart of accounts. In addition, there are transaction tables and other tables related to the LedgerTable, and hopefully you will gain an understanding of how some of these tables relate to each other by taking a look at the next entity schema:

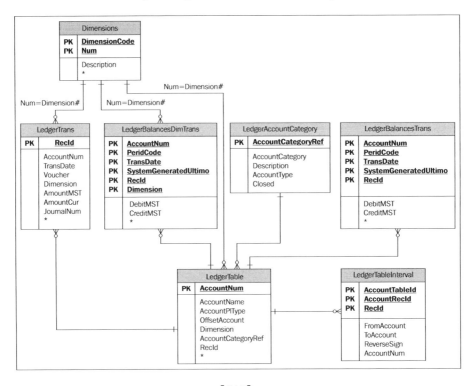

The next table gives a brief description of each of the tables shown in the Ledger entity schema:

TableName	Description
LedgerTable	The LedgerTable contains the definitions of the general ledger accounts, also called the chart of accounts.
LedgerTrans	The LedgerTrans table contains the posted general ledger transactions.
LedgerAccountCategory	The LedgerAccountCategory contains the financial categories that accounts fall into. The categories are assigned to accounts to allow easier grouping of accounts on financial statements.
Dimensions	The Dimensions table contains the dimension values for all of the defined dimensions. This is explained further later on.
LedgerTableInterval	The LedgerTableInterval table contains ranges of accounts associated with a Total ledger account.
LedgerBalancesTrans	The LedgerBalancesTrans table contains the posted ledger amounts per account and date.
LedgerBalancesDimTrans	The LedgerBalancesTrans table contains the posted ledger amounts per account, date, and dimension.

Ledger posting

There are two ways of posting ledger transactions:

- LedgerJournal: Enter data into a journal and post the journal using the LedgerJournalCheckPost class
- LedgerVoucher: Create a list of vouchers (LedgerVoucherObject) and post them using the LedgerVoucher class

Enter and post a ledger journal

The easiest way of posting ledger transaction is by using the LedgerJournal. The procedure is similar to the example in the previous section of this chapter, where you learned how to fill the inventory journal with data and then post the journal from code.

In the next example, we will do the same by filling LedgerJournalTable and LedgerJournalTrans with data and posting the journal using the LedgerJournalCheckPost class.

```
static void enterPostLedgerJournal(Args _args)
{
    LedgerJournalName        ledgerJournalName;
```

```
    LedgerJournalTable      ledgerJournalTable;
    LedgerJournalTrans      ledgerJournalTrans;

    LedgerJournalCheckPost  ledgerJournalCheckPost;
    NumberSeq               numberSeq;
    ;
    // You MUST have tts around the code or else
    // the numberSeq will generate an error while
    // trying to find the next available voucher
    ttsbegin;
    // Specify which ledger journal to use
    ledgerJournalName = LedgerJournalName::find("GenJrn");
    // Initialize the values in the ledgerJournalTable
    // from the ledgerJournalName and insert the record
    ledgerJournalTable.initFromLedgerJournalName
      (ledgerJournalName.JournalName);
    ledgerJournalTable.insert();

    // Find the next available voucher number from
    // number sequence setup with the journalName
    numberSeq = NumberSeq::
      newGetVoucherFromCode(ledgerJournalName.VoucherSeries);
    ledgerJournalTrans.voucher = numberSeq.voucher();

    // Set the fields necessary in the ledgerJournalTrans
    ledgerJournalTrans.JournalNum = ledgerJournalTable.JournalNum;
    ledgerJournalTrans.currencyCode = 'USD';
    ledgerJournalTrans.ExchRate =
      Currency::exchRate(ledgerJournalTrans.currencyCode);
    ledgerJournalTrans.AccountNum = '140550';
    ledgerJournalTrans.AccountType = ledgerJournalACType::Ledger;
    ledgerJournalTrans.AmountCurDebit = 1220.00;
    ledgerJournalTrans.TransDate = systemdateget();
    ledgerJournalTrans.Txt = 'Projector sold';
    ledgerJournalTrans.OffsetAccount = '401140';
    // Insert to records into the ledgerJournalTrans table
    ledgerJournalTrans.insert();

    // Use the LedgerJournalCheckPost class to
    // post the journal
    ledgerJournalCheckPost =
      LedgerJournalCheckPost::construct(LedgerJournalType::Daily);
    // Set the JournalId, tableId of the journalTable
    // and specify to post the journal (not only check it).
    ledgerJournalCheckPost.parmJournalNum
      (ledgerJournalTable.JournalNum);
    ledgerJournalCheckPost.parmPost(NoYes::Yes);
    ledgerJournalCheckPost.run();

    ttscommit;
}
```

You can also have AX validate the content of the journal before posting it. This is a good idea, especially when the data originates from a different solution, for instance, when migrating data from a previous ERP system to AX.

LedgerVoucher

Using the LedgerVoucher classes to post ledger transactions means that you have to first create vouchers before posting them. This is more controlled, and more similar to the traditional way of dealing with posting of ledger transactions.

The method is based on having a LedgerVoucher object where you can add multiple vouchers (LedgerVoucherObject). For each voucher you typically have 2 transactions (LedgerVoucherTransObject), one for debit and one for credit. You can, of course, have more transactions in a voucher. However, they have to reconcile. That means that if you add the amount of all of the credit transactions and all of the debit transactions, the result has to be 0.

When all transactions have been added to a voucher, and all vouchers has been added to the LedgerVoucher object, you can simply call the `ledgerVoucher.end()` in order to validate and post the voucher.

```
static void createAndPostLedgerVoucher(Args _args)
{
    LedgerVoucherTransObject      ledgerVoucherTransObjectCredit,
                                  ledgerVoucherTransObjectDebit;
    LedgerVoucherObject           ledgerVoucherObject;
    LedgerVoucher                 ledgerVoucher;
    NumberSeq                     numberSeq;
    ;
    // MUST use tts to make the numberSeq work
    ttsbegin;
    // Get a new voucher
    numberSeq = NumberSeq::
      newGetVoucher(LedgerParameters::numRefLedgerTempVoucher());
    ledgerVoucher = LedgerVoucher::
      newLedgerPost(DetailSummary::Detail, SysModule::Ledger,
        numberSeq.parmNumberSequenceCode());
    ledgerVoucherObject = LedgerVoucherObject::
      newVoucher(numberSeq.voucher());
    // Create a credit voucher transaction
    ledgerVoucherTransObjectCredit =
      LedgerVoucherTransObject::newCreateTrans(
                ledgerVoucherObject,
                LedgerPostingType::CustRevenue,
```

```
            '130100',              // Offset ledger account
            Dimensions::emptyDimension(),
            CompanyInfo::find().currencyCode,
            -5000,                 // Amount
            0,  // Reference to the originating table if any
            0); // Reference to the originating record if any
    // Add the credit transaction to the ledger voucher
    ledgerVoucher.addTrans(ledgerVoucherTransObjectCredit);

    // Create a debit voucher transaction
    ledgerVoucherTransObjectDebit =
      LedgerVoucherTransObject::newCreateTrans(
            ledgerVoucher.findLedgerVoucherObject(),
            LedgerPostingType::CustRevenue,
            '411200',              // Ledger account
            Dimensions::emptyDimension(),
            CompanyInfo::find().currencyCode,
            5000,                  // Amount
            0,  // Reference to the originating table if any
            0); // Reference to the originating record if any
    // Add the debit transaction to the ledger voucher
    ledgerVoucher.addTrans(ledgerVoucherTransObjectDebit);

    // Validate and post the ledgerVoucher
    ledgerVoucher.end();

    ttscommit;
}
```

Dimensions

The financial dimensions in AX (also called dimensions) are used to group financial transactions in greater detail. It does so using more than just the ledger account as reference, for a broader perspective. Using more references adds additional grouping and filtering in reports, inquiries, and when executing tasks on a set of transactions.

Standard AX comes with the following three default dimensions:

- Department
- Cost center
- Purpose

The name of these dimensions can easily be changed by changing the label of the values of the base enum SysDimensions, and also by changing the labels of the array elements of the following extended data types:

- Dimension
- DimensionAllocation

- DimensionCriteria
- DimensionExtCodeId
- DimensionKeepFromTransaction
- DimensionLedgerAllocCriteria
- DimensionLedgerJournal
- DimensionPriority
- MandatoryDimension

Using array elements in an extended data type means that when you drag-and-drop the extended data type into a table, you are actually adding several fields. The number of fields added to the table equals the number of array elements in the extended data type plus 1 field. The reason for the extra field is that the first array element is the extended data type itself.

In order to read or write data, from or to a dimension field, you have to keep in mind that dimensions are treated as arrays in X++.

```
static void dimensionArray(Args _args)
{
    LedgerTrans       lt;
    ;
    select firstonly lt
        where lt.Voucher == "INV-100628";
// Get dimensions
    info(strfmt("Department: %1",lt.Dimension[1]));
    info(strfmt("Purpose: %1",lt.Dimension[2]));
    info(strfmt("Costsenter: %1",lt.Dimension[3]));
// Set dimensions
    lt.Dimension[1] = "090";
    lt.Dimension[2] = "100";
    lt.Dimension[3] = "010";
}
```

The table that holds the valid dimension values is the Dimensions table. Here you can add all the different values that AX should be able to use when creating transactions.

Adding a new dimension

To add a new dimension in AX, you can simply run the Financial Dimension Wizard from the main menu **Tools | Development tools | Wizards | Financial Dimension Wizard** and follow the steps given next:

Before running the wizard you need to fix a small bug in AX:

- Open the AOT, go to the class **SysDimensionAddWizard,** and open the method **run()**

- Add the following line somewhere inside the **if** statement:

```
this.addElementToEDT(typeId(DimensionExtCodeId), labelDimension,
strFmt("External code type for converting %1", labelDimension));
```

- Then open the **versionControlCheckOut** method and add the following lines:

```
treeNode = treeNodeEDTPath.AOTFindChild("DimensionExtCodeId");
listTreeNodePaths.addEnd(treeNode.treeNodePath());
```

Now you are ready to run the wizard as specified next:

Type the name of the new dimension. The caption is set to the same as the name by default, but you can override it if you would like to. The caption will be created in the label file as specified. The enumeration value is defaulted to value 100 if it is the first dimension you are adding.

Click on the **Next** button when you are satisfied with the values entered.

 The number of dimensions that are available to add in AX are controlled by a license key. This means that you should make sure that the AX solution where you are adding dimensions have sufficient licenses for the number of dimensions needed.

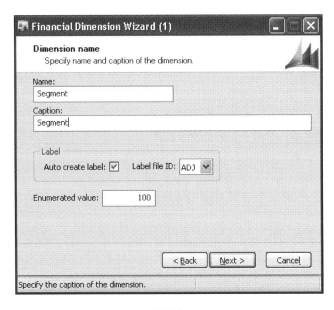

In the next step of the wizard, simply click on **Finish**.

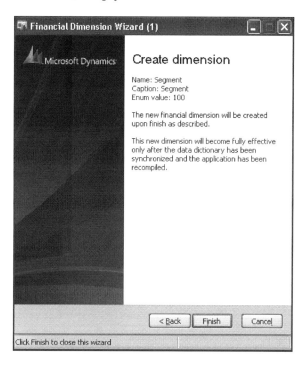

All changes needed in the code are done now, but you have to synchronize the Data Dictonary (right click on **DataDictionary** in the AOT and select **Synchronize**) to complete the change.

The result of this example and the dimension wizard hotfix are in the project Chapter8, included in the code bundle for this book.

Accounts Receivable / Accounts Payable

The Accouns Receivable (AR) and Accounts Payable (AP) modules in AX are very similar to one another. On one hand you have customers and sales orders, and on the other hand you have vendors and purchase orders. The examples in this chapter are only from the AR, but switching the example to AP should be no problem for you at this point.

As you can see from the next entity schema, the similarities between the tables on the different sides are taken to a common level using a table map in the in AOT. This enables you, as a developer, to write one class that can easily handle both AR and AP simultaneously when you reference the table map, instead of having two classes; one class to reference the AP tables and another class to reference the AR tables.

Entity schema: Base data and orders

This entity schema shows how the base data in the Accounts Receivable (AR) and Accounts Payable (AP) modules relate to one another. It also shows that the fields that are common in the AR and AP modules are put into **Maps** to enable one piece of code to refer to the MAP and have it work for both the AR and the AP modules.

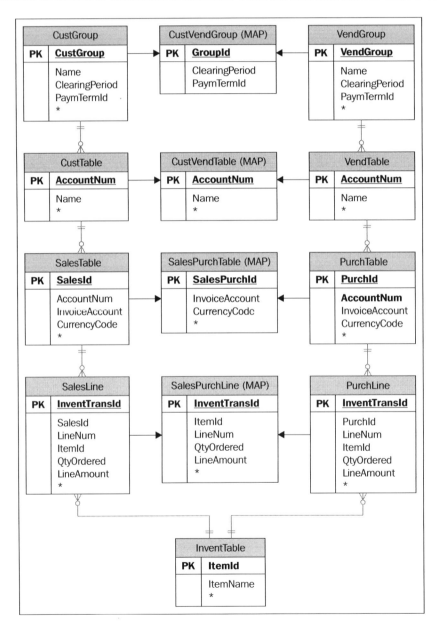

Again, this schema is very simplified since there are many more fields and other entities that also relate to the tables in the schema.

The following table gives a brief description of each of the tables shown in the previous entity schema:

TableName	Description
CustGroup	The CustGroup table contains a list of groups into which customers can be added. Every customer must specify a CustGroup with which it is associated. The group contains information such as default payment terms and settlement periods, and is also used for reporting.
VendGroup	The VendGroup table contains definitions of vendor groups.
CustTable	The CustTable table contains the list of customers for accounts receivable and customer relationship management.
VendTabel	The VendTable table contains vendors for accounts payable.
SalesTable	The SalesTable table contains all sales order headers, regardless of whether they have been posted or not.
PurchTable	The PurchTable table contains all purchase order headers, regardless of whether they have been posted or not.
SalesLine	The SalesLine table contains all sales order lines, regardless of whether they have been posted or not.
PurchLine	The PurchLine table contains all purchase order lines, regardless of whether they have been posted or not.

Entity schema: Transactions

The transactions entity schema shows how the customer and vendor transactions link to the settlement tables and the ledger transactions, and how all of these tables relate to the ledger dimensions.

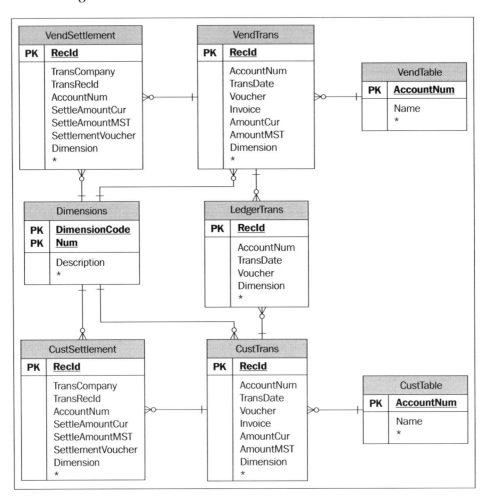

The following table gives a brief description of each of the tables shown in the transactions entity schema:

TableName	Description
CustTrans	The CustTrans table contains posted transaction information for the customer.
VendTrans	The VendTrans table contains posted transaction information for the vendor.
CustSettlement	The CustSettlement table contains information relating to the settlement or reverse settlement of two transactions. They are used to link a transaction with the transaction it was settled against.
VendSettlement	The VendSettlement table contains information relating to the settlement or reverse settlement of two transactions. They are used to link a transaction with the transaction it was settled against.

Trade agreements

The trade agreements module in AX is where prices and discounts are handled. An item can, for example, have a default sales price, discount, and so on, that is valid for all customers. This information is then stored in the InventTableModule table (see the InventTable entity schema under the *Inventory* section of this chapter).

At other times however times however, you would like to give either a certain customer, a group of customers or perhaps all customers, special prices or discounts on an item, a group of items, or all items. This is achieved by setting up trade agreements in the PriceDiscTable.

 A price can only be set for a specific item. You cannot set a price for a group of items or all items. You can however, set a discount on all items, a group of items, or on a specific item.

The trade agreements can also be combined so that, for example, multiple discounts are used to give the customer the correct price. This is done by checking the Find Next flag in the trade agreements form. Explaining all the details of the trade agreements in AX is beyond the scope of this book, but I suggest that you play around in AX to set up several different price agreements and try them out in a sales order to see the different effects they have.

Finding the price for an item for a specific customer

Finding the correct price for an item can be pretty messy if you start to write code that searches the `PriceDisc` table for the price. Luckily, you don't have to since this has already been taken care of in standard AX. The question is, however, how to use the code that is present in standard AX to get the correct prices when you write your code. The next example shows you how to find the correct price of an item with a specific item dimension for a given customer account.

```
static void findPrice(Args _args)
{
    PriceDisc           priceDisc;
    InventDim           inventDim;
    Price               price;
    CustTable           custTable;
    InventTable         inventTable;
    InventTableModule   sales;
    ;
    // Specify the inventDim that we would like
    // to get the price for
    inventDim.configId = "HD";
    inventDim.InventSizeId = "50";
    inventDim.InventColorId = "01";
    inventDim = InventDim::findDim(inventDim);

    // Specify the item and customer
    inventTable = InventTable::find("1003");
    custTable = CustTable::find("1101");
    sales = inventTable.inventTableModuleSales();

    // Create a new object of the PriceDisc
    // class with the specifications of parameters
    priceDisc = new PriceDisc(ModuleInventPurchSales::Sales,
                              inventTable.ItemId,
                              inventDim,
                              sales.UnitId,
                              systemdateget(),
                              1, // Quantity
                              custTable.AccountNum);
    // Find the price from PriceDiscTable if one exist
    // for the specification
    if (priceDisc.findPrice(custTable.PriceGroup))
        price = priceDisc.price();

    // If no record in PriceDiscTable matches, then
    // get the default item price
    else if (priceDisc.findItemPrice())
        price = priceDisc.price();

    info(strfmt("Price: %1", priceDisc.price()));
}
```

Posting and printing Sales/Purch updates

One of the most commonly used classes in AX are the FormLetter classes. The FormLetter classes define how to post different status updates against sales orders and purchase orders.

The next screenshot shows the class hierarchy of **FormLetter** with all its subclasses:

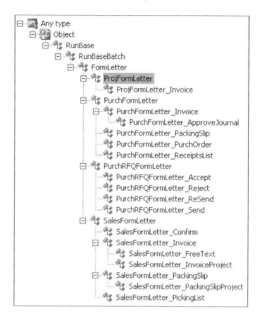

As you can see, there are four main operations on both the sales and the purchase side that are fairly similar:

Sales	Purch
Confirmation	Purchase order
Picking list	Receipt list
Packing slip	Packing slip
Invoice	Invoice

In addition, the class hierarchy contain classes for updating request for quotes and project invoices.

Since the process of posting orders can include several orders in one update, and also, only post parts of an order, AX uses parm tables that are filled with data before the actual posting. For example, on the sales side the SalesParmUpdate contains information regarding the update taking place and can be linked to several records in the SalesParmTable that again contains information regarding the sales orders being updated. The SalesParmLine is linked to the SalesParmTable and contain information regarding the lines being updated.

The normal flow when a posting is being performed is that the parm tables are populated with data, and then the update itself is performed.

Updating a single sales order is, however, a lot easier as the next example shows. It will of course, only update the one order and also update all the lines in the order.

```
static void postSalesInvoice(Args _args)
{
    // Define a classvariable according to the
    // type of posting being performed
    SalesFormLetter_Invoice      invoice;
    SalesTable                   salesTable;
    ;

    // Select the salesTable to update
    salesTable = SalesTable::find("SO-101297");

    // Create a new object of the SalesFormLetter_Invoice
    // by using the construct-method in SalesFormLetter
    invoice = SalesFormLetter::construct(DocumentStatus::Invoice);
    // Post the invoice
    invoice.update(salesTable,
                    SystemDateGet(),
                    SalesUpdate::All,
                    AccountOrder::None,
                    false,
                    true); // Set to true to print the invoice

}
```

Settlement

When a payment is made or received towards an invoice, either on the vendor side or on the customer side, the transactions have to settle against each other in order to close transaction. Obviously, the standard functionality in AX lets the users take care of this in a very neat way, using the payment journal form, where they can enter the payment into AX and mark the invoices to settle the payment against.

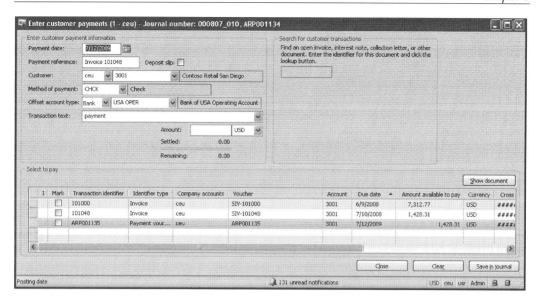

However, you might find yourself creating an integration that should take care of this automatically, and then it would be nice to know how to do this using X++, right?

Let us assume that a payment has been registered by the customer account shown in the previous form (**3001**), but the settlement hasn't been done yet. It is our task to write the code that takes care of it.

The following code should do the trick:

```
static void settlePayment(Args _args)
{
    CustTable custTable;
    CustTrans invCustTrans, payCustTrans;
    SpecTransManager    manager;
    CustVendTransData    custVendTransData;
    ;
    custTable = CustTable::find("3001");
    // Find the oldest invoice that hasn't been settled yet
    // for this customer
    select firstonly invCustTrans
        order by TransDate asc
        where invCustTrans.AccountNum == custTable.AccountNum &&
            invCustTrans.TransType == LedgerTransType::Sales &&
            !invCustTrans.LastSettleDate;
    // Find the oldest payment that hasn't been settled yet
    // for this customer
    select firstonly payCustTrans
        order by TransDate asc
        where payCustTrans.AccountNum == custTable.AccountNum &&
```

```
                payCustTrans.TransType == LedgerTransType::Payment &&
                !payCustTrans.LastSettleDate;
    ttsbegin;
    // Create an object of the CustVendTransData class
    // with the invoice transaction as parameter and mark
    // it for settlement
    custVendTransData = CustVendTransData::construct(invCustTrans);
    custVendTransData.markForSettlement(CustTable);
    // Create an object of the CustVendTransData class
    // with the payment transaction as parameter and mark
    // it for settlement
    custVendTransData = CustVendTransData::construct(payCustTrans);
    custVendTransData.markForSettlement(CustTable);
    ttscommit;
    // Settle all transactions marked for settlement for this
    // customer
    if(CustTrans::settleTransact(custTable, null, true,
       SettleDatePrinc::DaysDate, systemdateget()))
          info("Transactions settled");
}
```

Summary

In this chapter you have learned how to trigger standard functionality in AX that is normally done manually from code. Being able to automate processes and extending the standard functionality will most likely be something that you will do over and over again if you work with customer development.

You should now know how the main tables and the transactional tables in the inventory, ledger, accounts receivable, and accounts payable modules are related to each other.

In the inventory section you learned how to find an inventory dimension, how to find the current inventory stock for an item, how to find the inventory stock for an item by a specific date, and how to enter and post an inventory journal.

In the ledger section you learned how to add a new financial dimension, and how to enter and post a ledger journal.

In the AR and AP section you learned how to find an item price from the trade agreements for a specific customer, how to post a sales order invoice, and how to settle a payment against an invoice.

In the next chapter you will learn how to create and set up a new module in AX by creating number sequences, parameter tables, and configuring the security framework.

9
Creating a New Module

At some point in time you might have a great idea for a fantastic module in AX that solves some of the trouble your customers may be having. If so, there are a couple of things to keep in mind.

In this chapter you will learn about the following topics:

- Number sequences
- Parameter tables
- Security framework

As you learned in Chapter 4, *Data-User Interaction*, a module in AX should have its own area page that contains menu items added to the menu element for the module grouped by the following sub groups:

- Places
- Common forms
- Journals
- Reports
- Inquiry
- Periodic
- Setup

The places and common forms groups are added automatically based on the content of the menu; the rest of the groups have to be added manually.

After implementing the examples in this chapter, you should have an area page for the **Car Rental** module that looks like the next screenshot:

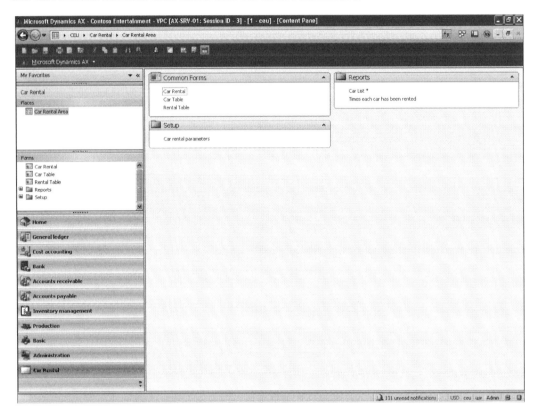

Setting up a number sequence reference

Number sequences are used to automatically create values for specific fields when a new record is created. They are typically used by identifier fields and can have prefix, infix, postfix, a number formatting, and a specification of how to increment an identifier field.

The number sequences that already exist in AX can be adjusted and set up using the **Number Sequence** form that is available under: **Main Menu | Basic | Setup | Number sequences | Number sequences**. New number sequences can also be created in this form, but in order to set up a new number sequence you will first have to:

- Create an extended data type to connect the number sequence to
- Create a number sequence reference that will be used by the extended data type RentalId
- Used RentalId as the unique identifier in the **RentalTable**

This example will demonstrate how to add a new module to the number sequences framework as well as adding a new number sequence reference. If you only need to add a new number sequence reference to an existing module, some of the following steps are obsolete:

1. The first thing to do in order to add a new module to the number sequence framework is to add a new element to the base enum **NumberSeqModule**.

2. We will add a new element that we call **CarRental**. We also create a new configuration key that we call `CarRental` as well. This configuration key will enable us to turn the module on and off in an AX installation.

3. Do this by right-clicking on the **Configuration Keys** under the **Data Dictionary** node in the AOT and selecting new **Configuration Key**. Then simply name the configuration key **CarRental** and change the label to **Car rental**.

> Beware that turning off a configuration key will drop the tables that use the configuration key. This means that all of the content in those tables will be deleted.

4. After the configuration key has been created, we will modify the **ConfigurationKey** parameter to **CarRental** on the following elements:

5. The next screenshot shows the **ConfigurationKey** parameter changed on the extended data type `RentalId`.

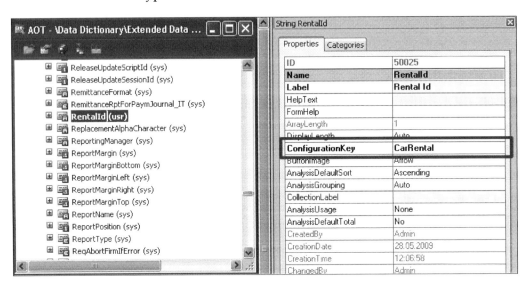

6. The next thing we need to do is to add a new class that extends the `NumberSeqReference` class. Our new class will be called `NumberSeqReference_CarRental` and will look like this:

```
public class NumberSeqReference_CarRental extends
NumberSeqReterence
{
}

public static client server NumberSeqModule numberSeqModule()
{
    return NumberSeqModule::CarRental;
}

protected void loadModule()
{
    NumberSequenceReference numRef;

    ;
    /* Setup CarRental numbers */
    numRef.DataTypeId = typeId2ExtendedTypeId(typeid(RentalId));
    numRef.ConfigurationKeyId = configurationkeynum(CarRental);
    // Use lable instead like this:
    // numRef.ReferenceHelp = literalstr("@SYS53946");
    numRef.ReferenceHelp =
      "Unique key for rental identification. The key is used
        when new rentals are created.";
```

```
        numRef.WizardManual = NoYes::No;
        numRef.WizardAllowChangeDown = NoYes::No;
        numRef.WizardAllowChangeUp = NoYes::No;
        numRef.SortField = 1;
        this.create(numRef);
    }
```

7. We also have to change the following methods in the `NumberSeqReference` class:

    ○ construct

    ○ moduleList

8. In the construct method, we add the following code inside the switch statement:

```
// CarRental
    case (NumberSeqReference_CarRental::numberSeqModule())
        : return new NumberSeqReference_CarRental(_module);
// CarRental
```

9. In the moduleList method, we add the following code before the return statement:

```
// CarRental
    moduleList += NumberSeqReference_CarRental::numberSeqModule();
// CarRental
```

10. In order to set up the number sequence reference, we also have to add a parameter that will link the number sequence reference to a number sequence created in the number sequence table. We will discuss the steps to do this in the next section of this chapter.

Parameter table

Most modules need a parameter-table that can only consist of one record. The values in the table specify general options for the module. They typically consist of the number sequences needed for the module and default values that are used throughout the module.

In the next example we create a parameter table for the **Car Rental** module.

First off, we will create a table in the same way that we did in Chapter 3, *Storing Data*, and name the table **CarRentalParameters** and set the label of the table to be **Car rental parameters**.

We then add a field to the parameter table that will work as the key for the parameter table, ensuring that a maximum of one record can exist in the table. In order to do this we open an additional AOT window and browse down to the extended data type named **ParametersKey**. Then we drag-and-drop it onto the **Fields** node of our newly created parameter table and change the name of the field in the table to **Key**. We also have to change the following properties of the **Key** field in the parameter table:

- AllowEditOnChange: No
- AllowEdit: No
- Visible: No

We also create an index that consists of this single field and call it **KeyIdx**, and set the parameter Allow Duplicates to No.

Then we add a field that will be used to hold the default file location for importing and exporting data in the module. This field is used in the example at the end of this section. We name this field **DefaultFilepath** and use it to extend the extended data type Filename.

The next thing we do is change some of the parameters of the **CarRentalParameter** table:

- TableContents: Base + default data
- MaxAccessNode: Edit
- CacheLookup: Found
- TableGroup: Parameter
- PrimaryIndex: KeyIdx
- ClusterIndex: KeyIdx
- ModifyDateTime: Yes
- ModifyBy: Yes

We will also create a find method for the table that will look something like this:

```
client server static CarRentalParameters find(boolean _forupdate =
false)
{
    CarRentalParameters parameter;
    ;
    // Try/catch added because of issues that
    // might occur during upgrade
    try
    {
        if (_forupdate)
            parameter.selectForUpdate(_forupdate);
```

```
        // Find the one and only record in
        // the table if any
        select firstonly parameter
            index KeyIdx
            where parameter.Key == 0;
        // If the record doesn't exist and
        // the table buffer used has not been
        // set as temporary, then create the record.
        if (!parameter && !parameter.isTmp())
            Company::createParameter(parameter);
    }
    catch (Exception::DuplicateKeyException,parameter)
    {
        retry;
    }
    return parameter;
}
```

The **CarRentalParameter** table should now appear in the AOT as follows:

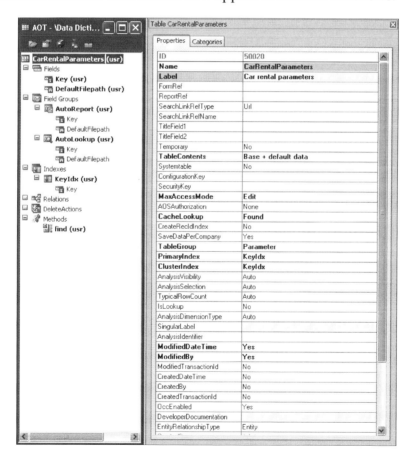

We can now use the parameter table in the `ImpExpFileDialog` class that we created in Chapter 7, *Integrate Data*. We will modify the dialog method and add the following code between the NEW comments:

```
public Object dialog()
{
    ;
    // Create a new object of the DialogRunbase class
    dialog = new DialogRunbase("Import data from file", this);
    // +++ NEW +++
    // Find the default filepath if it has been set
    // in the parameter table if the fileName variable
    // is empty (no value fetched while unpacking).
    if (!fileName)
        fileName = CarRentalParameters::find().DefaultFilepath;
    // --- NEW ---
    // Add the fields to the dialog and
    // set the initial value to be equal to
    // the value selected last time.
    dialogReadWrite =
      dialog.addFieldValue(typeid(ReadWrite), readWrite);
    dialogFileName =
      dialog.addFieldValue(typeid(FileName), fileName);
    dialogFileType =
      dialog.addFieldValue(typeid(FileType), fileType);
    dialogEntity = dialog.addFieldValue(typeid(FileEntity), entity);
    return dialog;
}
```

As we haven't created a form for the parameter table yet, you will have to use the table browser to change the parameter in order to test the import or export classes. Remember to delete the usage data after implementing the previous changes. If you don't, you will get the previously selected file location and filename instead of the current file location from the parameter table.

Setting up a number sequence

In the first section of this chapter you learned how to set up a number sequence reference by adding a new class that extended the `NumberSeqReference` class. You now have to create a number sequence and to link it to the number sequence reference by the following steps:

1. First, we need to create the number sequence from the number sequence form found at: **Main Menu | Basic | Setup | Number sequences | Number sequences.**

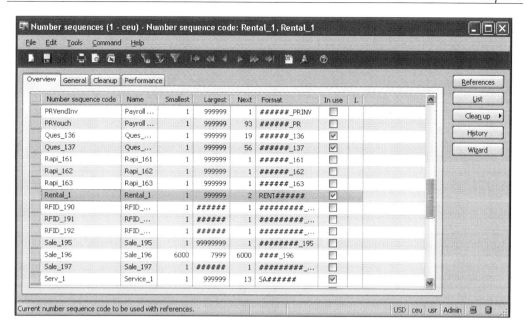

As you can see from the previous screenshot, I have created a new number sequence and called it **Rental_1**. I have also formatted the number sequence to have a prefix followed by six digits that can be anything from 1 to 999999. The General tab in the next figure shows that I have set up this number sequences as **Continuous** so that it will increment by one each time a new record Is created in the **RentalTable**.

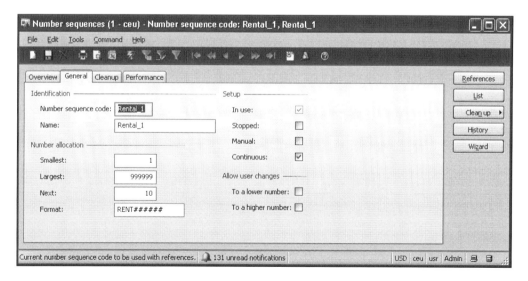

2. When we open the number sequence reference form found at **Main Menu | Basic | Setup | Number sequences | References**, we can now link the reference with the number sequence as shown in the next screenshot:

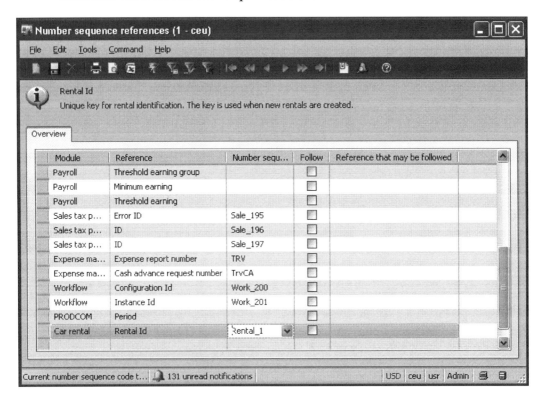

We can also do the same thing from a parameter form, but we first need to create our parameter table for the **CarRental** module.

3. We start off by creating a new form and adding the **CarRentalParameter** as the data source. We also add the **NumberSequenceReference** table as a data source and set the following parameters to it:

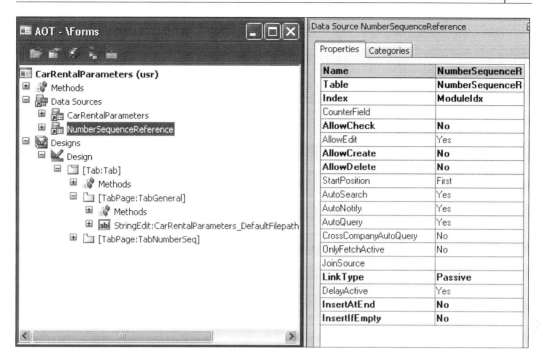

4. We now create the design of the form by adding a tab with two tab pages. We will call one **TabGeneral**, and the other **TabNumberSeq**.

5. To add the **DefaultLocation** field from the **CarRentalParameter** table, you simply drag the field from the **CarRentalParameter** datasource and drop it onto the **TabGeneral** tab page.

6. To add all the necessary fields in the **TabNumberSeq** tab page, simply copy from one of the other parameter forms and paste it onto the tab page in the **CarRentalParameters** form. I have copied the next layout from the **InventParameters** form:

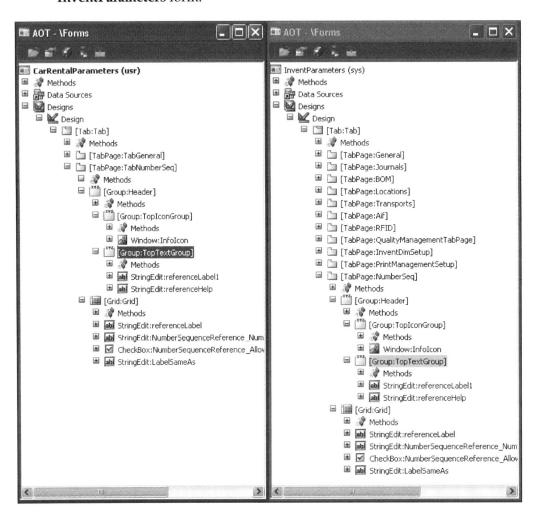

7. We now have to add some methods to the form for the setup to work properly:

```
public class FormRun extends ObjectRun
{
    NumberSeqReference      numberSeqReferenceCarRental;
    boolean                 runExecuteDirect;
    TmpIdRef                tmpIdRef;
}
```

```
void numberSeqPreInit()
{
    runExecuteDirect  = false;
    // Load the number sequences for the
    // specified module.
    numberSeqReferenceCarRental =
      CarRentalParameters::numberSeqReference();
    numberSeqReferenceCarRental.load();
    // Set the number sequences into the
    // tmp table TmpIdRef
    tmpIdRef.setTmpData(NumberSequenceReference::
      configurationKeyTableMulti(
        [CarRentalParameters::numberSeqModule()]));
}
public void init()
{
    this.numberSeqPreInit();
    super();
    CarRentalParameters::find();
}
```

We also have to add some code to the following methods in the `NumberSeqReference`
data source:

```
void executeQuery()
{
    if (runExecuteDirect)
    {
        super();
    }
    else
    {
        runExecuteDirect = true;
        this.queryRun(NumberSeqReference::buildQueryRunMulti(
            numberSequenceReference,
            tmpIdRef,
            [CarRentalParameters::numberSeqModule()]));
        numbersequenceReference_ds.research();
    }
}
void removeFilter()
{
    runExecuteDirect = false;
    numbersequenceReference_ds.executeQuery();
}
```

If you now open the parameter form and go to the second tab page, the form should look like the next screenshot:

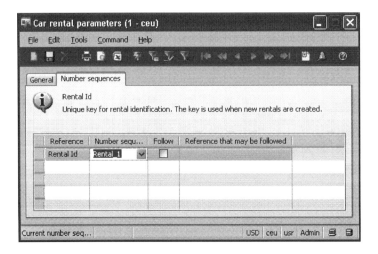

8. Also, remember to add a display menu item for this form and add it to the **CarRental** menu. The display menu item should also have the configuration key that you created earlier in this chapter, so that it looks something like the next screenshot:

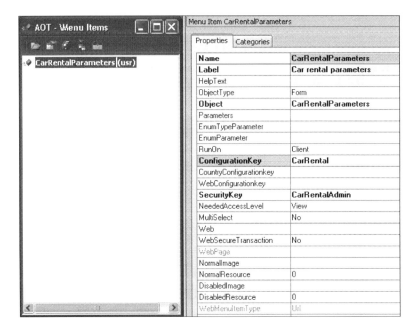

The security key that you see here will be added in the next section of this chapter.

Using the number sequence

There are a couple of steps you have to perform in order to use the number sequence as well. I will demonstrate the number sequence for `RentalId` in the **RentalTable** form:

1. We add a global variable in the **RentalTable** form to hold an object of the `NumberSeqFormHandler` class:

```
public class FormRun extends ObjectRun
{
    NumberSeqFormHandler    numberSeqFormHandler;
}
```

Also add a global method in the form that creates and holds the reference to the `numberSeqFormHandler` object:

```
NumberSeqFormHandler numberSeqFormHandler()
{
    if (!numberSeqFormHandler)
    {
        // Create a new object of the NumberSeqFormHandler
        // class by using the static method newForm
        numberSeqFormHandler = NumberSeqFormHandler::newForm(
            CarRentalParameters::numRefRentalId().NumberSequence,
            element,
            RentalTable_DS,
            fieldnum(RentalTable, RentalId));
    }
    return numberSeqFormHandler;
}
```

2. Next, you need to override the following methods on the **RentalTable** data source as shown below:

```
public void create(boolean _append = false)
{
    element.numberSeqFormHandler().
      formMethodDataSourceCreatePre();
    super(_append);
    element.numberSeqFormHandler().formMethodDataSourceCreate();
}
public void delete()
{
    element.numberSeqFormHandler().formMethodDataSourceDelete();
    super();
}
public void write()
{
    super();
    element.numberSeqFormHandler().formMethodDataSourceWrite();
}
```

3. Open the **RentalTable** form now and create a new record to create a new value for the **RentalId**, as shown in the next screenshot:

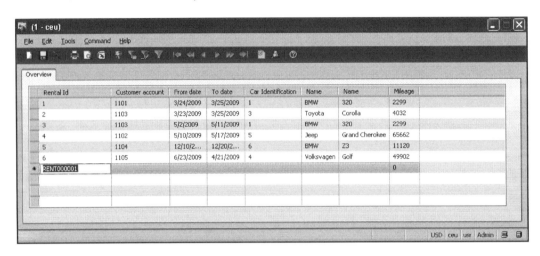

Security framework

The security framework in AX is used to ensure that the user experience is tailored to suit each users individual needs, filtering out functionality that may be irrelevant to the user.

To do this, AX uses three main areas of the security framework:

- License codes
- Configuration keys
- Security keys

License codes

The license codes give access to the different modules in AX. In a customer environment, the customer will have a customized set of license codes activated in AX depending on which modules they have bought.

Value Added Resellers (VAR) and **Independent Software Vendors (ISV)** get their own set of license codes that normally include most of the standard modules within AX.

You can look at the existing license codes in the AOT under **Data Dictionary | License keys,** but to get a new license code that works with the new license key that you create for your new module, you have to get the solution approved by Microsoft to have it available for all other partners and customers to purchase.

The set of license codes for an installation is called the **license letter** and can be viewed in the **License Information** form available at: **Main Menu | Administration | Setup | System | License Information.**

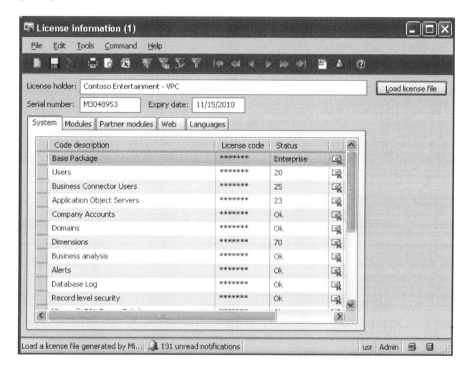

The form will tell you if the current solution has valid licenses for the different modules and how many of them (**Users, AOS, Dimensions, Details of license holder, Serial number,** and **Expiry date**) exist.

Configuration keys

In addition to the license codes, AX has a built in feature to turn parts of a module on and off. This is done from the **Configuration** form available at: **Main Menu | Administration | Setup | System | Configuration**.

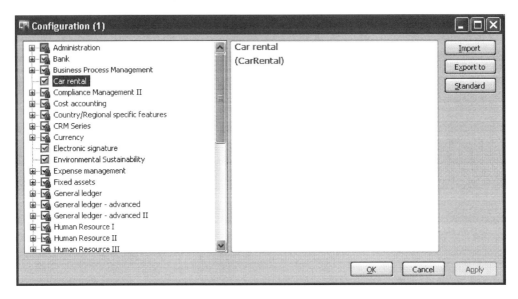

As you can see in the previous screenshot, the configuration key **Car rental** that we created earlier in this chapter is shown in the alphabetically sorted list of configuration keys.

If we turn a configuration key off, the tables using the configuration key will be dropped from the database and all AOT elements using the configuration keys will be disabled.

Configuration keys can also be linked to a license code. This means that the set of configuration keys available in the configuration form shown in the previous screenshot will be limited to those that have an active license code. If the configuration key is not linked to a license code, it will always be available in the previous form.

Configuration keys can also be linked to other configuration keys so that you can create a hierarchy of configuration keys.

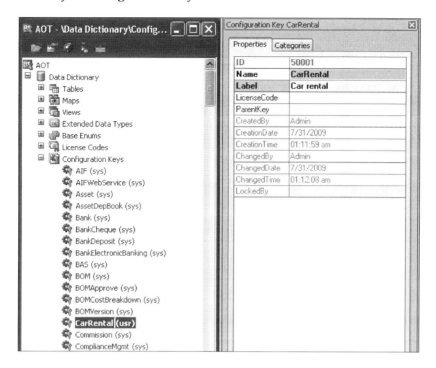

Security keys

Security keys enable us to give certain permissions to certain users in AX depending on which user group the users are members of, but before we can do this we have to create the security keys in the AOT.

Open an AOT and browse to **Data Ditionary | SecurityKeys**. Then right-click on the **SecurityKeys** node and select **New Security Key**.

We will create 3 security keys for our example:

Name	Label	ConfigurationKey	ParentKey
CarRental	Car rental	CarRental	
CarRentalClerk	Car rental clerk		CarRental
CarRentalAdmin	Car rental administrator		CarRental

As you can see, the security keys can also be created in a hierarchy or they can be attached to a configuration key. It is common to have the topmost security key in a hierarchy attached to a configuration key since you cannot set both the ParentKey and the ConfigurationKey parameters for a security key.

When the security keys are created, you need to attach the security keys to the elements that you want to limit access to.

In our example, we will change the following elements:

Element type	Name	Security key
Table	CarRentalParameters	CarRentalAdmin
Table	CarTable	CarRentalClerk
Table	RentalTable	CarRentalClerk
MenuItem\Display	CarRental	CarRentalClerk
MenuItem\Display	RentalTable	CarRentalClerk
MenuItem\Dispay	CarRentalParameters	CarRentalAdmin

You can now use this security setup to attach these settings, as well as the users, to the user groups.

The user group permission setup uses different access levels to control what access should be given to the different security keys.

Name	Description
No access	The user has no access to the features that link to the security key or any of the sub security keys.
View access	The user can view the features that link to the security key, but can't update, create, or delete data.
Edit access	The user is allowed to view and use the features that link to the security key.
Create access	The user is allowed to view and use the features that link to the security key and can also add new records where the security key applies to a table.
Full access	The user can view, edit, and even delete records in the specific table.

In our example, we will only use "No access" and "Full access".

To set the user group permissions for our example, go to the following menu location: **Main Menu | Administration | Setup | User groups**.

Create two user groups (**CR_Admin** and **CR_Clerks**), as shown here, and add some users to each of the groups by opening the **Users** tab page:

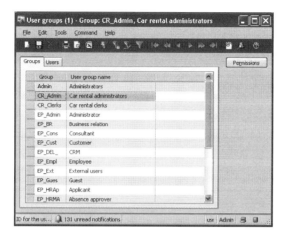

Select the **CR_Admin** group and click on the **Permissions** button.

In the form that opens, select the **Permissions** tab page and expand the **Car rental** node as shown in the next screenshot:

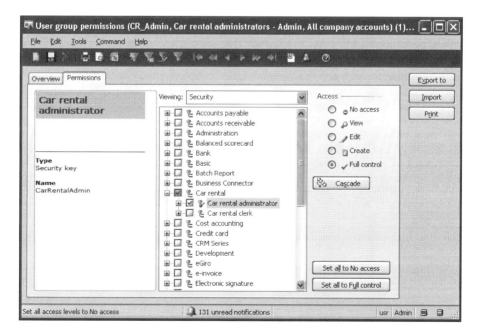

You have to do the same for the **CR_Clerks** user group, except that you will have to set the **Car rental** clerk **Security** key to **Full control** instead.

As you now have the user groups ready, you can add some users to each of the user groups. This is done from the **User** form available at: **Main Menu | Administration | Users**. Open the form and select a user. Then go to the **Groups** tab and add the groups you created, as shown in the next screenshot:

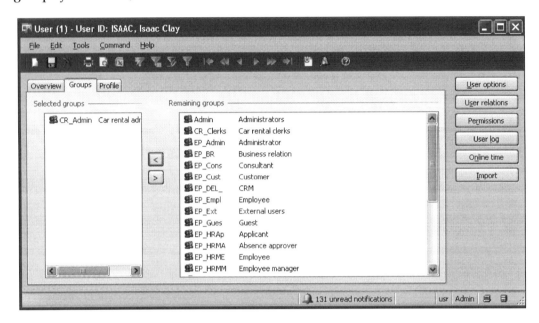

Summary

In this chapter, we have learned how to create a parameter table used to hold default values and other settings for your module. We also learned how to create a number sequence to be used with an identifier field and take advantage of the security framework within AX in order to lock down the module.

This should enable you to create a module in AX that follows the standard principles used by the rest of the modules in AX.

In the next chapter, we will learn how to use .NET assemblies in X++ and look at some of the possibilities the common language runtime gives us in AX.

We will also make some simple .NET programs that use the .NET Business Connector to execute functionality in AX and return the results.

10
Working with .NET and AX

When you are done with this chapter, you should be able to use .NET classes as reference classes in AX through the **Common Language Runtime** (**CLR**). The chapter will also guide you through the process of creating a .NET class in Visual Studio, and how to use it in AX. You will also learn how to use AX logic from external applications by using the .NET Business Connector.

The topics covered in this chapter are:

- A brief description of Common Language Runtime (CLR)
- Adding .NET references to classes in AX
- Using a .NET class in X++
- Adding references to the .NET Business Connector
- Using the .NET Business Connector in .NET classes

 All the Visual Studio examples in this chapter are written in C#.

Common Language Runtime

You might have done some .NET development before looking into X++ right? Maybe you're even a .NET expert? If so, you must have heard of CLR before. The CLR is a component of .NET that enables objects written in different languages to communicate with each other. CLR can be used in AX to combine functionality from .NET classes and libraries, including the ones you have yourself created in .NET. However, you cannot consume AX objects in .NET by using the CLR. Instead, you will then have to use the .NET Business Connector.

To learn more about the CLR, check out the following link:
http://msdn.microsoft.com/en-us/library/ddk909ch(VS.71).aspx

One very useful feature in AX when dealing with integration between AX and .NET is the way AX implicitly converts the most common data types. For the data types listed in the next table you do not need to convert the data manually. For all other data types, you will have to convert them manually.

.NET Common Language Runtime	X++
System.String	str
System.Int32	int
System.Int64	int64
System.Single	real
System.Double	real
System.Boolean	boolean
System.DateTime	date
System.Guid	guid

 Enums are stored as integers in AX and are treated as integers when they are implicitly converted between .NET and AX.

We prove this by executing the next example that shows the conversion between System.String and str. The same can be done for any of the other data types in the above table.

```
static void ImplicitDataConversion(Args _args)
{
    System.String netString;
    str xppString;
    ;

    // Converting from System.String to str
    netString = "Hello AX!";
    xppString = netString;
    info(xppString);

    // Converting from str to System.String
    xppString = "Hello .NET!";
    netString = xppString;
    info(netString);
}
```

X++ is case insensitive, except when dealing with CLR. This means that writing `System.string` in the previous example will result in a compile error, whereas writing `Str` instead of `str` will not.

The result will look like this:

Adding a reference to a .NET class in AX

To be able to use .NET classes in AX you have to make sure that the .NET assembly that you would like to use in AX exists under the **References** node in the AOT. If you can't find it there, you have to add it by adding a reference to the DLL file that contains the assembly in the AOT under **References**.

 When adding a reference node in the AOT you have to make sure that the DLL exists on all client computers. If there is a client computer in which the DLL does not exist, it will result in compile errors when compiling code on that client computer.

Assembly exist in the Global Assembly Cache

Follow these steps to add a reference that exists in the Global Assembly Cache:

1. If the DLL has been added to the Global Assembly Cache, you can right-click on the **Reference** node in the AOT and select **Add Reference**.

2. In the form that opens (see next screenshot), you should be able to find the desired DLL. Add it by clicking on the **Select** button.

3. When you have selected the desired reference, click on the **OK** button. The assembly has now been added to the AOT, and can be used when writing X++ code.

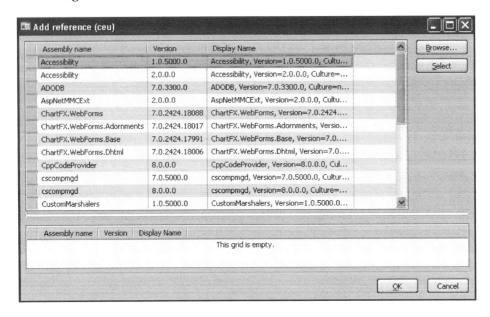

Assembly not in Global Assembly Cache

If the file does not exist in the Global Assembly Cache follow these steps:

1. Click on the **Browse** button in the **Add Reference** form shown above and find the DLL file.

2. Click on **Open**. If the DLL is a valid assembly it will be added to the AOT under **References**.

Another option is to add the DLL to the Global Assembly Cache first and select it as described in the previous section, *Assembly exist in the Global Assembly Cache*.

Using a .NET class in X++

After having added a reference to the .NET assembly you want to use in AX, you can start writing the X++ code that will use the assembly.

When referencing the classes in the assembly you will need to write the whole namespace and class name. In my example I'm using an assembly that has been added to the AOT in the SYS layer. The example shows a nice feature that enables AX to send info messages to the Windows Event Log.

This can be particularly useful when you would like to use the Windows Event Log to monitor AX batch Jobs.

First, we add a new static method called writeLogEntry to the Global class:

```
static void writeLogEntry(Exception e, str caller, int line, str text)
{
    // Use the standard .NET class EventLog from
    // the System.Diagnostics assembly
    System.Diagnostics.EventLog        eventLog;
    // Also use a .NET enumeration from the
    // System.Diagnostics assembly
    System.Diagnostics.EventLogEntryType        entryType;
    System.Exception        clrException;
    str stack;
    Batch batch;
    str batchInfo;
    ;

    try
    {
        // Create a new object of the EventLog class
        eventLog = new System.Diagnostics.EventLog();
        eventLog.set_Source("Dynamics AX");
        // Set the enumeration value based on the Exception
        // type in AX
        switch (e)
        {
            case Exception::Info :
                entryType =
                  System.Diagnostics.EventLogEntryType::Information;
                break;
            case Exception::Warning :
                entryType =
                  System.Diagnostics.EventLogEntryType::Warning;
                break;
            case Exception::Error :
                entryType =
                  System.Diagnostics.EventLogEntryType::Error;
                break;
        }
        // If the current user is running a batch job
        // we can assume that the info message came
        // from the batch job and add additional information
        // to the event log
```

```
        while select batch
            where batch.Status == BatchStatus::Executing &&
                batch.ExecutedBy == curuserid()
        {
            batchInfo += batch.GroupId + ': '+
              classid2name(batch.ClassNumber) + '\n';
        }

        if (batchInfo)
            eventLog.WriteEntry(strfmt("Batch info from AX: %1 \n\n
              The message originated from :%2 \nat line %3 \n\n
              Message: %4", batchInfo, caller, line, text),
              entryType);
        else
            eventLog.WriteEntry(strfmt("Info from AX: \n\n
              The message originated from :%1 \nat line %2 \n\n
              Message: %3", caller, line, text), entryType);
    }
    catch(Exception::CLRError)
    {
        // If not able to write the info to the eventlog
        // print an error in the print window instead.
        print "EventWriter:
          Unable to write entry to the windows eventlog";
    }
}
```

Then we add a line of code at the end of the add method in the Info class so that the end of the method will look like this:

```
        writeLogEntry(_exception, conpeek(packedAction,2) ,
          conpeek(packedAction,3), _txt);

        this.addSysInfoAction(_helpUrl, actionClassId, packedAction);
    }
    return super(_exception, (buildprefix?getprefix():'')+_txt);
}
```

To test the feature, simply create a new Job that prints something to the infolog:

```
static void TestEventLog(Args _args)
{
    ;
    info("This is a test");
}
```

You will now see an infolog message in AX, and if you open the Windows **Event Viewer** you should see the following message in the list:

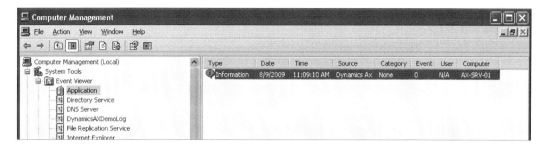

Double-clicking on the event will bring up information about the origin of the info and the message that was printed to the infolog in AX.

This example could easily be extended so you can enable or disable the feature for different users and select the level of messages to be sent to the EventLog.

.NET Business Connector

If you have external applications that need to integrate directly to AX logic you can easily achieve this by using the .NET Business Connector. A typical scenario can be that you would like your .NET application to execute some code in AX and have the result sent back to the .NET application.

 The .NET Business Connector requires additional licenses. Make sure that the AX installation in which you want to make use of the .NET Business Connector has the necessary licenses before you start developing the solution.

In standard AX, the .NET Business Connector is also used by the Enterprise Portal through the Web Parts in SharePoint so that they can expose AX data and logic directly to the Web. We will have a look at how this is achieved in Chapter 12, *Enterprise Portal*. It is also used by the standard **Application Integration Framework (AIF)**.

The way that the .NET Business Connector works is that it offers a set of .NET managed classes that .NET applications use in order to log on to AX and execute methods in AX classes.

Here is a list of the different managed classes that can be used in .NET when you want to integrate to AX through the .NET Business Connector. The list is taken from the Dynamics AX SDK.

Class name	Description
Axapta	The Axapta class contains methods that enable you to connect to AX, create AX objects, and execute transactions.
AxaptaBuffer	The AxaptaBuffer class contains methods that enable you to add data to, and retrieve data from an AX buffer.
AxaptaContainer	The AxaptaContainer class contains methods that enable you to read data from, and write data to, AX containers.
AxaptaRecord	The AxaptaRecord class contains methods that enable you to read, update, insert, and delete AX records. It also enables you to call table methods in AX.
AxaptaObject	The AxaptaObject class contains methods that enable you to call class methods in AX.

Add a reference to .NET Business Connector

In the next example, we create a new project in Visual Studio and add the reference to the project. You can skip this step if you already have a project where you would like to use the .NET Business Connector.

Open Visual Studio and create a new project as shown in the next screenshot:

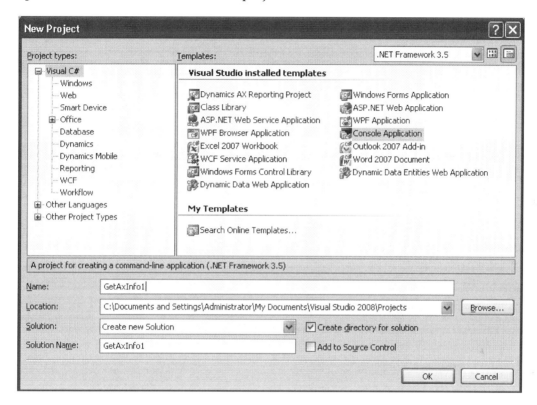

When you click on **OK**, you will have a new C# file called `Program.cs`. Before we start writing any code in the file, we have to add the .NET Business Connector as a reference.

In the **Solution Explorer** right-click on the **References** node and select **Add Reference**.

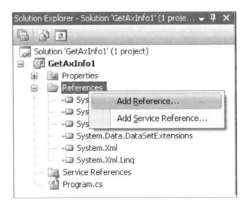

In the form that opens select **Microsoft.Dynamics.BusinessConnectorNet.dll** under the **Browse** tab.

The file is found in the Client\Bin catalog of your AX installation. The default path is:

```
C:\Program Files\Microsoft Dynamics Ax\50\Client\Bin
```

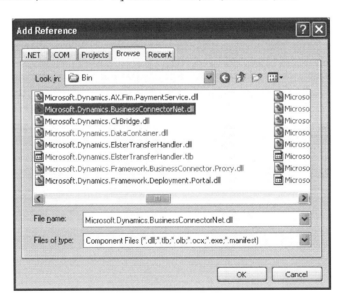

Click on **OK** and note that the reference has now been added under the **References** node in the **Solution Explorer**.

Using the .NET Business Connector in .NET classes

In the next sections of this chapter we will look at some examples that show how we can use methods in the .NET Business Connector to call AX methods, insert data into AX tables, and read data from AX tables.

Calling a static class method in AX

You now have to go back to AX, open the AOT and find the **Global** class. Add the following method to the **Global** class:

```
static str AxHelloWorld()
{
    return "HelloWorld!";
}
```

In the Visual Studio project we open the `Program.cs` file again and enter the following code that will create a connection to AX through the .NET Business Connector. We then call the method we created in the Global class before it prints the result to the console:

```
using System;
using Microsoft.Dynamics.BusinessConnectorNet;

namespace GetAxInfo1
{
    class Program
    {
        /// <summary>
        /// This class connects to AX throught the
        /// .NET Business Connector and call the static method
        /// AxHelloWorld in the Global class in AX.
        /// The result is sent to the console (command prompt).
        /// </summary>
        /// <param name="args"></param>
        static void Main(string[] args)
        {
            Axapta ax;
            Object axObject;
            try
            {
                // Create a new Axapta object.
                ax = new Axapta();
                // Logon using the default settings
```

```
                            // in the AX configuration for the .NET
                            // Business Connector
                            ax.Logon(null, null, null, null);
                            // Call the static method and return the
                            // result to the axObject variable
                            axObject =
                               ax.CallStaticClassMethod("Global", "AxHelloWorld");
                            // Print the result to the console
                            Console.WriteLine("The message from AX is {0}",
                               axObject.ToString());
                            ax.Logoff();
                        }
                    catch (Exception e)
                    {
                            Console.WriteLine(e.Message);
                    }
                    Console.ReadKey();
                }
            }
        }
```

Execute the program by pressing *Ctrl + F5*. You should now see the following result in the console (command prompt) that opens up:

If you get a different result it might be because you haven't set up the .NET Business Connector correctly. If so, please refer to the installation guide to set it up properly. Also, check the Windows Event Viewer to see if there are any error messages that can lead you in the right direction.

Insert data into an AX table

As mentioned earlier in this chapter, you can use the methods in some of the marshaled classes in the .NET Business Connector to manipulate data. However, it is better to avoid this and instead have AX handle all data selection and manipulation. It would be even better to have your .NET application call a method in AX that does the job and returns the results back to the .NET application again. However, this is not always feasible, for instance, when you would like to insert records from your .NET application to an AX table. The next section will guide you through the steps needed to achieve this.

First, you should create a new project in Visual Studio as we did earlier in this chapter. In this example, we will call the new project "InsertAxRecord".

Then you have to add a reference to the .NET Business Connector.

In the `Program.cs` file (or whatever you call your file), you write something like this:

```
using System;
using Microsoft.Dynamics.BusinessConnectorNet;

namespace InsertAxRecord
{
    class Program
    {
        static void Main(string[] args)
        {
            Axapta ax;
            AxaptaRecord record;

            try
            {
                // Create AX object and logon to AX
                ax = new Axapta();
                ax.Logon(null, null, null, null);

                // Create a new AxaptaRecord object with
                // the name of the table as input parameter
                using (record = ax.CreateAxaptaRecord("CarTable"))
                {
                    // Remember to clear the tablebuffer if
                    // you are inserting inside a loop
                    record.Clear();
                    record.InitValue();
                    // Set the fields in the table
                    record.set_Field("CARID", "XXX1");
                    record.set_Field("MODELYEAR", 1998);
```

```
                            record.set_Field("CARBRAND", "FORD");
                            record.set_Field("MODEL", "F1");
                            record.set_Field("MILEAGE", 89378);
                            // Insert the record
                            record.Insert();
                    }
                    // End the AX session
                    ax.Logoff();
            }
            catch (Exception e)
            {
                    Console.WriteLine(e.Message);
            }
        }
    }
}
```

If you open the table browser and look at the contents of **CarTable** in AX now (find the table in the AOT and pressing *Ctrl + O* to open the table browser) you should see that the record has been added.

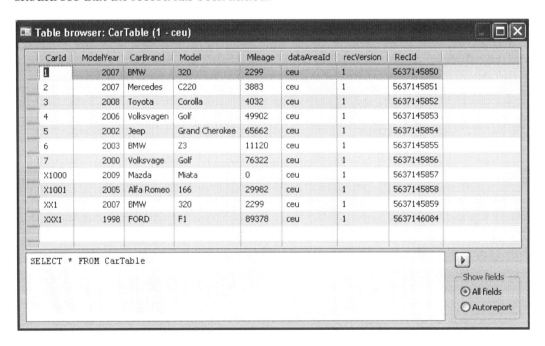

Read data from an AX table

For our next example we will repeat the procedure from the previous example, except that now we will read data from the table instead of writing to the table.

Start off by creating a new project and add the .NET Business Connector as a reference to the solution.

Enter the following code into the `Program.cs` file (or whatever you call your program):

```
using System;
using Microsoft.Dynamics.BusinessConnectorNet;

namespace ReadAxRecord
{
    class Program
    {
        static void Main(string[] args)
        {
            Axapta ax;
            AxaptaRecord record;
            Object carId, carBrand, model, modelYear, mileage;

            try
            {
                // Create AX object and logon to AX
                ax = new Axapta();
                ax.Logon(null, null, null, null);

                // Create an AxaptaRecord object from the
                // table that will be used
                using (record = ax.CreateAxaptaRecord("CarTable"))
                {
                    // Execute the statement entered as parameter
                    record.ExecuteStmt("select * from %1
                      where %1.CarBrand like 'BMW'");

                    // Loop through the result of the statement.
                    while (record.Found)
                    {
                        // Set our local variables to be
                        // equal to the fields in the table
                        // for the current record.
                        carId = record.get_Field("CARID");
                        carBrand = record.get_Field("CARBRAND");
                        model = record.get_Field("MODEL");
                        modelYear = record.get_Field("MODELYEAR");
```

```
                        mileage = record.get_Field("MILEAGE");

                        // Write the result to the console
                        Console.WriteLine(carId + "\t" +
                                             carBrand + "\t" +
                                             model + "\t" +
                                             modelYear + "\t" +
                                             mileage);

                        // Go to the next record in the result set
                        record.Next();
                    }
                    // End the AX session
                    ax.Logoff();

                    // Make sure the console stays up
                    // until a key is pressed
                    Console.ReadKey();
                }
            }
            catch (Exception e)
            {
                Console.WriteLine(e.Message);
            }
        }
    }
}
```

Execute the program by pressing *Ctrl* + *F5* and take a look at the result. It should look something like this:

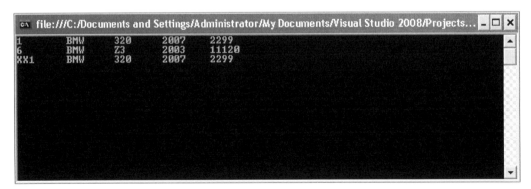

Exception classes

The .NET Business Connector also consists of a number of exceptions that AX can raise. These exceptions are controlled by exception classes that will help you determine further actions if an exception occurs. In the previous example I have only used the standard .NET exception class, but if you would like to write solid code you should consider using the exceptions from the .NET Business Connector instead.

The information in the next table is taken from the Dynamics AX SDK and shows all of the exception classes that exist within the .NET Business Connector.

Exception	Description
AlreadyLoggedOnException	Thrown when logon to AX fails because the user is already logged on.
AxBufferNotValidException	Thrown when the AX buffer being referenced is not valid.
AxContainerNotValidException	Thrown when the AX container being referenced is not valid.
AxObjectNotValidException	Thrown when the AX object being referenced is not valid.
AxRecordNotValidException	Thrown when the AX record being referenced is not valid.
BusinessConnectorException	Thrown when an unexpected error has occurred with the Business Connector.
ConnectionLostException	Thrown when the connection to the AOS is lost.
DebuggerStopException	Thrown when the AX debugger has been stopped.
ExecutionErrorException	Thrown when an unexpected system exception has occurred.
FatalErrorLoggedOffException	Thrown when the AX session is closed due to an error.
InitializationFailedException	Thrown when the .NET Business Connector fails to initialize.
InvalidReturnValueException	Thrown when a return value is invalid.
LogonAsGuestNotSupportedException	Thrown when trying to logon as Guest from a non-web (IIS) scenario, for example, directly through .NET Business Connector.
LogonFailedException	Thrown during an AX logon failure.
LogonSystemChangedException	Thrown when logon to AX fails due to logon parameters not matching those currently in use for the Business Connector.

Exception	Description
LogonUserLockedOutException	Thrown when the user attempting a logon is locked out due to exceeding the maximum number of logon attempts.
MethodUnknownException	Thrown when the method being referenced is not known by the system.
NoIISRightsException	Thrown when logon to AX fails because the user has not been granted the proper IIS rights.
NoSecurityKeyException	Thrown when a requested operation fails because the required security key does not exist.
NotLoggedOnException	Thrown when a requested operation cannot be performed because the user is not logged on.
PermissionDeniedException	Thrown when permission to execute an operation is denied.
ServerCommunicationErrorException	Thrown when communication between the client computer and the server fails.
ServerOutOfReachException	Thrown when communication with the server cannot be established.
ServerOutOfResourcesException	Thrown when the server terminates the session due to the server not having enough free resources.
ServerUnavailableException	Thrown when the server is unavailable. AX will attempt to connect to other servers listed in the client configuration.
SessionTerminatedException	Thrown when the server terminates the session.
UnknownClassHandleException	Thrown when the class being referenced does not exist.
UnknownRecordException	Thrown when the record being referenced does not exist.
UnknownTextException	Thrown when an unknown text exception has occurred.
UnknownXPPClassException	Thrown when an unknown X++ exception has occurred.
XppException	Thrown when an X++ exception has occurred.

Summary

You should now be able to use .NET classes in AX and also use AX code in .NET classes.

When using .NET classes in AX you had to add the reference to the .NET class first and then use the code in the .NET class from X++ code. AX makes this possible by using a bridge to the Common Language Runtime.

When you want to use AX functionality in your .NET classes you first had to add a reference to the .NET Business Connector. Then you had to use the marshalled classes that the .NET Business Connector consists of in your .NET code in order to call class methods, manipulate data or read data from AX.

For more examples on how to use the .NET Business Connector to create cool features in other programs, take a look at the **Microsoft Dynamics Snap** for AX: http://www.codeplex.com/axsnap

The Microsoft Dynamics Snap for AX are free applications that exemplifies how Microsoft Office applications like Excel, Word, and Outlook can be used to integrate with AX.

One of the applications is Business Data Lookup. It enables users that work in Word, Excel, and Outlook to lookup information in AX and paste data back to the Microsoft Office application.

In the next chapter we will look at how to create a webservice that expose AX logic and how to publish it to Internet Information Services (IIS).

We will also look at how we can make AX consume a webservice.

11
Web Services

A **Web Service** is defined by the W3S as *a software system designed to support interoperable machine-to-machine interaction over a network*. We have already looked at how we could create a file and store it on a disk so that another application can read it. This is all fine, but what if the other application was in a different network somewhere else in the world without any access to the disk area where the file was stored? We could solve this issue by sending the files using FTP. In some cases though, we might need to ask to get data instead of sending data, or retrieve data at certain intervals. As long as the size of the data being transferred is limited, using Web Services would be a good alternative.

You should know the basics of a Web Service before reading this chapter, and some good starting points are:

- `http://www.w3schools.com/webservices/default.asp`
- `http://www.w3.org/TR/ws-arch/`

After reading this chapter, you will learn how to:

- Create a Web Service that exposes AX logic
- Publish a Web Service to IIS
- Consume a web service from AX

Expose AX logic using web services

Before we have a look at how to expose AX logic by using a Web Service, let's look at how the AX logic is triggered by the external application.

What we would like is to have an external application (can also be internal) to execute a method in a Web Service and have that Web Service start a method in AX. The result is sent back through the same flow by which the methods were triggered.

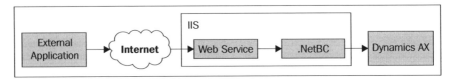

As you can see in the previous conceptual diagram, the request is sent from an external application through the Internet to a Web Service that runs on a Microsoft Internet Information Services (IIS) Web server. The Web Service uses the .NET Business Connector to create a session in AX and to execute a method in AX. When the result is returned from AX, it is passed back to the calling application the same way the request arrived.

Creating a Web Service that expose AX logic

In our example we will create a web service in .NET that will use the .NET Business Connector to log on to AX and to execute business logic within AX.

Our Web Service will contain two methods, one that returns the physical on-hand quantity of one specific item. The other method returns on-order quantity (what we expect to receive).

1. First, we have to open Visual Studio and create a new project as shown below:

    ○ Select **Web** under **Visual C#** in the **Project types** tree and select **ASP.NET Web Service Application** under the Visual Studio installed templates.

    ○ Give the project a descriptive name and click on **OK**.

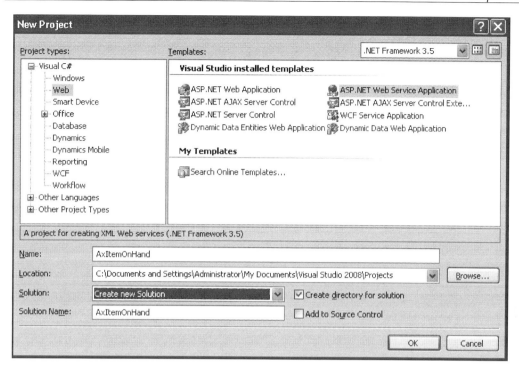

2. The next thing we need to do is to add a reference to the .NET Business Connector. This is done the exact same way as we did in the previous chapter under the *Add a reference to .NET Business Connector* section.

3. We now have to add the reference to the .NET Business Connector by adding it to the "using" list.

4. We then add a new private method that will log on to AX and create a new web user session and another private method that we use to log off the web user session from AX.

5. Then we have to create the two methods that we would like to expose in our Web Service. We create one called `AvailableNow` and another one called `AvailableInclOrdered`. They are very similar except that they call two different methods in the AX class InventOnHand.

The previous steps are implemented in the following code example:

```csharp
using System;
using System.Collections.Generic;
using System.Linq;
using System.Web;
using System.Web.Services;
using Microsoft.Dynamics.BusinessConnectorNet;

namespace AxItemOnHand
{
    /// <summary>
    /// This web service will return OnHand information regarding a
    /// given item
    /// </summary>

    // Autogenerated code -->
    [WebService(Namespace = "http://tempuri.org/")]
    [WebServiceBinding(ConformsTo = WsiProfiles.BasicProfile1_1)]
    [System.ComponentModel.ToolboxItem(false)]
    // To allow this Web Service to be called from script
    // using ASP.NET AJAX, uncomment the following line.
    // [System.Web.Script.Services.ScriptService]
    // Autogenerated code <--
    public class ItemOnHand : System.Web.Services.WebService
    {
        Axapta   ax;
        string output;

        [WebMethod]
        public string AvailableNow(string itemId)
        {
            AxaptaObject     inventOnHand;
            // Logon to AX
            this.Logon();
            // Create a new AxaptaObject of the InventOnHand class
            // by executing the static method newItemId
            inventOnHand =
                (AxaptaObject)ax.CallStaticClassMethod("InventOnHand",
                                                       "newItemId",
                                                       itemId);
            // Call the method availPhysical to get the qty
            // and convert it to a string
            output = inventOnHand.Call("availPhysical").ToString();
            // Release the object to the garbage collection
            inventOnHand.Dispose();
```

```
            // Logoff to release the webuser session in AX
            this.Logoff();
            // Return the output
            return output;
        }
        [WebMethod]
        public string AvailableInclOrdered(string itemId)
        {
            AxaptaObject inventOnHand;
            this.Logon();
            inventOnHand =
               (AxaptaObject)ax.CallStaticClassMethod("InventOnHand",
                                                      "newItemId",
                                                      itemId);
            output = inventOnHand.Call("availOrdered").ToString();
            inventOnHand.Dispose();
            this.Logoff();
            return output;
        }
        private void Logon()
        {
            try
            {
                ax = new Axapta();
                ax.Logon("ceu", "", "", "");
            }
            catch(Exception e)
            {
                output = e.Message;
            }
        }
        private void Logoff()
        {
            try
            {
                ax.Logoff();
            }
            catch (Exception e)
            {
                output = e.Message;
            }
        }
    }
}
```

The next **On-hand** form screenshot shows us what we expect to see when we execute our web methods. The `AvailableNow` method will return the **Available physical** value and the `AvailableInclOrdered` will add the **Ordered in total** to the available physical stock.

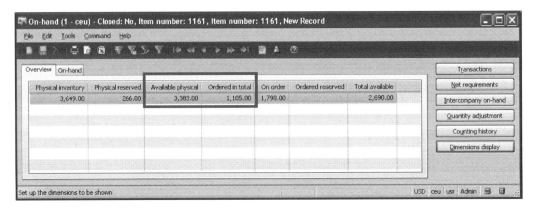

To test the Web Service, simply press *F5* in Visual Studio and you should get a web page that looks like the next screenshot:

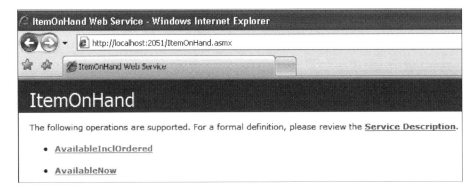

Click on the **AvailableNow** link and type an item number as shown here:

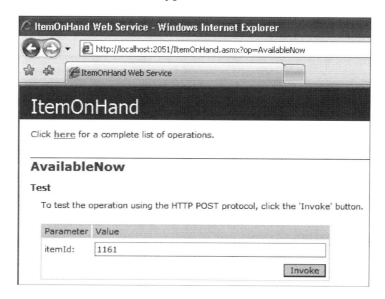

When you click on **Invoke**, you execute the web method and a new browser window will open to display the following result:

By executing the `AvailableInclOrdered` method, and using the same **itemId**, we get the following result:

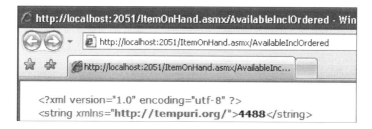

The result is correct as 3383 + 1105 = 4488.

Publishing a Web Service to IIS

Now that our Web Service is created and tested we have to publish it to a web server so that other applications will be able to use it.

As we live in a Microsoft world, the web server we use is the Internet Information Services, also known as IIS. This means that you have to make sure that the server where the web service should be published to has IIS installed. The server also has to have the .NET Business Connector and all its prerequisites installed.

1. To open the IIS, press the **Windows Key** and go to **Administrative Tools | Internet Information Services (IIS) Manager**.

2. In the tree on the left-hand side expand the **Server** node and then the **Application Pools** node. Right-click on the **Application Pools** node and select **New | Application Pool**.

3. Enter a name for the application pool that describes the applications that will be used by the pool.

4. Now that the application pool has been created, we have to set the identity of the pool to the user that has been set up as the .NET Business Connector Proxy. You can find or set this user in the following form in AX:

    Main Menu | Administration | Setup | Security | System service accounts.

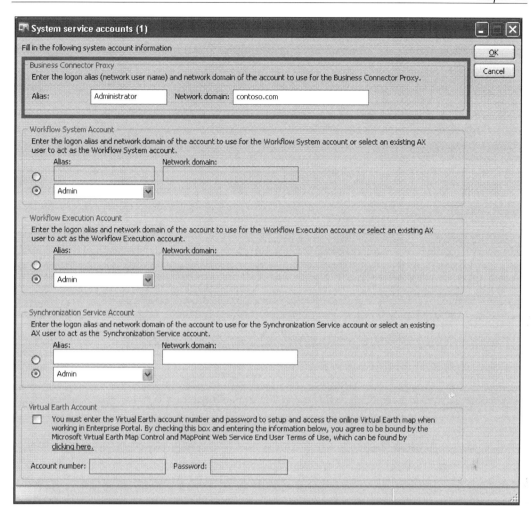

5. As we can see from the previous form, the user we have to set up for our application pool is the **contoso.com Administrator**.

6. Go back to the IIS management tool and right-click on the application pool you just created and select properties. In the form that opens go to the **Identity** tab page and change to a **Configurable** user and enter the **User name** and **Password** as shown in the next screenshot, and click on **OK**:

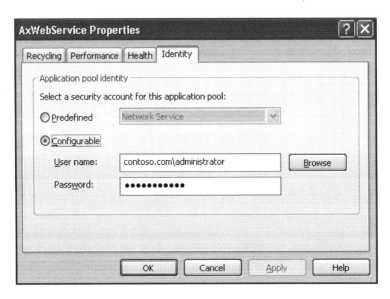

7. After confirming the password in the pop-up that will appear, click on the **OK** button.

8. The next thing to do is to create a website that uses this application pool. This is done by right-clicking on the **Web Sites** node in the tree in the IIS management tool and selecting **New | Web Site**.

9. A wizard starts up and you are prompted for a name of the website, an IP address, port number, and a host header for the website. In this example we enter the name and just select port 200 since it's a port that is not already in use. Then click on **Next**.

10. Now we are prompted for the path where the website resides and since we haven't published the Web Service yet, we create a new folder from Windows Explorer and use this folder in the wizard prompt. Typically, this folder will be under `C:\Inetpub\wwwroot`, so let's create the folder `AxWebService` here.

11. After we click on **Next** we have to set the website access permissions. In order to make the Web Service work we have to allow Active Server Pages (ASP) scripts to run.

12. After the site has been created you need to set the application pool for the site. This is done by right-clicking on the website and selecting Properties. In the window that opens, go to the **Home Directory** tab page and select the **Application pool** as shown in the next screenshot:

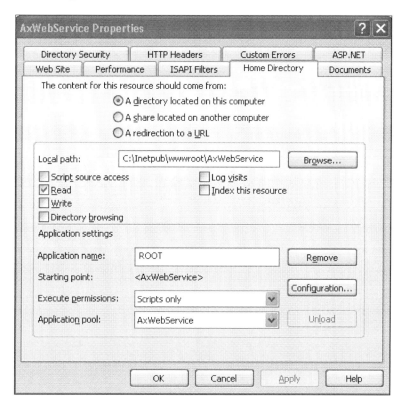

14. Now that the website is created, you can go back to the Web Services project in Visual Studio and select **Build | Publish.** Here you can enter the name of your project.

15. In the window that opens you have to specify the website that you have created. This can be done either by entering the URL if you know where it is, or you can click on the lookup button with the three dots as seen in the next screenshot:

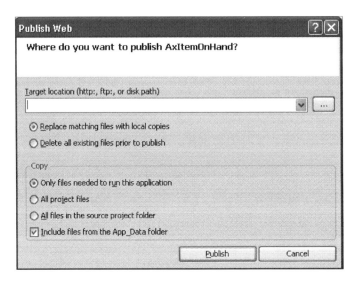

16. A new window comes up where you can select the folder, or website, where you want to publish the Web Service. Select **Local IIS** on the left-hand side of the window if your web server is on the same computer as the Visual Studio installation. Next, select the website on the right-hand side of the window and click on **Open**.

17. Now you will see that the **Target Location** is filled out in the **Publish Web** form and you can click on the **Publish** button.

When the status field in Visual Studio (lower left-hand side corner) shows that the publish was successful, you can check if the Web Service is found at the address by typing the full URL in a web browser and press *Enter*.

In this example the full URL would be `http://localhost:200/ItemOnHand.asmx` and it would present the following webpage:

Accessing logic in an external Web Service

Now that we have seen how we can make other applications trigger AX logic by exposing AX logic to Web Services, we will turn the other way around and see how we can make AX use web services that expose logic from external applications.

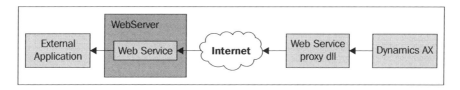

In the conceptual diagram above we see that AX uses a Web Service proxy that is created specifically for the Web Service that it is about to call. The Web Service proxy lets AX know everything it needs to know in order to call the Web Service through the Internet. The Web Service, in turn, will return a result from the external application and pass it back to AX.

A lot of the examples on the Web will show you how you can ask a Web Service to convert from one currency to another, check if an e-mail address is valid, and some others that are most likely less useful to your AX customers.

Sometimes, however, you will find that your AX customers have several other applications that AX should integrate with to get additional information. Maybe they even integrate with their vendors to get updated product information automatically from their vendors' applications. If these applications can have web services that trigger actions within these applications, you can consume these web services in AX so that AX can ask for data or trigger some event in the other application.

To exemplify how to achieve this we will continue to use the previous example. Our Web Service will then return a result from AX, but it could have been a result returned from any other application that supports web services as well.

Creating a service reference

The first thing we need to do is to add a service reference to our Web Service.

When we perform this action in AX, we are actually creating a new DLL that will work as a proxy class between AX and the Web Service. It is created in .NET automatically by reading the service description of the Web Service and adding all the methods and data types that the Web Service exposes.

To do this, simply open the AOT and go to the **References** node. Right–click on it and select **Add service reference**.

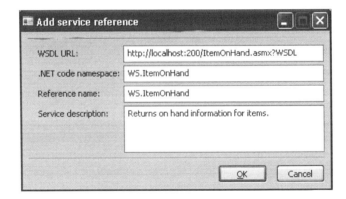

The **WDSL URL** is the location where the service description of the Web Service resides.

The **.NET code namespace** is the namespace that the proxy class will have. The proxy DLL will also be put in a directory corresponding with the .NET namespace.

The **Reference name** is the name of the reference to the proxy that we will use in AX. It will typically be the same as the .NET code namespace to have the same naming in the proxy class and in AX.

The **Service description** is just a simple description of the service so that other people easily will recognize what this service is used for in AX.

After filling out the required information in the box click on **OK**. After a little while, you should see an Infolog with information regarding the creation of the proxy class. There should be no errors or warnings in the Infolog.

Creating a class that consumes the Web Service

We can now create a class in AX that uses the Web Service.

1. Create a new class and call it OnHand. Add a new method that looks like this:

```
public static server str getOnHand(str itemId)
{
    // Reference the class in the WS.ItemOnHand namespace
    // Remember that the namespace and its classes are case
    // sensitive
    WS.ItemOnHand.ItemOnHandSoapClient      soapClient;
    str ret;
    ;
    try
    {
        // Make sure that we get permission to use the clr interop
        new InteropPermission(InteropKind::ClrInterop).assert();

        // Create a new object of the ItemOnHandSoapClient class
        // The endpoint configuration must be equal to the
        // wsdl:portType name value in the WSDL file
        soapClient = new WS.ItemOnHand.
                    ItemOnHandSoapClient('ItemOnHandSoap');
        // Execute one of the method in the web service
        ret = soapClient.AvailableNow(itemId);
        // Revert the clr interop access when we are done
        // using it.
        CodeAccessPermission::revertAssert();
    }
    catch (Exception::CLRError)
    {
        throw error(AifUtil::getClrErrorMessage());
    }

    return ret;
}
```

The method that creates and executes methods in an object that requires ClrInteropPermission must be executed on the server by a static method.

2. We also create a main method as a starting point of our class:

```
static void main(Args args)
{
    str itemId;
    ;
    itemId = "1161";
    info (strfmt("On-hand for item %1: %2", itemId,
                        OnHand::getOnHand(itemId)));
}
```

When we execute this class we get the same result as we did when we were testing the Web Service directly from the web browser earlier in this chapter:

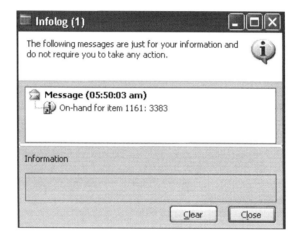

Summary

You have now learned how to let other applications access AX functionality by creating web services that expose AX logic. You should also be able to create a new website in IIS and publish web services to a website in IIS.

You have also seen how we can add a service reference in AX so it can consume web services.

The next chapter will guide you through the process of creating AX User Controls that expose AX data to the Enterprise Portal. You will also learn how to create a wizard that enables users to enter new records into an AX table.

12
Enterprise Portal

After reading this chapter you will know how to create `.aspx` pages in SharePoint based on the templates that come with the **Enterprise Portal**. You will also learn how to create **Dynamics AX User Controls** that will expose data from AX to the **Enterprise Portal**.

Dynamics 2009 has taken a huge step in regards to development of web content. In previous versions of AX you could publish web content using web parts defined in AX. These web parts are now being phased out and will no longer be available in the next version of AX. That means that everything you see in the AOT under **Web** will be gone. This makes it even more important to learn how to use the new **Enterprise Portal** development framework for AX.

This chapter will not focus on the old AX web parts, but rather look ahead at the new way of exposing data and functionality to the Web using the new .NET based **Enterprise Portal** framework in AX.

You will learn the basics so that you can explore the wonderful world of web development for Dynamics AX on your own. You will not become fluent in **Enterprise Portal** development simply by reading this chapter, but you will get a sense of how to work with it, and how the different elements are tied together.

To learn more about **Enterprise Portal** development, please refer to the Dynamics AX 2009 SDK.

In this chapter, we will look at the following topics:

- Creating a dataset containing the **RentalTable**
- Creating a webpage that displays a grid consisting of the records from the **RentalTable**
- Creating a wizard (also known as a tunnel) that is used to create a new record in the **RentalTable**

- Creating a toolbar with a menu item that is used to start the wizard
- Converting existing **WebForms** defined in the AOT to .NET **User Controls**

Creating a dataset

First of all, let's have a look at how we create datasets in AX that we will later use by the .NET controls.

The datasets defined in the AOT are used by the **AxDatasource** control in ASP.NET to fetch data from AX and send data back again when updated in a data binding enabled ASP.NET control.

A dataset can be considered a replacement of the **Datasource** node in the web forms and web reports. As web forms and web reports will eventually be phased out from AX, we should now use a dataset to connect the fields in our .NET forms to fields in AX tables.

1. To create a dataset, open the AOT and browse to **Data Sets**. Right-click on **Data Sets** and select **New Data Set**.

2. Right-click on the new dataset and select **Properties** to show the properties window. Then change the **Name** property to **RentalDataSet**.

3. Go to the **Data Sources** node under the dataset and add a new data source by right-clicking on the **Data Sources** node and selecting **New Data Source**. Open the properties window for the new data source and change the table and name property to **RentalTable**.

The dataset should now look like the next screenshot:

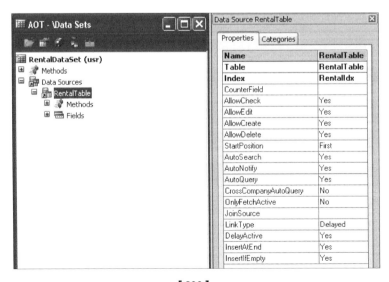

Creating a new Visual Studio project

Before you start creating a Visual Studio project, make sure that the Enterprise Portal development tools are installed on the same computer as Visual Studio.

1. To create a new project in Visual Studio, open Visual Studio and select **File | New | Web Site**.

2. In the form that opens, select **Dynamic Data Web Site**, change the name, and click on the **OK** button.

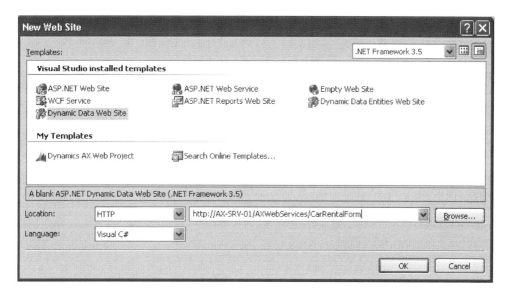

You are now good to go with a new web site project in Visual Studio. You will use this project for the rest of the examples in this chapter.

Creating a grid

Follow these steps to create a grid control in ASP.NET that retrieves data:

1. Right-click on the website in the **Solution Explorer** in Visual Studio and select **Add New Item**.

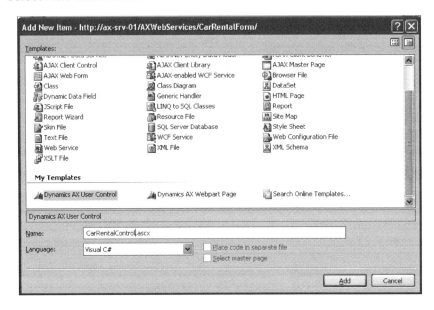

2. Select **Dynamics AX User Control** and give it a name that makes sense.
3. Now that the control has been created, right-click on it in the **Solution Explorer** and select **Add to AOT**.

4. When that is done, the control is saved in the AOT under **Web | Web files | Web controls**. This step has to be performed in order to use the user control from the SharePoint page.

5. Open the user control and add an **AxDataSource** control to the user control simply by dragging it into the design view.

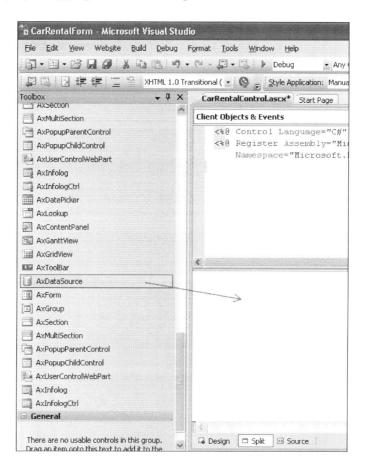

6. Click on the arrow to the right-hand side of the **AxDataSource** control in the design view and change the **DataSet Name** property to the dataset you just created in AX.

7. You can also do this by right-clicking on the control and selecting **Properties**
    to open the properties window. From here you can also change the rest of the
    parameters, as shown in the next screenshot.

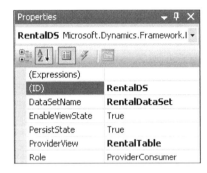

8. Now, go to the toolbox and drag the **AxGridView** control onto the
    design view.

9. Click on the arrow to the right of the control to select the most
    important properties.

10. The next thing to do is to set the **Data Source** property to the data source that
    you have just created.

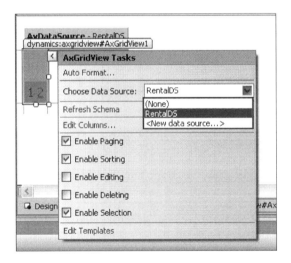

11. Also, if you would like the users to be able to edit or delete records from the grid, you have to check the **Enable Editing** or **Enable Deleting** checkboxes.

12. You can't insert records from a grid by using the AxGridView control. Instead you can add action in a toolbox that opens a tunnel or wizard that lets the user create a new record.

13. Next, click on the **Edit Columns** link to select the columns from the data source that you want to use in the grid.

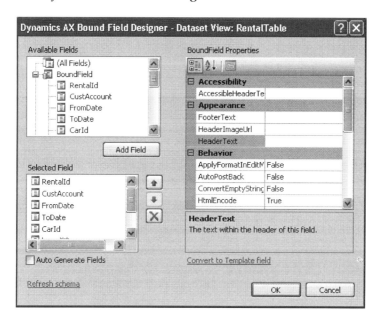

14. Available display and edit methods are also shown in the list of fields. Select all the fields in the list except the **dataAreaId**, **TableId**, and **RecId**. Then click on the **OK** button.

The grid is now ready to be used by a web part page.

Creating a new Web Part page

To create a web part page, make sure you have installed and set up **Enterprise Portal**.

1. Start by opening the **Enterprise Portal** in a web browser. Click on the **Site Actions** button in the upper-right corner, and then click on the **Create** button, as shown in the next screenshot.

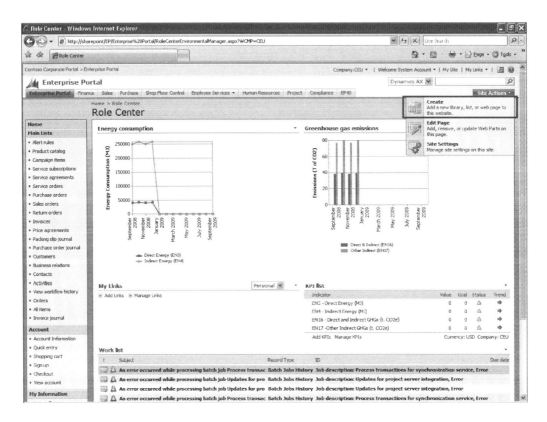

2. In the page that opens, click on the **Web Part** page under the **Web Pages** group.

3. The next page will ask you for the name of the page, what template you would like to use, and in which document library you would like the page to be stored in.

   Name the page **CarRental** and select the template called **Header, Left Column, Body** and store the page in the **Enterprise Portal** document library.

4. The page will now open in edit mode where you can add web parts. Add a new web part by clicking on the **Add a Web Part** button under the body section.

5. In the window that opens, find and select the **Dynamics User Control Web Part** and click on the **Add** button.

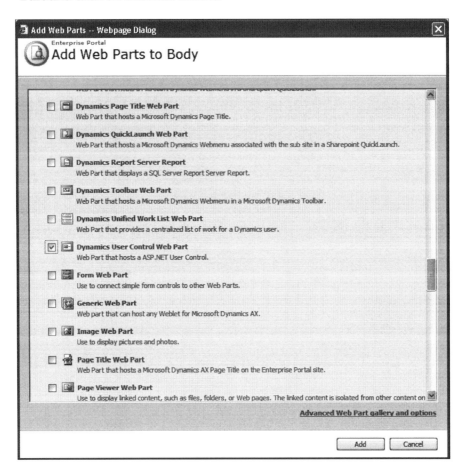

6. When you are back in edit mode, click on the **Edit** button in the new web part and select **Modify Shared Web Part**.

7. In the property window, you will find the user control you created in the list of **Managed content item** as shown in the next screenshot:

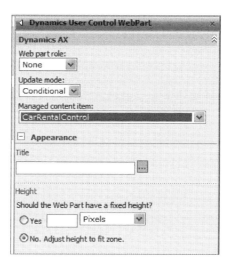

8. Once you have selected it, scroll down to the bottom and click on the **OK** button. Back in the edit mode, you can click on the **Exit edit mode** link in the top-right corner to see what the page looks like.

The web part page should now look something like the next screenshot:

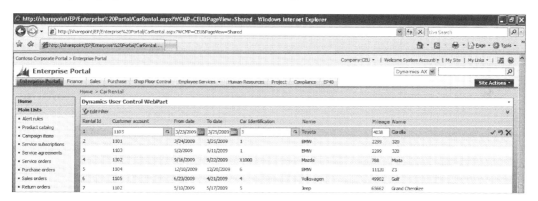

You have now created a **SharePoint** page with a grid that lists records from the **RentalTable** where users can edit and delete records.

The next thing to do is enable users to enter new records as well. From a user point of view, I would say that I should have been able to do this directly from the grid, but since that won't work we can create a **tunnel** (also known as a wizard) to achieve this.

Creating a tunnel or wizard

Follow these steps to create a tunnel that enables users to create a new record in the **RentalTable**.

1. Open the Visual Studio project that you worked with in the previous user control example and create a new **Dynamics AX User Control** like you did with the grid. Name this user control **CarRentalCreateTunnel** and click on **OK** in the **Add New Item** form.

2. Next, add the new control to the AOT by right-clicking on it and selecting **Add to AOT**.

3. Open the user control in design mode and add an **AxDataSource** the same way we did with the previous user control example. This data source should also point to the **RentalDataSet**.

4. Next, drag an **AxForm** element from the **Toolbox** and drop it onto the design view.

5. Make sure that the properties for the form are as follows:

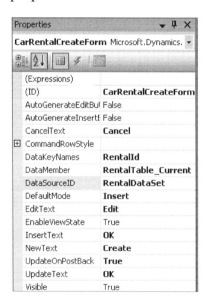

6. The next thing you need to do is to drag a **Wizard** control from the **Toolbox** and drop it onto the **AxForm** in the design view. The **Wizard** is not a Dynamics AX component but it can be found under the **Standard ASP** controls in the **Toolbox**.

7. Next, you have to set some of the properties of the wizard. Begin with defining the steps that the wizard should consist of. In our example, we create 3 steps:

   ° Select the customer

   ° Select the car to be rented

   ° Select the from-date and to-date and click on the **Finish** button

To define these steps, click on the arrow to the right of the control and bring up the **Wizard Tasks** window, as seen in the next screenshot:

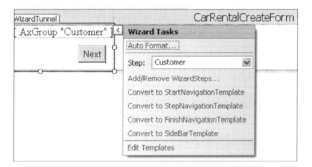

8. In the **Wizard Tasks** window, click on **Add/Remove WizardSteps** to bring up the window shown in the next screenshot:

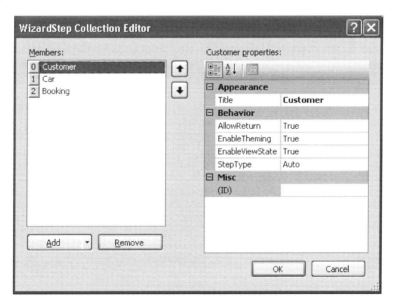

9. Click on **Add** to add the steps and give each step a title. Click on **OK** to return to the design view when you are done.

10. Next, click on the **Source** button at the bottom of the edit window (next to **Design** and **Split**) to see the source code of the control. The source code is an XML file that you now have to modify, as shown in the following code:

```
<asp:Wizard ID="WizardTunnel" runat="server" ActiveStepIndex="0"
        onfinishbuttonclick="WizardTunnel_FinishButtonClick">
    <WizardSteps>
        <asp:WizardStep runat="server" title="Customer">
            <dynamics:AxGroup ID="Customer" runat="server"
              FormID="CarRentalCreateForm">
                <Fields>
                    <dynamics:AxBoundField
                       DataField="CustAccount"
                       DataSet="RentalDataSet"
                       DataSetView="RentalTable"
                       AutoPostBack="true" />
                </Fields>
            </dynamics:AxGroup>
        </asp:WizardStep>
        <asp:WizardStep runat="server" title="Car">
            <dynamics:AxGroup ID="Car"
              runat="server"
              FormID="CarRentalCreateForm">
                <Fields>
                    <dynamics:AxBoundField DataField="CarId"
                       DataSet="RentalDataSet"
                       DataSetView="RentalTable"
                       AutoPostBack="true" />
                </Fields>
            </dynamics:AxGroup>
        </asp:WizardStep>
        <asp:WizardStep runat="server" Title="Booking">
            <dynamics:AxGroup ID="Booking"
              runat="server"
              FormID="CarRentalCreateForm">
                <Fields>
                    <dynamics:AxBoundField
                       DataField="FromDate"
                       DataSet="RentalDataSet"
                       DataSetView="RentalTable"
                       AutoPostBack="true" />
                    <dynamics:AxBoundField
                       DataField="ToDate"
                       DataSet="RentalDataSet"
```

```
                    DataSetView="RentalTable"
                    AutoPostBack="true" />
                </Fields>
            </dynamics:AxGroup>
        </asp:WizardStep>
    </WizardSteps>
</asp:Wizard>
```

In this XML file we add groups of fields from the data source into each step of the Wizard. As you can see from the first step, it will have a `dynamics:AxGroup` that consists of a `Fields` node, that contains the actual bound fields. For example, the `CustAccount` field from the `RentalTable DataSetView` in the `RentalDataSet`

```
<dynamics:AxBoundField
   DataField="CustAccount"
   DataSet="RentalDataSet"
   DataSetView="RentalTable"
   AutoPostBack="true" />
```

Also notice that I have added a reference to an event called `onFinishButtonClick`. The method I want to execute when this event occurs is `WizardTunnel_FinishButtonClick`. To see the code of this event, open the code behind the file by double-clicking on the wizard element in the design view. As we have created the project as a C# project, the code behind is a `.cs` file.

When the user clicks on the **Finish** button, we want the record to be saved and the user to be redirected to the grid form again.

This is achieved by first getting a handle to the data source view, then saving the content of that view by executing the `EndEdit` trigger.

The redirect is done by creating a new object of the `AxUrlMenuItem` that points to the URL menu item in AX that opens the desired **SharePoint** page. This is the **CarRentalList** URL menu item in our case. Next, we simply use the `Response` class to redirect to the URL of that menu item.

The steps to do this are shown in the code below:

```
using System;
using System.Collections;
using System.Web;
using System.Web.Security;
using System.Web.UI;
using System.Web.UI.WebControls;
using System.Web.UI.WebControls.WebParts;
using System.Web.UI.HtmlControls;
using Microsoft.Dynamics.Framework.Portal.UI.WebControls;
using Microsoft.Dynamics.Framework.Portal.UI.WebControls.WebParts;
```

```
public partial class CarRentalCreateTunnell :
System.Web.UI.UserControl
{
    protected void Page_Load(object sender, EventArgs e)
    {
    }
    protected void WizardTunnel_FinishButtonClick(object sender,
      WizardNavigationEventArgs e)
    {
        AxDataSourceView rentalTableView =
          this.RentalDataSet.GetDataSourceView("RentalTable");
        if (rentalTableView != null)
           rentalTableView.EndEdit();
        AxUrlMenuItem carRentalsMenuItem =
          new AxUrlMenuItem("CarRentalList");
        Response.Redirect(carRentalsMenuItem.Url.ToString());
    }
}
```

Now you can create a new **SharePoint** page like you did in the previous section of this chapter. Name the new page **CarRentalCreateTunnel** and apply the same template used earlier. You can also store this page in the **Enterprise Portal** document library.

Next, add the **CarRentalCreateTunnel** user control to this page and exit the edit mode to see what the page looks like. The first wizard page should look something like the next screenshot:

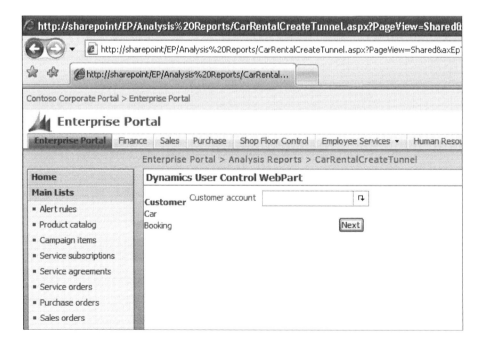

Note that the fields are already connected to the correct lookup forms so that you can easily find what you are looking for.

By filling in the **Customer account**, clicking on the **Next** button, and filling in all the information in all of the steps and finally clicking on the **Finish** button, a new record will be created in the **RentalTable** and you will be brought to the **CarRental.aspx** page again as specified by the `Response.Redirect` in the `FinishButtonClick` event.

Creating a toolbar

Now that we have created a wizard that enables the users to create a new record in the RentalTable, it would be nice to have this function available from the grid page that we created first. A nice way of doing this is to add a toolbar to the SharePoint page where one of the buttons opens the wizard.

1. First, we have to create a Web Menu Item in the AOT that points to the SharePoint page where the wizard has been added. Browse the AOT to **Web | Web Menu Items | URLs**.

2. Right-click on the **URLs** node and select **New URL**.

3. Name the new web menu item **CarRentalCreateTunnel**; add a label in the **Label** field saying something like **create new rental**.

4. Click on the lookup button to the left in the **URL** field. You will then get a window where you can find the SharePoint page that you want this link to point to.

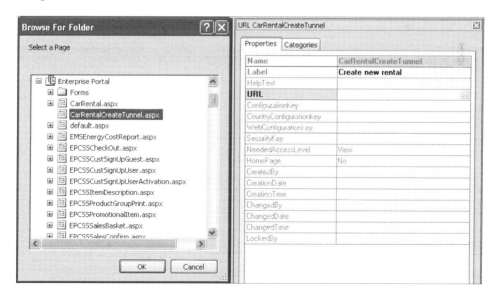

5. Our page was called **CarRentalCreateTunnel.aspx** so we select that one and click on the **OK** button.

6. Next, we need to create a new **Web Menu** in the AOT. Browse the AOT to **Web | Web Menus** and right-click on the **Web Menus** node and select **New Web Menu**.

7. Name the menu **CarRentalMenu** and add a describing label, like **Car Rental**.

8. Right–click on the web menu and select **New Submenu** to create an extra level in the menu in case you are adding more functions later. Call the submenu **Actions**.

9. Then drag the web menu item into the submenu.

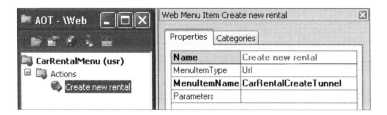

10. The next thing we need to do is to create a new **Dynamics AX User Control**. Again, we create it in the Visual Studio project we have used earlier in this chapter. Name this user control **CarRentalToolbar** and drag the **AxToolbar** control from the **Toolbox** and drop it onto the design view.

11. Change the name of the toolbar to **CarRentalMenu** and change the property **Dynamics AX Web Menu** to point to the web menu you just created in AX (**Car Rental Menu**). Also, remember to add this user control to the AOT from the Visual Studio Solution Explorer.

12. We can now add this toolbar to the first SharePoint page we created. To do that, we have to browse to that page in our web browser and select **Site Actions | Edit Page**.

13. You are now in the edit mode. Click on the **Add a Web Part** button in the **Body** section of the page, select the **Dynamics User Control Web Part** from the window that opens, and click on the **Add** button.

14. You are now back in the edit mode and should now see two **Dynamics User Controls**. Click on the **Edit** button at the top as shown in the next screenshot, and select **Modify Shared Web Part**.

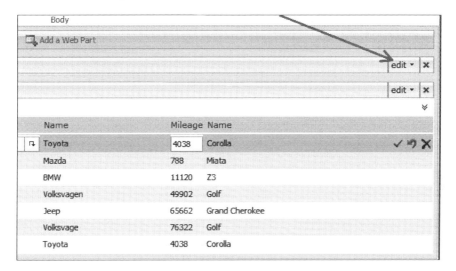

15. In the properties window that opens to the right-hand side, select the **CarRentalToolbar** that you have just created.

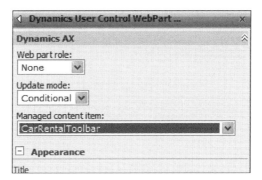

16. Click on **OK** at the bottom of the properties window and exit the edit mode.

Your page should now have a toolbar menu that looks like this:

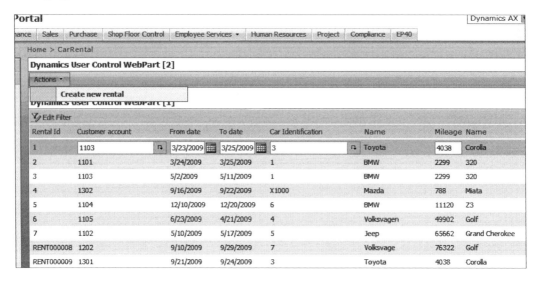

The menu item should take you to the wizard for creating a new rental, and it should create the rental and take you back to the list when you click on the **Finish** button.

Converting WebForm to .NET user controls

One very nice feature that is only semi-implemented in Dynamics AX 2009 is the conversion of regular WebForms created in the AOT to .NET User Controls.

When I say semi-implemented, it is because the class that does this (SysEPWebFormConverter) does not exist in AX. It does, however, exist in the SDK available at http://msdn.microsoft.com/en-us/library/cc615339.aspx

It is also included in the examples of this chapter.

To get it into your AX solution, you have to save the text as an XPO file and import it into AX. You then have to edit the getFormsToConvert method to include the web forms that you want to convert. When executing the class, it will generate a new project and put all of the elements that are created in it. This includes the data sets, web menus, and user controls.

Summary

In this chapter, you have learned how to create Dynamics User Controls from Visual Studio, have them use data sets created in the AOT to retrieve data, and to put that data into a grid that is displayed to the users. You have also seen how to create a wizard that enables the users to insert new records and how to create a toolbar that consists of elements defined in a web menu in AX.

You should now be able to "webify" simple forms in AX and hopefully, you will also have enough knowledge to start experimenting with the other AX elements that are available in Visual Studio for you to play with.

You have also seen how to convert WebForms to .NET User Controls, a feature that can be very nice to use if you are converting an AX solution from version 4.0 to AX 2009.

A
Links

Throughout this book there are references to websites and help files in AX. This appendix will structure these links so that it easier for you to find them again later. Other useful links are also added in this appendix.

All of the links can be imported into your browser by downloading a file from the book page at `http://www.packtpub.com/support`.

Websites

The following tables contain links to some of the websites that you will be familiar with after a while and other ones that can serve as references if you would like to delve deeper into things. The tables are divided into:

- Official Microsoft websites
- Blogs
- Other relevant websites

Official Microsoft websites

The following are links to the official Microsoft websites:

Description	URL
Dynamics AX community	`https://community.dynamics.com/ax/home.aspx`
Dynamics AX at MSDN	`http://msdn.microsoft.com/en-us/dynamics/ax/default.aspx`
Dynamics AX 2009 SDK	`http://msdn.microsoft.com/en-us/library/dd448627.aspx`
Dynamics AX Technical Newsgroups	`https://community.dynamics.com/content/axnewsgroups.aspx?groupid=21`
Dynamics AX VPC from Partnersource	`https://mbs.microsoft.com/partnersource/deployment/documentation/howtoarticles/presalesdemokitmdax2009.htm?printpage=false&stext=AX 2009 VPC`
Dynamics AX VPC from Customersource	`https://mbs.microsoft.com/customersource/downloads/servicepacks/vpcimageax2009sp1.htm?printpage=false&stext=ax2009 vpc`

Blogs

The following is a list of the technical AX blogs that you might find interesting:

Description	URL
Erlend Dalen's blog	`http://msdynamicsax.wordpress.com`
Harish Mohanbabu's blog	`http://www.harishm.com/Mis/blog.htm`
Michael Fruergaard Pontoppidan's blog	`http://blogs.msdn.com/mfp/default.aspx`
Arijit Basu's blog	`http://daxguy.blogspot.com/`
Ivan Kashperuk's blog	`http://kashperuk.blogspot.com/`
Issues concerning X++	`http://blogs.msdn.com/x/`
Enterprise Portal blog	`http://blogs.msdn.com/epblog/`

Other relevant websites

The following are miscellaneous links where you can find specific information about AX, .NET, and other technologies:

Description	URL
List of all standard shortcut keys in AX	`http://kashperuk.net/DynamicsAX/AX%20 2009%20Keyboard%20Shortcuts.docx`
Axaptapedia	`http://www.axaptapedia.com/Main_Page`
Dynamics AX 2009 System Requirements	`http://www.microsoft.com/dynamics/en/ us/using/ax-system-requirements-2009. aspx`
Web services Architecture	`http://msdynamicsax.wordpress.com`
Web services Tutorial	`http://www.harishm.com/Mis/blog.htm`
SysEPWebFormConverter – Class that converts old AX WebForms into .NET User Controls	`http://blogs.msdn.com/mfp/default. aspx`
Codepages supported by Windows	`http://daxguy.blogspot.com/`
Common Language Runtime	`http://kashperuk.blogspot.com/`
.NET Framework 3.5 SDK	`http://blogs.msdn.com/x/`
Microsoft Dynamics Snap for Microsoft Dynamics AX	`http://blogs.msdn.com/epblog/`
Dynamics AX naming conventions	`http://msdn.microsoft.com/en-us/ library/aa632638.aspx`

B
Debugger

In the first chapter of this book it was briefly mentioned that the debugger was one of the most important tools when programming in AX. This appendix is written as a quick guide on how to use the debugger.

The debugger is installed as a separate application and can be opened directly from Windows or you can open it from AX. There are two ways of opening the debugger in AX. You can open it before you start executing whatever you would like to debug by pressing the Microsoft Dynamics AX button (*Alt + M*) and then navigate to **Tools | Development Tools | Debugger**.

The debugger is also started automatically when the code execution hits a breakpoint. If you are trying to debug code that is executed through the .NET Business Connector there are certain steps you have to follow. Learn more about these steps here: `https://community.dynamics.com/blogs/axdilip/archive/2009/03/17/how-to-debug-enterprise-portal-code-in-dynamics-ax-2009.aspx`

If the code you would like to debug runs on the server you will need to enable server-side debugging in the AX 2009 Server Configuration Tool.

To actually debug a piece of code simply press *F9* to add a breakpoint in the code. Try to do this somewhere in the Job Collection_Set that we created in Chapter 2, *X++ language*. You can also modify the code and write the statement `breakpoint;` to set a breakpoint. This can be especially helpful when debugging form controls.

 Make sure that the debugger is installed on your client computer and that debugging is enabled for your user by navigating to the **Options** form (Microsoft Dynamics AX button (*Alt+M*), followed by **Tools | Options**). Navigate to the **Development** tab and make sure that the **Debug Mode** field is set to **When Breakpoint**.

When you execute the Job it will stop at your breakpoint and it will look like the following screenshot (without the red numbers that are put there for explanation):

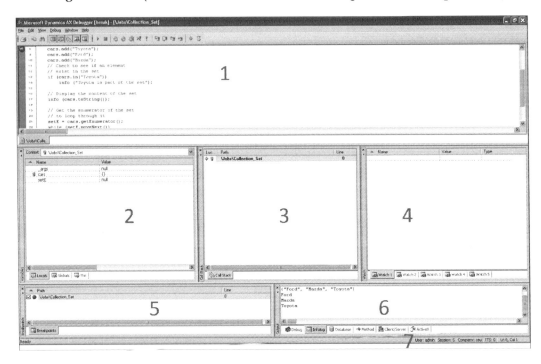

The following is the description of the screen in the previous screenshot:

1. **Code** window: This window displays the code that is being executed. The red bullet to the left of the line numbering indicates a breakpoint. The yellow arrow on top of the breakpoint indicates the line that is about to be executed.

2. **Variable** window: The variables that are in the selected context are shown here. The variable window is divided into the following three tabs:

    ◦ **Local**: Shows the variables in the current execution scope

    ◦ **Globals**: Shows variables from the objects that are always created when AX runs (InfoLog, VersionControl, Classfactory, and Appl)

    ◦ **This**: Shows the class member variables

3. **Call Stack** window: This window displays the methods that have been executed in order to get to the current code. Therefore, when method A calls method B which in turn calls method C, they will be listed in this window where method C is on the top and method A is at the bottom. You can also double-click on a path in the call stack to see that method's code in the code window.

4. **Watch** window: In this window you can look for certain variables regardless of their context. If they are in the current context then a value will be shown if they have any. You can mark a variable in the **Code** window and drag it to the **Watch** window to add it to the watch list.

5. **Breakpoints** window: This window shows all the breakpoints you have set in AX. You can also set new breakpoints and remove breakpoints directly in the debugger.

6. **Output** window: This window will display different kinds of output as follows:

    ◦   **Debug**: You can write statements in the code, such as the following and have them traced in this window:
        ```
        Debug::printDebug("Test something");
        ```

    ◦   **Infolog**: All messages sent to the infolog

    ◦   **Database, Method, Client/Server, ActiveX**: Any traces generated by these if their flags have been switched on in the **Options** form (Microsoft Dynamics AX button (*Alt + M)* and navigate to **Tools | Options**)

7. **Info bar**: This part of the debugger shows the following information related to the current session:

    ◦   **User**: The user executing the current session

    ◦   **Session**: The identifier of the current server session

    ◦   **Company**: The three lettered ID of the current company account

    ◦   **TTS**: The transaction level for the current session

    ◦   **Ln, Col**: Line number and Column of the cursor in the code window

The following are the main operations of the debugger (see a full list of shortcuts in the *List of all standard shortcut keys in AX* link in Appendix A, *Links*):

- Step over - *F10*: Executes the current line without debugging methods called by the statement if any.

- Step into - *F11*: Steps into the method called by the current line. If more than one method is called the innermost will have the top priority, then the first one to the left-hand side of the line, and then rightmost.

- Step out - *Shift + F11*: Steps out of the current method and moves back to the caller method (previous method in the stack).

- Go back: Drag the yellow arrow to a previous line of code in the current method to go back. Remember that the variables will not automatically be reset to the state they had when that line executed for the first time.

- Run - *F5*: Continue the execution and jump to the next breakpoint if any.

- Run to cursor - *Ctrl + F10*: Continue to execute and break at the line where the cursor is in the code window.

- Stop debugging - *Shift + F5*: Stop executing the code. None of the lines after the current execution position will be executed.

Index

I

InventTable table 207
InventTrans table 207
VendTable table 207
InventUpdate classes 208
Io class
  about 176
  AsciiIo class 177
  CommaIo classes 177
  CommaTextIo class 177
  TextIo class 177

J

jobs, AOT 11
join mode, data sources
  exists join 132
  inner join 132
  noexists join 132
  outer join 132
join parameters, select statement
  exists join 151
  inner join 149
  notexists join 152
  outer join 150

L

labels 18
ledger
  about 214
  dimension, adding 219, 221
  dimensions 218
  Ledger entity schema 214, 215
  posting 215
ledger dimensions
  about 218, 219
  default 218
Ledger entity schema
  about 214
  dimensions table 215
  LedgerAccountCategory 215
  LedgerBalancesTrans table 215
  LedgerTable 215
  LedgerTableInterval table 215
  LedgerTrans table 215
ledger journal
  transaction, entering 215, 216
  transaction, posting 215, 216

ledger posting 215
LedgerVoucher 217, 218
license codes, security framework 246
license letter 247
list pages
  about 123, 124
  creating 124, 125
lookup form
  creating 106
lookup form, creating
  in lookup method 108, 109
  new form, adding in AOT 107, 108

M

macros 69
Macros, AOT 10
main class hierarchies, inventory
  about 207
  InventAdj classes 209
  InventMovement class 207
  InventSum classes 209
  InventUpdate classes 208
main method 64
menu items, AOT 11
menu items, AX
  about 120
  action menu items 120
  creating 121
  display menu items 120
  output menu items 120
  types 120
  using, as button 121, 122
menus, AOT 11
menus, AX 125-127
method access 57
methods, AX reports
  about 110
  dialog 110
  fetch 110
  init 110
  print 110
  prompt 110
  run 110
  send 110
methods, forms
  about 92

modified, created By/Date Time/TransId
  78
name 78
PrimaryIndex 78
ReportRef 78
security key 78
TableGroup 78
temporary 78
TitleField 78

Q

queries
  about 129
  dynamic query, creating 134, 135
  static query, creating 130
  using 135-137
queries, AOT 11
query object model
  working 134

R

range operators, queries
  , 130
  ! 131
  ? 131
  .. 131
  * 131
  < 131
  = 130
  > 131
RDL 116
real data type
  about 38
  num2str function 39
  str2num function 39
record-based data manipulation
  about 162
  delete 166
  insert 163
  update 164, 165
relational operators
  like operator 55
  && operator 55
  ! operator 55
  != operator 55
  < operator 55

<= operator 55
== operator 55
> operator 55
>= operator 55
|| operator 55
relations 88, 89
RentalTable table
  fields 81
Report Definition Language. *See* RDL
reporting services 116
report libraries, AOT 11
reports, AOT 10
reports, AX
  about 109
  reporting services 116
resources, AOT 12
revertAssert() method 178
rich client 30
RunBase framework 64
RunOn property 58

S

sales/purch updates, AR/AP
  operations 227
  posting 227, 228
  printing 227, 228
security framework
  about 246
  configuration keys 248
  license codes 246, 247
  security keys 249-252
security keys, security framework 249-252
select statement
  about 140
  aggregate select statements, writing 153
  CarTable 141
  CustTable 142
  join, using 149
  RentalTable 142
  sort order, using 147
  writing 142-146
services, AOT 11
set-based data manipulation
  about 167
  delete_from operator, using 172
  insert_recordset operator, using 167, 168

**Thank you for buying
Microsoft Dynamics AX 2009
Programming: Getting Started**

About Packt Publishing

Packt, pronounced 'packed', published its first book *"Mastering phpMyAdmin for Effective MySQL Management"* in April 2004 and subsequently continued to specialize in publishing highly focused books on specific technologies and solutions.

Our books and publications share the experiences of your fellow IT professionals in adapting and customizing today's systems, applications, and frameworks. Our solution based books give you the knowledge and power to customize the software and technologies you're using to get the job done. Packt books are more specific and less general than the IT books you have seen in the past. Our unique business model allows us to bring you more focused information, giving you more of what you need to know, and less of what you don't.

Packt is a modern, yet unique publishing company, which focuses on producing quality, cutting-edge books for communities of developers, administrators, and newbies alike. For more information, please visit our website: www.packtpub.com.

Writing for Packt

We welcome all inquiries from people who are interested in authoring. Book proposals should be sent to author@packtpub.com. If your book idea is still at an early stage and you would like to discuss it first before writing a formal book proposal, contact us; one of our commissioning editors will get in touch with you.

We're not just looking for published authors; if you have strong technical skills but no writing experience, our experienced editors can help you develop a writing career, or simply get some additional reward for your expertise.

Programming Microsoft Dynamics NAV 2009

ISBN: 978-1-847196-52-1   Paperback: 620 pages

Develop and maintain high performance NAV applications to meet changing business needs with improved agility and enhanced flexibility

1. Create, modify, and maintain smart NAV applications to meet your client's business needs

2. Thoroughly covers the new features of NAV 2009, including Service Pack 1

3. Focused on development for the three-tier environment and the Role Tailored Client

Quality Assurance for Dynamics AX-Based ERP Solutions

ISBN: 978-1-847192-91-2   Paperback: 168 pages

Verifying Dynamics AX customization to the Microsoft IBI Standards

1. Learn rapidly how to test Dynamics AX applications

2. Verify Industry Builder Initiative (IBI) compliance of your ERP software

3. Readymade testing templates

Please check **www.PacktPub.com** for information on our titles

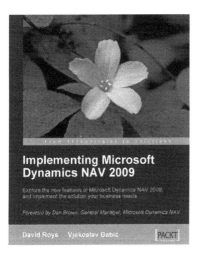

Implementing Microsoft Dynamics NAV 2009

ISBN: 978-1-847195-82-1   Paperback: 552 pages

Explore the new features of Microsoft Dynamics NAV 2009, and implement the solution your business needs

1. First book to show you how to implement Microsoft Dynamics NAV 2009 in your business

2. Meet the new features in Dynamics NAV 2009 that give your business the flexibility to adapt to new opportunities and growth

3. Easy-to-read style, packed with hard-won practical advice

Programming Microsoft® Dynamics™ NAV

ISBN: 978-1-904811-74-9   Paperback: 480 pages

Create, modify, and maintain applications in NAV 5.0, the latest version of the ERP application formerly known as Navision

1. For experienced programmers with little or no previous knowledge of NAV development

2. Learn as quickly as possible to create, modify, and maintain NAV applications

3. Written for version 5.0 of NAV; applicable for all versions

Please check **www.PacktPub.com** for information on our titles

Made in the USA
Lexington, KY
09 December 2011